THE Knowledge Economy AND POSTSECONDARY EDUCATION

Report of a Workshop

MW00724156

Committee on the Impact of the Changing Economy
on the Education System

Patricia Albjerg Graham and Nevzer G. Stacey, Editors

Center for Education
Division of Behavioral and Social Sciences and Education
National Research Council

NATIONAL ACADEMY PRESS
Washington, DC

NATIONAL ACADEMY PRESS • 2101 Constitution Avenue, N.W. • Washington, D.C. 20418

NOTICE: The project that is the subject of this report was approved by the Governing Board of the National Research Council, whose members are drawn from the councils of the National Academy of Sciences, the National Academy of Engineering, and the Institute of Medicine. The members of the committee responsible for the report were chosen for their special competences and with regard for appropriate balance.

This study was supported by Grant No. ESI-0002231 between the National Academy of Sciences and the National Science Foundation. Any opinions, findings, conclusions, or recommendations expressed in this publication are those of the author(s) and do not necessarily reflect the views of the organizations or agencies that provided support for the project.

Library of Congress Control Card Number 2002103034

International Standard Book Number 0-309-08292-7

Additional copies of this report are available from National Academy Press, 2101 Constitution Avenue, N.W., Lockbox 285, Washington, D.C. 20055; (800) 624-6242 or (202) 334-3313 (in the Washington metropolitan area); Internet, http://www.nap.edu

Printed in the United States of America

Suggested citation: National Research Council. (2002). *The knowledge economy and postsecondary education: Report of a workshop.* Committee on the Impact of the Changing Economy on the Education System. P.A. Graham and N.G. Stacey (Eds.). Center for Education. Division of Behavioral and Social Sciences and Education. Washington, DC: National Academy Press.

THE NATIONAL ACADEMIES

National Academy of Sciences
National Academy of Engineering
Institute of Medicine
National Research Council

The **National Academy of Sciences** is a private, nonprofit, self-perpetuating society of distinguished scholars engaged in scientific and engineering research, dedicated to the furtherance of science and technology and to their use for the general welfare. Upon the authority of the charter granted to it by the Congress in 1863, the Academy has a mandate that requires it to advise the federal government on scientific and technical matters. Dr. Bruce M. Alberts is president of the National Academy of Sciences.

The **National Academy of Engineering** was established in 1964, under the charter of the National Academy of Sciences, as a parallel organization of outstanding engineers. It is autonomous in its administration and in the selection of its members, sharing with the National Academy of Sciences the responsibility for advising the federal government. The National Academy of Engineering also sponsors engineering programs aimed at meeting national needs, encourages education and research, and recognizes the superior achievements of engineers. Dr. Wm. A. Wulf is president of the National Academy of Engineering.

The **Institute of Medicine** was established in 1970 by the National Academy of Sciences to secure the services of eminent members of appropriate professions in the examination of policy matters pertaining to the health of the public. The Institute acts under the responsibility given to the National Academy of Sciences by its congressional charter to be an adviser to the federal government and, upon its own initiative, to identify issues of medical care, research, and education. Dr. Kenneth I. Shine is president of the Institute of Medicine.

The **National Research Council** was organized by the National Academy of Sciences in 1916 to associate the broad community of science and technology with the Academy's purposes of furthering knowledge and advising the federal government. Functioning in accordance with general policies determined by the Academy, the Council has become the principal operating agency of both the National Academy of Sciences and the National Academy of Engineering in providing services to the government, the public, and the scientific and engineering communities. The Council is administered jointly by both Academies and the Institute of Medicine. Dr. Bruce M. Alberts and Dr. Wm. A. Wulf are chairman and vice chairman, respectively, of the National Research Council.

COMMITTEE ON THE IMPACT OF THE CHANGING ECONOMY ON THE EDUCATION SYSTEM

PATRICIA ALBJERG GRAHAM (*Chair*), Graduate School of Education, Harvard University

DAVID W. BRENEMAN, Curry School of Education, University of Virginia

PETER CAPPELLI, Wharton School, University of Pennsylvania

MARTHA DARLING, Education Policy Consultant, Ann Arbor, MI

ARNE L. KALLEBERG, Department of Sociology, University of North Carolina

RONALD M. LATANISION, Department of Materials Science and Engineering, Massachusetts Institute of Technology

Speakers

CHARLES ABELMANN, The World Bank

CLIFFORD ADELMAN, U.S. Department of Education

ESTELA BENSIMON, University of Southern California

BRANDON DOBELL, Credit Suisse First Boston

THOMAS DUFFY, Cardean University

WILLIAM GRAVES, Eduprise

IRVING HAMER, New York City Schools Board of Education

LISA LYNCH, Tufts University

DAVID STERN, University of California

ROBERT ZEMSKY, University of Pennsylvania

National Research Council Staff

NEVZER G. STACEY, *Study Director*

MARGARET HILTON, *Program Officer*

LINDA DEPUGH, *Administrative Assistant*

Preface

Americans have witnessed and participated in an extraordinary decade of economic volatility and educational reform. The National Academy of Sciences, through its Center for Education in its Division of Behavioral and Social Sciences and Education of the National Research Council (NRC), recognized this tumult. It responded by appointing the Committee on the Impact of the Changing Economy on the Education System in fall 2000. The committee's charge was to organize a workshop, held in May 2001, to explore how the various participants in the postsecondary sector were or were not changing their practices. Funding was provided by the National Science Foundation.

An underlying assumption of the workshop, albeit one that several participants debated, was that the economy was a powerful force influencing postsecondary education. As the indicators of U.S. economic vitality have altered during the preparation of this document, we have maintained our focus upon the postsecondary system itself, rather than attempt to explain the manner in which the U.S. economy influences higher education. That important and challenging issue we commend to another National Academy of Sciences group.

This report is the result of the committee's deliberations, the discussions at the workshop, and most importantly, the papers prepared for the workshop, which form the body of this document. Such work is inevitably collaborative, and the committee is deeply indebted and appreciative of the participation of the authors and attendees at the workshop. We are also very grateful for the reviewers' comments on our draft document. Finally, we especially thank Nevzer Stacey, our program officer at the National Academy of Sciences, and her colleagues, Linda DePugh and Margaret Hilton, for their attentiveness, incisive observations, and support. Michael Feuer, director of the Center for Education, gave us our initial charge, and we believe that this report helps to advance understanding of the dynamics of today's postsecondary environments.

This report has been reviewed in draft form by individuals chosen for their diverse perspectives and technical expertise, in accordance with procedures approved by the NRC's Report Review Committee. The purpose of this independent review is to provide candid and critical comments that will assist the institution in making its published report as sound as possible and to ensure that the report meets institutional standards for objectivity, evidence, and responsiveness to the study charge. The review comments and draft manuscript remain confidential to protect the integrity of the deliberative process. We wish to thank the following individuals for their review of this report:

Kristin Conklin, National Governors Association
Robert I. Lerman, The Urban Institute
Roy Radner, New York University

Although the reviewers listed above have provided many constructive comments and suggestions, they were not asked to endorse the final draft of the report before its release. The review of this report was overseen by Kenneth I. Wolpin, University of Pennsylvania. Appointed by the NRC, he was responsible for making certain that an independent examination of this report was carried out in accordance with institutional procedures and that all review comments were carefully considered. Responsibility for the final content of this report rests entirely with the authoring committee and the institution.

Patricia Albjerg Graham, *Chair*
Committee on the Impact of the Changing
Economy on the Education System

Contents

PART I: WORKSHOP REPORT

The Knowledge Economy and Postsecondary Education

INTRODUCTION

During the last quarter century, the American economy has undergone profound changes, initially in business leadership's confidence in the ability of its institutions to compete effectively internationally, then in a comprehensive restructuring of its organizations, and finally in the remarkable growth in the use of new technologies. These efforts have challenged the institutions with primary responsibility for formal education, schools and colleges, to supply workers who are able to assist their employers in meeting their new business goals. Initially in the 1980s and 1990s, the focus was on schools and their limitations in providing graduates who could successfully undertake this work. An argument made forcefully in 1983 by the National Commission on Excellence in Education in *A Nation at Risk* alleged that the entire country was threatened by the inadequacies of the American school system. The resurgence of the American economy in the 1990s suggested that the connection between schooling and subsequent worker productivity, while important, was not as direct or linear as had seemed to the authors of *A Nation at Risk,* because the increase in academic performance of American school children was considerably more modest than the rate of growth of the economy and the performance of the stock market in the late 1990s.

Today the focus has shifted in the United States and, as the World Bank has observed, internationally, to the ability of the postsecondary education system to prepare workers both effectively and efficiently to meet the demands of organizations whose job requirements appear both more complex and less static than previously. Beginning in the 1980s, baccalaureate graduates' employment became much better paid than that of individuals with only some college, only high school, or only grade school experience (Hudson, this volume; Juhn, Murphy, and Pierce, 1993). Further, the wages of males with grade school or high school only were no longer enough to keep a family above the poverty line, as they had been in earlier decades. Coincident with these recognitions, or perhaps because of them, U.S. college enrollment rates grew for much of the population, particularly for women (Hudson, this volume). The easy assumption was that going to college, and especially completing a degree, led to a job that paid better than the job one would get without a college degree. The solution seemed simple: more education equals more money. But what was the college education really buying? What essence of the college experience made graduates better compensated employees? Could other institutions besides colleges provide that essence?

The Committee on the Impact of the Changing Economy on the Education System held a two-day workshop to discuss the implications of emerging trends and their relevance to the U.S. postsecondary education system. Participants in the workshop on May 14-15, 2001, sponsored by the National Research Council of the National Academy of Sciences, discussed these issues, assisted by the presentation of six papers on various aspects of these matters. The first session of the workshop generated a discussion that was not addressed by any of the papers. (See Appendix A, Workshop Agenda, for the chronology of presentations at the workshop.) Central questions raised later on in this introduction reflect the workshop participants' concerns as well as the issues in the workshop papers. These papers form the essence of this volume. As intended for workshops in which an issue is to be explored, the papers' authors, assigned discussants, and invited participants did not find themselves in immediate unanimity in determining the significance of changes in the amorphous and shifting "system" that encompasses postsecondary education. The influence of the economy on these changes, while acknowledged, was not the focus of the discussion.

American colleges and universities, believing themselves to be world leaders in education, are finding that indeed other providers and alternative modes of instruction are supplanting their traditional curricula and course organization with their characteristic faculty autonomy and lack of assessment of student learning. Workshop participants noted that many colleges and universities, particularly those without academically selective admissions criteria, are moving to modify their curricula to what they perceive as desirable by potential students and their employers. The institutions' agility in making these adjustments is questioned by many critics, some from within academe and some from other sectors.

Several workshop participants also acknowledged that the apparent monopoly of colleges and universities in providing postsecondary education is over, if, in fact, it ever existed. Even the term "postsecondary" simply defines experiences that occur after high school. It does not identify the organizations or institutions that provide them. Traditionally, employers and unions have also provided instruction, both explicit and implicit, in what one needed to know and be able to do to be successful in the unique culture of a particular institution. Today it is less clear what the mix of providers of postsecondary education will be and what means they will utilize to provide that education. The "postsecondary education system" appears very unsystematic.

Debate continues, particularly in the precincts of colleges and universities, about what the balance between job skills training and broader academic learning ought to be and for whom these opportunities should be provided. Traditional definitions of colleges' missions have given only limited attention to job training, though all have argued that the overall experience would enhance one's employment prospects. At the beginning of the 20th century, most U.S. colleges required a common curriculum with individual concentration in an academic major subject. Now at the beginning of the 21st century, colleges offer curricula with highly differentiated studies often aligned with apparent job skills. Ironically, the dominant call for reform in elementary and secondary schools pushes those institutions to demonstrate through assessments that their students have met "academic standards" in various subjects, thus pushing toward a common curriculum, while colleges move toward increased specialization without much assessment. What, in fact, are employers paying for when they hire college graduates for higher wages?

Some of the explanation for lack of agreement among workshop participants on these matters was based upon a difference in fundamental principles regarding the role of higher education in the United States, particularly alternative views of its purpose. For example, the participants recognized that they would not on this occasion resolve the difference between those who sought public support for colleges and universities that provide excellent education for both employment and citizenship at costs affordable to all and those who believed that students (and their families) assume primary financial responsibility for their education in order to enhance their employment prospects. The degree to which strong postsecondary education benefits the nation as a whole as well as the persons who participate in it, and what the balance of the relative benefit to society and to the individual should be, underlay much of the discussion about specific proposals.

STRUCTURE OF THE REPORT

What follows the Workshop Report (Part I) are the Workshop Papers (Part II). In organizing the workshop and soliciting papers for it, the committee believed that, first, members needed the best available demographic data to learn who was participating in different kinds of postsecondary education. Lisa Hudson's paper, presented as Chapter 1 in this volume, supplies this information. Second, we believed that it was important to look at the traditional higher education sector—colleges and universities—to ascertain the degree to which different parts were modifying their programs and instruction to adapt to the apparent changing skill requirements of employers. Thomas Bailey's paper (Chapter 2) concentrates upon community colleges, traditionally the higher education sector most immediately responsive to employer needs. Carol A. Twigg (Chapter 3) surveys the ways in which four-year institutions are attempting to modify their curricular offerings and their pedagogy, often utilizing the resources of the Internet, to adapt their offerings in ways that they and their students believe will be more useful. In the paper presented here as Chapter 4, Brian Pusser, on the other hand, reminds participants of the public's broader interests in higher education, challenging the acceptance of the primacy of job preparation for the individual and of the "market" metaphor as an appropriate descriptor of American higher education.

The discussion stimulated by these papers raised many issues about both the desirability of these changes in traditional colleges and universities and the likelihood that these institutions would, in fact, change significantly. Other providers, particularly for-profit organizations with significant capacities for distance or virtual learning, recognize great opportunities for developing programs to serve students' need for immediate focused instruction that will enhance job skills. During the workshop, Brandon Dobell, who follows the business fortunes of these companies for Credit Suisse First Boston, explained the popularity of such organizations on Wall Street: their excellent customer service, good business models, and effective management permit them to meet their earnings estimates regularly.

The committee believed that it would be helpful to look in some detail at one example of a for-profit company that was providing instruction necessary for workers in its industry. Richard Murnane, Nancy Sharkey, and Frank Levy investigated the experience of Cisco Systems with its Networking Academies, which prepare students in high school and community colleges to earn certificates testifying to their information technology skills. Their findings are presented in Chapter 5. Finally, the committee concluded that changes in postsecondary education must be based on a deeper understanding of how learning occurs and how it can be encouraged, particularly in cyberspace. John Bransford and his colleagues, Nancy Vye and Helen Bateman, addresses these issues in their paper, which appears here as Chapter 6.

FIVE MAJOR DISCUSSION QUESTIONS

Five central questions emerged from the workshop presentations and the discussions resulting from them:

1. How are job skills changing?
2. How does learning occur best?
3. Can we assess learning adequately?
4. What structural and organizational changes are taking place in the provision of postsecondary education?
5. Who is participating and to what effect in postsecondary education?

How Are Job Skills Changing?

What is the nature of these assumed changes in skills? Very little evidence is cited that supports what is, in fact, a widespread public conviction that such changes have occurred. Most discussions focus upon increasing needs for technological skills, such as those in demand in the information technology field. Many participants pointed to requirements for much stronger literacy skills for understanding written and oral instructions. Still others at the workshop stressed that demand for effective workplace communication and cooperative team member participation, often called "soft skills," has become ubiquitous. On the other hand, recognition exists that certain skills are no longer in high demand, such as the ability to compute change due or to add a bill mentally, having been replaced by computers and other technology. Undoubtedly job skill demands are shifting, as the economy and jobs within it shift, but the nature of these changes and the impact of them upon future preparation of workers are not well understood.

How Does Learning Occur Best?

Traditionally colleges and universities have addressed this question by engaging in discussions about curriculum, course requirements, and syllabi, and occasionally pedagogy, triggering familiar arguments about the value of the 50-minute lecture versus seminar discussion. Several participants noted that demand for admission to highly selective institutions has risen steadily in recent years, presumably at least partially on the basis that students there will benefit from regular contact with others who have been similarly selected. These institutions tout their pedagogy, but few engage in rigorous examination of their students' learning. As John Bransford and his co-authors note in their paper, recent advances in cognitive science married to emerging knowledge of the uses of technology to enhance learning are creating an important new opportunity to engage this issue. They observe that the topic is shifting from pedagogy to learning. The focus, they argue, has appropriately become the students and how they, each of them, will master the material. Formerly, the focus was upon the instructors and how they delivered the material. Other workshop participants also cited the importance of more complicated under-standing of how we learn, how elements of learning can be isolated or "modularized," and how learning in one setting can be utilized in a different one. These are all part of the fundamental new investigations that focus upon learning itself.

Can We Assess Learning Adequately?

As many participants noted, assessment (a more comprehensive term than "testing") is achieving a new salience in postsecondary education. Already the subject of contentious discussion for elementary and secondary schools, assessment is emerging as a major issue for the postsecondary community as well. Formerly, the college degree itself was thought to be assessment enough. Today the demand for the degree or some other credential increasingly is supplemented by some indication that the person has actually learned what the degree or credential attests. This is not a novel development. Lawyers must still pass bar exams, doctors who want recognition as specialists must pass board exams, and elementary and secondary teachers, who became licensed through examinations until the 1920s, are again increasingly facing certification examinations. Institutions whose students fail the teacher examinations in large numbers are being threatened by powerful sanctions. Thus, assessment is creeping into institutions themselves, rather than simply being the responsibility of the students to master the material themselves, either through good pedagogy, self-study, or some combination of both.

As Carol A. Twigg observes in her paper and as others noted in discussion, systematic assessments are vastly enhanced by the imaginative use of technology with immediate response to student effort. Such careful and immediate analysis of student work is still relatively rare but is clearly growing in both its accuracy and its applicability. Several participants observed that one of the most profound effects of the distance education and virtual learning movements, as well as the for-profit providers of education, has been the increased use of and attention to assessment. Since the traditional modes of college experience (and the public confidence of accountability that the four-year residential college provided) are not available to them, these organizations have had to devise means to show that students were benefiting from their experiences. The benefit was documented learning, a new idea for most traditional colleges and universities. An additional point made by many of the workshop participants is that while attention to assessment has increased substantially throughout postsecondary education recently, given the stimulus of the growth of cognitive science, technology, distance learning, and the for-profit education providers, the adequacy of these new assessments remains a subject for additional investigation and research.

What Structural and Organizational Changes Are Taking Place in the Provision of Postsecondary Education?

For-profit institutions and nonresidential instruction dominated discussions at the workshop of the organization of postsecondary education. Yet what is most striking to the committee is the enormous increase in the last 50 years in enrollments at U.S. colleges and universities, both from U.S. citizens and from foreign nationals. Higher education has experienced tremendous growth, traditionally believing itself to be a separate species from the corporate sector. How separate are they? Many at the workshop argued that a convergence is occurring with traditional colleges and universities becoming more like companies.

This phenomenon is often described as an acceptance of the "market model" for higher education and hence a renunciation of its traditional isolation in an "ivory tower." Both descriptions caricature reality, but the advent of unionized graduate student assistants; "revenue-centered" budgeting in colleges; outsourcing of many staff functions, such as the police or food service; and the provision of publicly subsidized college courses designed to serve specific industries all suggest to the committee an erosion of the eleemosynary nature of higher education. An important dilemma raised at the workshop was the determination of appropriate distinctions between for-profit institutions, maximizing value to shareholders, and educational institutions, enabling learning and investigations for the benefit of students and society.

Who Is Participating and to What Effect in Postsecondary Education?

Although the tremendous growth in participation rates in U.S. higher education in the last 50 years is well documented by Lisa Hudson and others, the explanations for the differing participation rates by gender, ethnicity, and age are not. Workshop participants raised the question: Why have women, particularly White and Black, increased their participation rates so markedly? Do women need the degree or credential more than men? What is happening with the category termed "Hispanic," whose participation rates in higher education seem to be falling? "Hispanics," of course, include immigrants, multigenerational U.S. citizens, rich, poor, and various racial mixes. Since the 18–22 year olds devoting full-time to their college studies (the traditional undergraduate population) now constitute considerably less than half of all undergraduates, the balance of enrollees is important but little understood. Workshop participants raised questions such as:

• Do the remainder think of themselves primarily as employees taking a few courses or students working to pay for their education? If difficulty occurs in understanding enrollees in colleges and universities, then the problem in identifying and understanding the motivation for persons enrolled in nontraditional forms of postsecondary education, particularly distance learning and emerging for-profit and nonprofit organizations that supply instruction, is immensely greater. Several participants familiar with current U.S. government data collection methods report that data from such institutions are difficult to encompass in surveys, yet those activities are vital to our committee's understanding of the skill sets that individuals seek.

• Who will have access and at what cost to the emerging technologies, such as the benefits from the auction of the electromagnetic spectrum?

• Finally, who is paying the costs of these educational activities? Are individuals from low-income families increasingly attending courses and institutions that limit their job options and ultimate economic mobility, as the data for non-Asian minorities concentrated in two-year community colleges would suggest (Hudson, this volume)? Has the shift in U.S. financial aid policies over the last 25 years from fewer grants to more loans had the effect of diminishing educational opportunities to those living in low-income families who are understandably fearful of debt? Is stratification by family wealth increasing in U.S. postsecondary education? Would it matter if it were?

The five questions formed the heart, but not the entire body, of the workshop discussion. To explore the issues further, we commend the papers themselves and the sources they cite.

REFERENCES

Juhn, C., Murphy, K.M., and Pierce, B. (1993). Wage inequality and the rise in returns to skill. *Journal of Political Economy* 101(June): 410–442.

National Commission on Excellence in Education. (1983). *A nation at risk: The imperative for educational reform.* Washington, DC: U.S. Government Printing Office.

PART II: WORKSHOP PAPERS

1

Demographic and Attainment Trends in Postsecondary Education

*Lisa Hudson**

"More people are going to college!" is hardly an attention-grabbing headline, as it describes a long-standing trend in American education. This trend reflects continued increases in the skills required by the labor market and by society in general. Within this world of increasing skill demands, America's public and private postsecondary education institutions have firmly maintained their role and mission. In recent years, however, these postsecondary institutions have faced growing competition. In particular, the growth of alternative providers (such as for-profit institutions, "virtual" universities, and corporate universities) and alternative credentials (such as company-based certificates) have called into question the efficacy of the traditional postsecondary institution and its ability to continue its dominant role as the (nearly) exclusive provider of postcompulsory education.

Other chapters in this volume examine alternative postsecondary education providers and pedagogies and the ways in which traditional postsecondary institutions are adapting to changing conditions. This chapter provides a context for the remainder of the volume, by providing a broad overview of trends within postsecondary education, as well as trends in the civilian labor market and the military that may affect the demand for postsecondary education. These three activities (postsecondary education, civilian work, and military service) constitute the three main career options available to those leaving high school. To put these options in perspective, among students who were eighth-

*Lisa Hudson is an education statistician at the National Center for Education Statistics in the U.S. Department of Education. The views in this paper are those of the author. No official support by the U.S. Department of Education is intended or should be inferred.

graders in 1988 (and thus expected to graduate in 1992), 74 percent were working for pay or looking for work in 1994, and 53 percent were in a postsecondary education program. (About 35 percent were engaged in both activities.) Only 3 percent of these former students were in the military, and 7 percent were full-time homemakers (Berktold, Geis, and Kaufman, 1998).

STRUCTURE OF THE CHAPTER

Although this chapter examines all three postsecondary school activities, the main emphasis is on postsecondary education. The chapter begins by examining characteristics of the young adult population. A number of aspects of postsecondary education are then examined, including trends in postsecondary enrollment levels and rates, the composition of students in postsecondary education, the number and types of degrees awarded, and student financial aid. The chapter then presents a brief overview of trends within the military and the labor market that may influence participation in postsecondary education. The final section reviews the limitations of current data sources for monitoring changes in postsecondary education and suggests areas for improvement.

This chapter focuses primarily on trends within the past three decades, from 1970 to 2000, although shorter time periods are used when data are not available for all 30 years. Throughout, the chapter relies on analyses of federal data, particularly data collected by the U.S. Department of Education's National Center for Education Statistics (NCES). NCES data are a rich source of relatively objective, reliable data with which to describe postsecondary education. They do, however, have some limitations. First, the national portrait provided by these data necessarily masks differences that exist among states and regions of the country (e.g., enrollment trends among Hispanic students are likely to differ in the Southwest compared to the Midwest). These more detailed analyses were beyond the scope of this chapter.[1] Also, for reasons discussed at the end, existing national data primarily describe "traditional" postsecondary institutions and the attainment of "traditional" postsecondary education credentials. Finally, because of both the reliance on national data and the broad scope of this chapter, many topics could not be covered in depth, and many of the complex issues raised by these data received admittedly cursory treatment.

YOUNG ADULT POPULATION TRENDS

Although about 40 percent of college students are over age 24, young adults aged 18–22 are often considered the key constituency

---

[1]The reader interested in state-level data is referred to publications produced by the State Higher Education Executive Officers (SHEEO) and the National Center for Public Policy and Higher Education (e.g., *Measuring Up 2000*).

for postsecondary education. This population of young adults has fluctuated in size over the past three decades, increasing in the 1970s (as the baby boomers reached college age) and declining during the 1980s and early 1990s. The number of young adults increased from 23.7 million in 1970 to 30.2 million in 1981, then declined to a low of 24.8 million in 1996. Since 1996, the size of the 18-24-year-old cohort has increased to 26.0 million in 1999, and it is expected to continue to grow in size over the next five decades (U.S. Census Bureau, 1996, 2000).

Because the federal government did not separate out Hispanics in its data collections until the mid-1970s, trend data on the racial/ethnic composition of the young adult cohort are more limited. Over the roughly two decades from 1980 to 1999, the proportion of young adults who are White[2] declined from 78 percent to 66 percent. At the same time, the proportion of Blacks increased slightly from 13 percent to 14 percent, the proportion of Hispanics increased from 8 percent to 15 percent, and the proportion of other minorities (Asians and Native Americans) increased from 2 percent to 5 percent (U.S. Census Bureau, 1996, 2000). As will be seen later, these changes in the racial/ethnic composition of the young adult population are reflected in changes in the college student population over time.

Looking at a slightly older group of adults, those aged 25–29, shows that the education level of adults has increased over time, as more individuals have completed high school, enrolled in college, and earned a college degree (Figure 1-1). From 1971 to 1999, the percentage of adults aged 25–29 who completed high school increased from 78 percent to 88 percent; the percentage who had at least some college education increased from 44 percent to 66 percent; and the percentage who had at least a bachelor's degree increased from 22 percent to 32 percent (NCES, 2000). The proportion of these adults completing at least some college has increased faster than the proportion completing high school, suggesting that the college enrollment rate has been increasing. As will be discussed later, this rate has indeed been rising. But before students can go to college, they must leave high school.

High School Dropout and Completion Rates

Completing high school increases a student's chances of attending college, and completing high school through a regular diploma rather than an alternative route increases a student's chances of both going on to college (Snyder, 2001) and of completing college once he or she has started (Boesel, Alsalam, and Smith, 1998). Thus, to maximize their opportunity to enter and complete college, students should

---

[2]Throughout this paper, "White" refers to non-Hispanic Whites and "Black" refers to non-Hispanic Blacks.

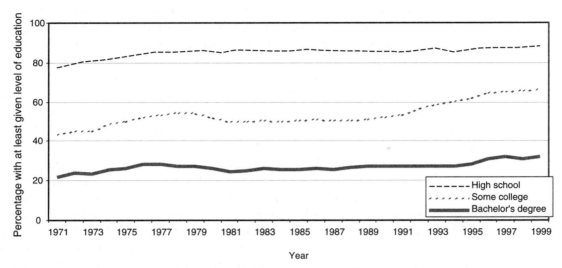

FIGURE 1-1 Percentage of 25–29 year olds who have completed at least high school, some college, or a bachelor's degree: 1971–1999.

SOURCE: Data from National Center for Education Statistics (2000, pp. 154–156).

ideally graduate from high school with a regular high school diploma.[3] While most high school students do this, many do not. For example, in 1999, 86 percent of 18–24 year olds who were not enrolled in high school had completed high school, 77 percent by graduating from high school and 9 percent through an alternative means such as the General Educational Development (GED) test. Thus, 23 percent of these young adults had failed to graduate from high school through the traditional path.

These figures represent a decline in high school dropout rates and corresponding increase in completion rates since the 1970s. Eleven percent of 16–24 year olds were dropouts[4] in 1999, down from over 14 percent in 1972 (Kaufman, Kwon, Klein, and Chapman, 2000). However, while dropout rates have declined since the early 1970s, they were fairly steady during the 1990s; similarly, the high school completion rate has increased slightly since the early 1970s, but remained flat in the 1990s.

---

[3]High school graduation maximizes other opportunities as well: Graduating from high school with a regular diploma is also related to lower levels of unemployment and higher wages, compared to not completing high school or completing through an alternative program (Boesel et al., 1998).

[4]This measure of dropouts includes all young adults aged 16–24 who are not in school and have not earned a high school credential. This measure undercounts school dropout rates, since some of these young adults may have dropped out of high school but subsequently earned a credential.

These trends are occurring along with increased academic course taking among high school students (Levesque, Lauen, Teitelbaum, Alt, and Librera, 2000) and relatively steady or increasing academic achievement on national standardized tests (NCES, 2000; Smith, 1996). Taken together, these findings suggest that school reform and accountability efforts in the past few decades may have improved learning outcomes for many high school students, although, at least in recent years, they seem to have had little effect on high school completion rates. It is not clear to what extent these trends have affected postsecondary education—for example, it is not (yet) known whether these learning gains have reduced the need for remediation at the college level or to what extent they account for increasing enrollments at the postsecondary level.

Immediate Transition to College and SAT Scores

The most successful route to a college degree is to enter college immediately after high school graduation (NCES, 1997). The percentage of high school completers who make this immediate transition remained relatively constant at about 50 percent from 1972 to 1980 but then increased to 66 percent by 1998 (NCES, 2000). The number of students who took the SAT also increased from 1975 to 1999 (College Board, 2000c). This increase has occurred despite a declining cohort of 17 year olds, so that in 1975 the number of SAT-takers was 23 percent of the number of 17 year olds, while in 1999, SAT-takers were 31 percent of the 17-year-old population. Most of this increase occurred during the 1980s; by 1987, SAT-takers were 29 percent of the 17-year-old population (Snyder and Hoffman, 1991; College Board, 2000c; Snyder, 2001).

At the same time that more high school graduates are going directly to college and more students are taking the SAT, SAT scores have been holding steady or increasing (Snyder, 2001). Average verbal SAT scores declined from 507 to 505 from 1986 to 1987 but have remained constant at 505 since then (up to 1999). However, over this same time period, verbal SAT scores *increased* for each racial/ethnic group except Hispanics, whose scored dropped. These within-group trends suggest two reasons for the lack of an overall increase in verbal scores. The first reason is the drop in scores among Hispanics; the second reason is the increasing percentage of minorities attending college. Since all minority groups have lower verbal scores than Whites, this enrollment increase lowers the overall average score. Average math SAT scores increased from 501 to 514 from 1986 to 1999. Part of this increase may be due to increasing enrollments of Asian students, who have higher average math scores than other racial/ethnic groups, but it also reflects an increase in scores among each racial/ethnic group.

These positive trends reflect a high school student body that appears to be, on average, better prepared to enter college. The next sections take a closer look at college enrollment trends in general and the students who are enrolling in college.

COLLEGE ENROLLMENTS

The number of students enrolled in college has been increasing for at least the last three decades (Figure 1-2). This growth has been fueled by increasing college enrollment rates among high-school graduates and among adults in general (Figure 1-3), rather than from increases in the number of high school graduates or college-age adults (defined as adults aged 18–24). In fact, enrollment increases have occurred *in spite of* a declining cohort of college-age adults over most of the last two decades and relatively constant high school graduation rates.

The increase in college enrollment was particularly steep during the 1970s, when community colleges were expanding. Interestingly, however, the college enrollment rate of 18–24 year olds was fairly constant over this period. During the 1970s, college enrollment growth appears to have resulted from enrollment rate increases among older adults (aged 25–34, see Figure 1-3) combined with a growing cohort of adults in this age category (U.S. Census Bureau, 2000).

Enrollment growth continued throughout the 1980s, fueled primarily by an increasing enrollment rate among college-age adults. Since 1992, however, enrollment appears to have leveled off, and the increase in the enrollment rate of college-age adults has slowed. The apparent leveling off of enrollment does not appear to be due to changes in the

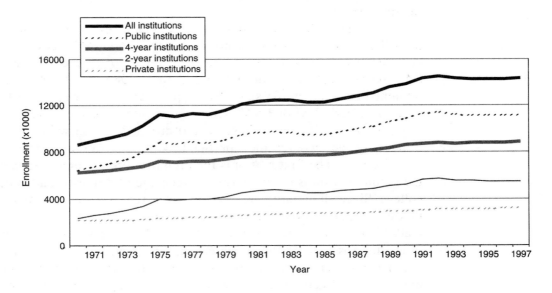

FIGURE 1-2 Total fall enrollment in degree-granting postsecondary institutions, by control and level of institution: 1970–1997.

SOURCE: Data from Snyder (2001, p. 203).

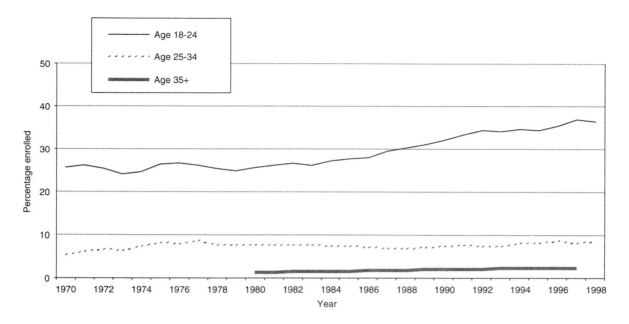

FIGURE 1-3 Percentage of the population enrolled in postsecondary education, by age group: 1970–1998.

SOURCES: Data from National Center for Education Statistics (2000, pp. 114-115) and U.S. Census Bureau, (2000, p. 167).

size of the college-age population. Although this cohort became smaller during the 1990s, it shrank less during the 1990s than in previous decades, when enrollment grew. Data on the wage premiums associated with college education may provide one clue as to why growth in enrollment rates and levels may be slowing.

College Wage Premiums

College enrollment rates can be viewed as an indicator of labor market demand for a college education; when demand is high, the enrollment rate increases, and vice versa. Another indicator of labor market demand for a college education is the wage premium associated with a college education. This measure indicates how much a college-educated worker earns compared to a worker who has only a high school education (Figures 1-4a and 1-4b).

Comparing the trend in Figure 1-3 with the trends in Figures 1-4a and 1-4b shows that the enrollment rate among adults aged 18–24 began to increase a few years after the wage premium for a college education began to rise. Throughout most of the 1980s, both the relative returns to a college education and young adult enrollment rates increased, suggesting a strong labor market increase in the demand for a college education during that decade. In the 1990s, however, the wage premium for a college education leveled off and college enroll-

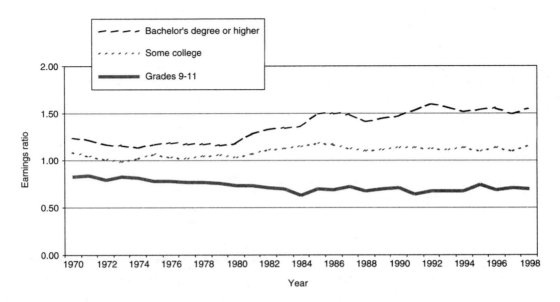

FIGURE 1-4a Ratio of median annual earnings of male wage and salary workers aged 25–34 whose highest education level was grades 9–11, some college, or a bachelor's degree or higher, compared to those whose highest education was a high school diploma or GED: 1970–1998.

SOURCE: National Center for Education Statistics (2000, p. 144).

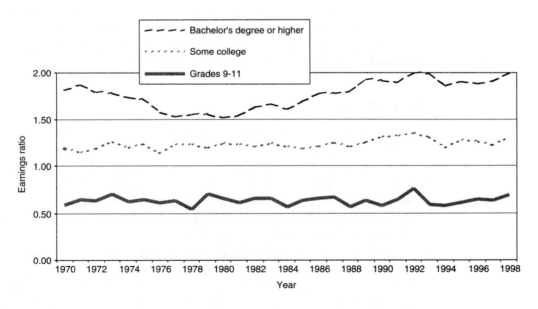

FIGURE 1-4b Ratio of median annual earnings of female wage and salary workers aged 25–34 whose highest education level was grades 9–11, some college, or a bachelor's degree or higher, compared to those whose highest education was a high school diploma or GED: 1970–1998.

SOURCE: National Center for Education Statistics (2000, p. 144).

ment rates fluctuated, suggesting that the labor market may have (at least temporarily) met its demand for college-educated workers. Of course, many factors in addition to the wage premium can affect college enrollment rates, and some factors (such as a growing high-skill economy) may drive both measures in the same direction. Nonetheless, these trends seem to suggest that labor market demand for a college education was particularly strong during the 1980s and *may* have leveled off in the late 1990s.

Enrollments Among Types of Postsecondary Institutions

The overall increase in college enrollments in the last three decades has occurred within public institutions, private institutions, four-year institutions, and two-year institutions (see Figure 1-2). During the 1970s, as the community college system grew, enrollment increases were larger at public rather than private institutions and at two-year rather than four-year institutions. As a result of these changes, from 1970 to 1980, public institution enrollments increased from 75 percent to 78 percent of all postsecondary enrollments, and four-year institution enrollments decreased from 73 percent to 63 percent of all enrollments. Since 1980, the share of enrollments at four-year institutions has dropped only slightly to 62 percent, and the share at public institutions has not changed. Thus, the last decade has been characterized by fairly stable enrollment shares across public and private institutions and across four-year and two-year institutions.

Table 1-1 provides a more detailed look at enrollments in the four major types of postsecondary institutions—public four-year, public two-year, private four-year, and private two-year—in 1981 and 1998. (This time period was selected because the criteria NCES uses to define the two-year sector have changed over time, such that data on two-year institutions before 1981 are not comparable with data in the

TABLE 1-1 Fall Enrollments in Postsecondary Institutions and Distribution of Enrollments among Institutions, by Type of Institution: 1981 and 1998

Type of institution	1981		1998	
	Enrollment	% Distribution	Enrollment	% Distribution
Public 4-year	5,166,324	41.8	5,903,837	40.6
Public 2-year	4,480,708	36.2	5,272,347	36.2
Private 4-year	2,489,137	20.1	3,128,908	21.5
Private 2-year	235,503	1.9	244,097	1.7
All institutions	12,371,672	100.0	14,549,189	100.0

SOURCE: Snyder (2001, p. 203).
NOTE: The 1998 data are for degree-granting institutions. Data in 1981 were not available for degree-granting institutions, so data in this year represent two-year and four-year institutions of higher education. In any given year, enrollment estimates for these two types of institutions differ by about 1 percent.

1990s.) This table shows, first of all, that enrollments at public institutions are almost evenly split between those at the four-year level and those at the two-year level, while enrollments at private institutions are heavily concentrated at the four-year level. From the other perspective, public four-year institutions enroll about twice as many students as private four-year institutions, while public two-year institutions enroll more than 10 times as many students as their private counterparts.

From 1981 to 1998, there was little change within the two-year sector; public institutions' share of enrollments increased only slightly from 95 percent to 96 percent. Over the longer time period from 1970 to 1997, there was a shift within the four-year sector from public institutions to private institutions, resulting in a decline in public institutions' share of four-year enrollments from 74 percent to 65 percent. This relative growth in the private four-year sector is somewhat surprising, since private four-year institutions have had higher tuition increases in the past three decades than have public institutions. However, the shift from public to private institutions occurred only during the 1970s and 1990s, not the 1980s. It was during the 1980s that private four-year institutions increased in tuition costs relative to public four-year institutions; their relative costs have declined since 1990-1991 (see Snyder, 2001, and Table 1-10 later in this chapter). So the public-to-private shift seems to reflect a combination of increasing interest in attending private four-year institutions combined with the mitigating influence of relative costs.

In sum, except for a shift from public to private four-year institutions, there has been little change in the past two decades in the type of institution in which students (in general) enroll. If past trends are any guide, private four-year institutions may increase their enrollments relative to public four-year institutions in the future *if* their relative tuition costs do not increase.

Who Enrolls in College[5]

The modal college student in 1970 was a young (under age 24) White male who attended school full-time; today the modal college student looks much the same, except she is female. Attending school along with today's modal student is a more diverse student body. College students vary more now than they did during the 1970s in age (as the population has aged and more older students have enrolled in college), minority composition (reflecting population changes and enrollment growth among some minorities), and attendance status (as more students have enrolled part-time). Most of these changes in the composition of the student body occurred during the 1970s, rather than during the 1980s or 1990s.

---

[5]All data in this section are student counts. Except for Table 1-2, all enrollment data are from the U.S. Department of Education's Integrated Postsecondary Education Data System (IPEDS). IPEDS includes all students enrolled in for-credit courses; it excludes students enrolled *only* in noncredit or continuing education courses.

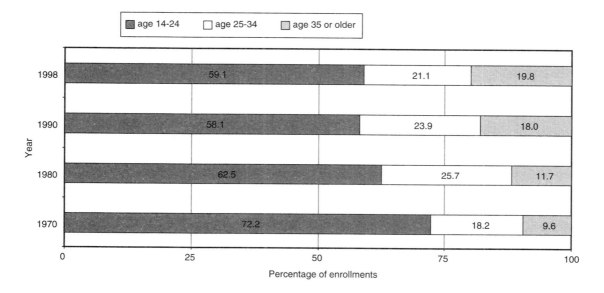

FIGURE 1-5 Distribution of fall enrollments in degree-granting institutions, by age group: 1970, 1980, 1990, and 1998.

SOURCE: Data from Snyder (2001, p. 204).

As shown in Figure 1-5, the proportion of young college students (under age 25) declined from 72 percent to 63 percent during the 1970s. This change was driven by increasing enrollment rates among older students and by the changing age distribution of the population. Although this proportion declined further (to 58 percent) during the 1980s, by 1998 the proportion of young college students had increased slightly to 59 percent (reflecting primarily the strong increases in enrollment rates among recent high school graduates seen earlier in Figure 1-3).

The projected increases in the size of the college-age population (discussed above as the "young adult population") and increasing enrollment rates among these college-age adults (Figure 1-3) suggest that future college enrollment growth may be concentrated among younger students rather than older students, as was the case during earlier decades. But labor market trends, discussed in a later section, may increase the enrollments of older students, *assuming* postsecondary institutions are seen as a viable alternative for worker training; this is a more difficult trend to predict.

The 1970s also saw a relatively large shift in enrollments from male to female and from full-time to part-time (Figures 1-6 and 1-7). Female enrollments rose from 41 percent to 51 percent of all enrollments during this decade, while part-time enrollments increased from 32 percent to 41 percent. Since 1980, however, the proportion of students who are female has increased only from 51 percent to 56 percent, and the proportion of students attending part-time has remained

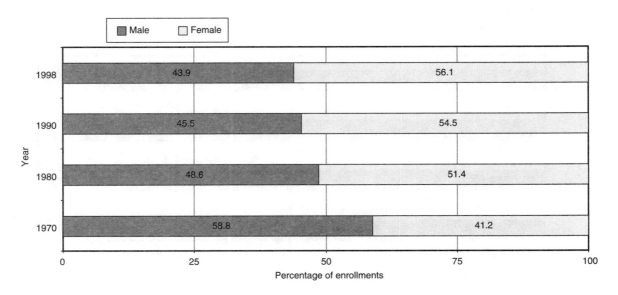

FIGURE 1-6 Distribution of fall enrollments in degree-granting institutions, by sex: 1970, 1980, 1990, and 1998.

SOURCE: Data from Snyder (2001, p. 204).

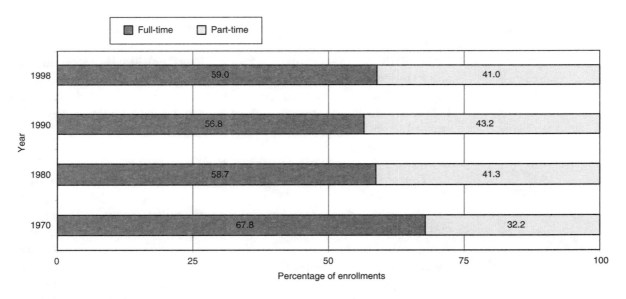

FIGURE 1-7 Distribution of fall enrollments in degree-granting institutions, by attendance status: 1970, 1980, 1990, and 1998.

SOURCE: Data from Snyder (2001, p. 204).

fairly constant. Thus, in terms of age, sex, and attendance status, there has been relatively little change in the student body over the last two decades, even as enrollments have increased.

The growing predominance of females in college has created concern in some quarters about the absence of males (e.g., Mortenson, 1999). A closer look at the enrollment rates of males and females in postsecondary education suggests that males are increasingly less likely than females to enroll in college (Table 1-2), but it is unclear how this finding should be interpreted. Male college enrollment rates were artificially high during the late 1960s and early 1970s, when young men could receive a draft deferment by enrolling in college. The 1970s also ushered in the women's movement, with changing mores that have, over time, made it more acceptable for young women to postpone marriage and childbearing in order to further their education. So the higher enrollment rates of males relative to females in the 1970s reflect both an inflated rate for males caused by the Vietnam War, and a deflated rate for women caused by more traditional mores.

While both male and female enrollment rates have been increasing since 1980 (for females since 1970), the increase has been larger for females than for males, so that by 1999, females' enrollment rate was 1.4 percentage points higher than the rate for males. One might assume that "equal access" implies that male and female college participation rates should now be equal. However, to the extent that the labor market provides good-paying jobs that do not require a college education in traditionally male-dominated fields (such as construction), the labor market may serve as a greater deterrent to college attendance for males than for females. Differences in pay between males and females may also encourage females to obtain more education in order to have earnings that match those of males. (In 1998, among those with income, males aged 16–24 and 25–34 earned more than females in the same age groups [U.S. Census Bureau, 2000].) In sum, it is difficult to tell whether sex differences in pay or job opportunities (or job interests) lead to these differential participation rates, or whether the lower rate of males reflects a more systemic educational problem facing males in today's society. These uncertainties about the causes and interpretations of these trends make it difficult to predict whether and to what extent females' participation rate will continue to outstrip that of males.

TABLE 1-2 Enrollment in Two- and Four-Year Colleges of Persons Aged 14–34, by Sex: October 1970, 1975, 1980, 1990, and 1999

Sex	1970	1975	1980	1990	1999
Male	14.6	14.9	13.0	13.6	15.0
Female	9.2	11.6	12.8	14.4	16.4

SOURCES: *Current Populations Survey*, October supplement, 1999; U.S. Census Bureau, special tabulations.

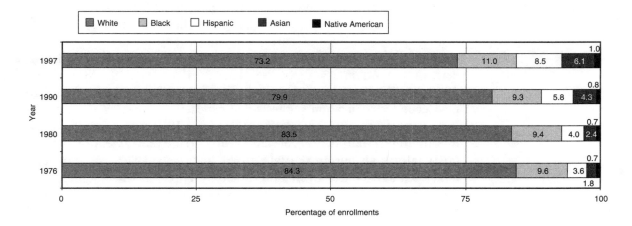

FIGURE 1-8 Distribution of fall enrollments in degree-granting institutions, by race/ethnicity: 1976, 1980, 1990, and 1997.

SOURCE: Data from Snyder (2001, p. 236).

The racial/ethnic composition of the student body *has* changed significantly during the last two decades (Figure 1-8).[6] From 1980 to 1997, White students aged 14–34 declined from 84 percent to 73 percent of all enrollments; this decline was accompanied by increases among all minority groups, but particularly among Hispanics and Asians. For example, from 1980 to 1997, the proportions of students who were Black or Native American increased only slightly (from over 9 percent to 11 percent, and from 0.7 percent to 1 percent, respectively), while the proportions who were Hispanic or Asian each more than doubled.

These changes in student-body composition partly reflect changes in the young adult population. Over the same time period, the proportion of 14–34 year olds who were White declined from 81 percent to 66 percent, the proportion of Blacks increased from 10 percent to 13 percent, and the proportion of Hispanics and other minorities more than doubled. The increases for Blacks and other non-Hispanic minorities also reflect increasing college participation rates over time. In fact, the proportion of Black students enrolled in postsecondary education did not increase until the 1990s, the decade in which their participation rate increased (Table 1-3). Among other non-Hispanic minorities,[7] representation in postsecondary education and participation rates increased

---

[6]Since Hispanics were not separately identified in federal data collections until the mid-1970s, data by race/ethnicity cannot be provided for 1970.

[7]The *other minority* category in Table 1-3 includes Asians and Native Americans. In 1980, 72 percent of this combined group consisted of Asians; by 1999, 82 percent of the group consisted of Asians.

TABLE 1-3 Enrollment in Two- and Four-Year Colleges of Persons Aged 14–34, by Race/Ethnicity: October 1975, 1980, 1990, and 1999

Race/ethnicity	1975	1980	1990	1999
White	13.7	13.5	14.8	16.6
Black	10.7	10.4	10.7	14.6
Hispanic	9.9	8.2	6.7	9.6
Other minority	17.3	17.0	18.8	23.0

SOURCES: *Current Populations Survey,* October supplement, 1999; U.S. Census Bureau, special tabulations.

during both the 1980s and 1990s. The participation rate for Hispanics, however, did not increase during these decades, suggesting that their increased representation in postsecondary education reflects only their increased representation in the population.

The stagnant participation rate of Hispanics in postsecondary education may be due partly to changes in the size and composition of the immigrant population over time. The main areas from which the United States attracts Hispanic immigrants are Mexico, Cuba, the Dominican Republic, Central America, and South America (Guzmán, 2001). The rate of immigration from these countries grew dramatically during the 1980s and 1990s, from 147,880 annual immigrants in the 1970s to 405,737 annual immigrants in the 1990s (U.S. Census Bureau, 1992, 2000). As a result, the percentage of the U.S. Hispanic population that is foreign born increased from 25 percent in 1980 to 39 percent in 2000. Hispanic immigrants are also increasingly likely to come from Mexico and Central America, rather than other countries. During the 1970s, immigrants from Mexico and Central America comprised 52 percent of immigrants from the countries listed above; during the 1990s (up to 1998), they comprised 72 percent of these immigrants (U.S. Census Bureau, 1992, 2000).

The net result of these racial/ethnic group trends suggests mixed progress in minority participation in postsecondary education. To summarize this progress, Table 1-4 presents an indicator of the extent to which each racial/ethnic group was overrepresented or underrepresented in postsecondary education in 1975 and 1999. As the table shows, Blacks have achieved a more equitable participation in postsecondary education over time, as their underrepresentation has shrunk in size, and Asians (the predominant group in the *other minority* category) have increased their overrepresentation in postsecondary education. Hispanics, however, not only remain underrepresented in postsecondary education but also were more underrepresented in 1999 than in 1975.

Finally, Table 1-5 shows that the increase in female enrollments from 1976 to 1997 reflects increases in female participation among all racial/ethnic groups. However, the nature of the increase varies by racial/ethnic group. Among Blacks, enrollments have been predomi-

TABLE 1-4 Index of Degree, Those Aged 14–34, Racial/Ethnic Groups are Over- or Underrepresented in Two- and Four-Year Colleges: 1975 and 1999

| | Index | |
Racial/ethnic group	1975	1999
White	0.04	0.07
Black	−0.19	−0.08
Hispanic	−0.25	−0.41
Other minority	0.29	0.43

SOURCES: *Current Population Survey*, October supplement, 1999; U.S. Census Bureau, special tabulations.
NOTE: An index value greater than 0 signifies overrepresentation in two- and four-year colleges; a value lower than 0 signifies underrepresentation. The index was calculated by dividing the proportion of college students aged 14–34 who are in a racial/ethnic group by the proportion of the population aged 14–34 in the racial/ethnic group and subtracting one from that value.

TABLE 1-5 Percentage of Fall Enrollments in Degree-Granting Institutions Who Are Male, by Racial/Ethnic Group: 1976, 1980, 1990, and 1997

Race/ethnicity	1976	1980	1990	1997
White	53.0	48.5	45.3	44.3
Black	45.5	41.9	38.9	37.3
Hispanic	54.6	49.1	45.2	43.2
Asian	54.8	52.8	51.5	48.6
Native American	50.6	45.1	41.9	41.5

SOURCE: Snyder (2001, p. 237).

nantly female since at least 1976 and have become more so over time. Among Native Americans, enrollments have shifted from a fairly equitable sex division to enrollments that are predominantly female. Finally, among Whites and Hispanics, enrollments have shifted from predominantly male to predominantly female, while among Asians the shift has been from predominantly male enrollments to a fairly equitable sex division. The net result is that as of 1997 females were overrepresented among the enrollments of all racial/ethnic groups except Asians. While equity concerns typically focus on females, in this situation it is the continued and significant underrepresentation of Black males in postsecondary education—relative to other racial/ethnic groups as well as to females—that is particularly troubling. This underrepresentation seems to reflect larger problems in the lives of American Black males that are not, by this indicator, being resolved over time. (Also see the *Annuals of the American Academy of Political and Social Science,* 569, May 2000, a special issue devoted to the American Black male.)

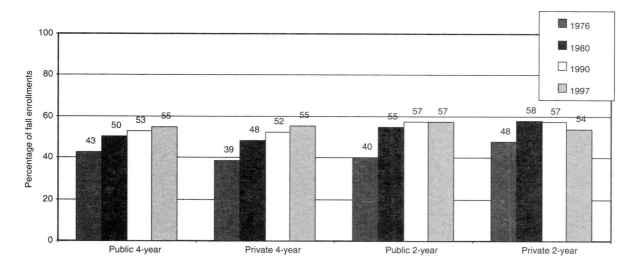

FIGURE 1-9 Percentage of fall enrollments in degree-granting institutions who are female, by institution type: 1970, 1980, 1990, and 1997.

SOURCE: Data from Snyder (2001, p. 208).

Trends Among Institutions

Looking more closely at enrollments in the four basic types of postsecondary institutions helps clarify the nature of the trends noted above. This section examines patterns and trends in the gender and racial/ethnic composition of students in each type of institution.

The percentage of females enrolled does not vary much among different types of institutions, although enrollments at public two-year institutions are slightly more female than are enrollments at other types of institutions (57 percent versus 54–55 percent, respectively; as shown in Figure 1-9). Although the percentage of students who are female increased within each type of institution from 1970 to 1997—with the largest increases in each case occurring during the 1970s—it is only among four-year institutions that female enrollments continued to increase (relative to male enrollments) during the 1990s. Among two-year institutions, the proportion of female students remained constant or declined during the 1990s. It is not clear why the proportion of female enrollments leveled off in two-year institutions; this leveling off could reflect (among other things) a movement of females from two-year to four-year programs and/or a shift in offerings within two-year institutions toward courses and programs that are more appealing to males than to females.

Two-year institutions, in accordance with community colleges' mission of opening access to postsecondary education (e.g., through lower tuition rates, greater geographic accessibility, and more relaxed admissions standards), enroll a higher proportion of minority students

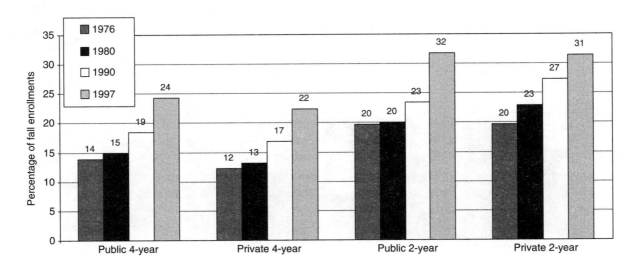

FIGURE 1-10 Percentage of fall enrollments in degree-granting institutions who are minority, by institution type: 1976, 1980, 1990, and 1997.

SOURCE: Data from Snyder (2001, p. 236).

than do four-year institutions (31–32 percent versus 22–24 percent, respectively; as shown in Figure 1-10). However, within the four-year and two-year sectors, public and private institutions enroll roughly equivalent percentages of minority students. This overall enrollment pattern has not changed over time, as increases in minority representation have been roughly equivalent across all four types of institutions.

Looking at specific minority groups (Figures 1-11 through 1-13) shows that within the four-year sector, public and private institutions enroll similar proportions of Black, Hispanic, and Asian students, currently and over time.[8] But within the two-year sector, minority group enrollments vary among public and private institutions. Private two-year institutions enroll a larger proportion of Black students than do public two-year institutions, while the opposite is true for Hispanic and Asian students. Taken together, these data show that the higher representation of minority students in the two-year sector is limited to the higher representation of Black and Hispanic students within these institutions—in particular, to the relatively high representation of Blacks in private two-year institutions and Hispanics in public two-year institutions.

As noted above, minority enrollments increased during both the 1980s and 1990s. For Hispanics and Asians, this trend appears to result from their increased representation in all types of institutions

---

[8]Because of their low representation in postsecondary education, Native American students are not examined separately in this section.

DEMOGRAPHIC AND ATTAINMENT TRENDS IN POSTSECONDARY EDUCATION

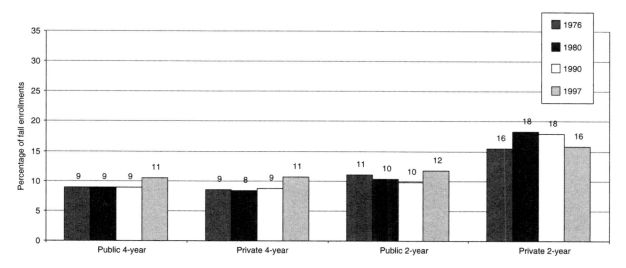

FIGURE 1-11 Percentage of fall enrollments in degree-granting institutions who are Black, by institution type: 1976, 1980, 1990, and 1997.

SOURCE: Data from Snyder (2001, p. 236).

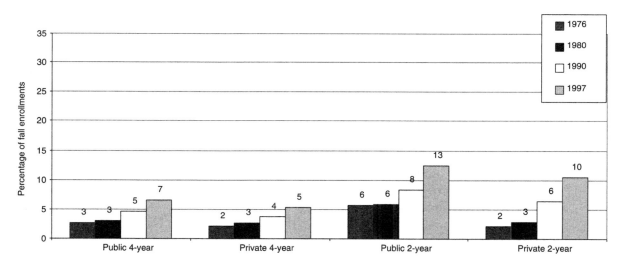

FIGURE 1-12 Percentage of fall enrollments in degree-granting institutions who are Hispanic, by institution type: 1976, 1980, 1990, and 1997.

SOURCE: Data from Snyder (2001, p. 236).

during both decades, but with an especially large increase in the representation of Hispanics within both public and private two-year institutions (Figures 1-12 and 1-13). Figure 1-11 also shows that the overall increase in the proportion of Black enrollments during the 1990s reflects an increasing representation of Black students in four-year institutions and public two-year institutions. The proportion of

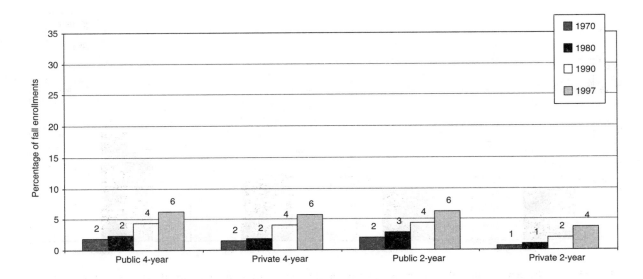

FIGURE 1-13 Percentage of fall enrollments in degree-granting institutions who are Asian, by institution type: 1976, 1980, 1990, and 1997.

SOURCE: Data from Snyder (2001, p. 236).

students enrolled in private two-year institutions who were Black *declined* during the 1990s, suggesting that during this decade Black student enrollments may have shifted from private two-year institutions to public two-year and four-year institutions.

In summary, over the past two to three decades, changes in college enrollments have largely reflected the changing minority composition of the American population. However, the increasing representation of women, Blacks, and Asians reflects both an increasing rate of participation among these groups and (for the two minority groups) their growing representation in the adult population. The growth of Hispanics in postsecondary education, on the other hand, reflects only their increase in the population, not an increasing rate of participation in postsecondary education. Increases also occurred at different points in time for each group. While the 1970s was the primary decade of enrollment growth for women, the 1980s and 1990s were growth decades for Hispanics and Asians, and only the 1990s were a decade of growth for Blacks.

Regardless of their race or sex, most of these students enrolled in postsecondary education to earn a degree. Degree awards are examined next.

DEGREES AWARDED

Bachelor's degrees made up 52 percent of all degrees awarded by postsecondary institutions in 1997–1998. The next most commonly awarded degree was the associate degree, constituting 24 percent of

DEMOGRAPHIC AND ATTAINMENT TRENDS IN POSTSECONDARY EDUCATION

all degrees, followed by the master's degree (19 percent), first professional degrees (3 percent), and doctoral degrees (2 percent). Overall, public institutions award the majority of degrees, 67 percent of all degrees in 1997–1998. With the exception of doctoral degrees, the proportion of degrees awarded by public institutions compared to private institutions declined as the level of the degree increases. For example, in 1997–1998, public institutions awarded 81 percent of associate degrees, 66 percent of bachelor's degrees, 55 percent of master's degrees, and 40 percent of first professional degrees. As will be seen below, this is a change from past decades, when public institutions awarded about two-thirds of all master's degrees.

As one would expect given rising enrollments, the number of degrees awarded increased from the 1970s through the 1990s (Table 1-6), with an overall increase of 65 percent from 1970–1971 to 1997–1998. (Over the same time period, enrollments increased 67 percent.) The marked growth in associate degrees over this period (121 percent) is the result of both the expansion of the community college system during the 1970s and the addition of for-profit private schools to

TABLE 1-6 Number of Degrees Awarded by Degree-Granting Postsecondary Institutions and Percentage Change in Number of Degrees Awarded, by Type of Institution and Level of Degree: 1970–1971, 1982–1983, and 1997–1998

Institution and degree type	Number of degrees awarded in:			% change in number of degrees, 1982–1983 to 1997–1998
	1970–1971	1982–1983	1997–1998	
All institutions				
Associate degree	252,311	449,420	558,555	24
Bachelor's degree	839,730	969,510	1,184,406	22
Master's degree	230,509	289,921	430,164	48
Doctoral degree	32,107	32,775	46,010	40
First professional degree	37,946	73,054	78,598	8
Total degrees	1,392,603	1,814,680	2,297,733	27
Public institutions				
Associate degree	215,645	377,617	455,084	21
Bachelor's degree	557,996	646,317	784,296	21
Master's degree	151,603	176,246	235,922	34
Doctoral degree	20,788	21,186	29,715	40
First professional degree	16,139	29,757	31,233	5
Total degrees	962,171	1,251,123	1,536,250	23
Private institutions				
Associate degree	36,666	71,803	103,471	44
Bachelor's degree	281,734	323,193	400,110	24
Master's degree	78,906	113,675	194,242	71
Doctoral degree	11,319	11,589	16,295	41
First professional degree	21,807	43,297	47,365	9
Total degrees	430,432	563,557	761,483	35

SOURCE: Snyder (2001, p. 306).

NCES' postsecondary data collection system. Since the second factor artificially inflates counts of associate degrees and private institutions' share of these degrees, trends by degree level are examined in Table 1-6 starting in 1982–1983, the year after for-profit schools were fully incorporated into the data system.

The trend data from 1982–1983 to 1997–1998 show that the number of degrees awarded over this time period increased 27 percent. Although increases occurred at all degree levels and at both public and private institutions, increases were most notable in the private sector and among master's and doctoral degrees. The greater growth in degree awards within the private sector is due primarily to relatively large increases in the number of associate and master's degrees awarded by these institutions. From 1982–1983 to 1997–1998, the number of associate degrees awarded by public institutions increased 21 percent while the number awarded by private institutions increased 44 percent. Similarly, the number of master's degrees awarded by public institutions increased 34 percent, compared to 71 percent in private institutions. As a result, public institutions' share of associate degrees declined over this period from 84 percent to 81 percent, and their share of master's degrees declined from 61 percent to 55 percent (Table 1-7). Because of these declines, the total percentage of degrees awarded by public institutions declined slightly from 69 percent to 67 percent from 1982–1983 to 1997–1998.

As shown below, business degrees account for much of the increase in awards at the master's degree level, and employers are particularly likely to financially support students in these programs. Thus, this relatively large increase in the private sector may result from an increase in employers' willingness to pay for their employees to attain MBAs (making private institutions more affordable to individuals) or because private institutions are increasingly targeting their programs to local business needs. The relatively strong growth among private institutions in associate degrees (which are largely vocational in nature) lends support to the second hypothesis.

TABLE 1-7 Percentage of All Degrees Awarded by Degree-Granting Institutions That Were Awarded by Public Institutions, by Level of Degree: 1982–1983 and 1997–1998

Level of degree	1982–1983	1997–1998
Associate degree	84	81
Bachelor's degree	67	66
Master's degree	61	55
Doctoral degree	65	65
First professional degree	41	40
All degrees	69	67

SOURCE: Snyder (2001, p. 306).

TABLE 1-8 Number of Associate, Bachelor's, and Master's Degrees Conferred by Degree-Granting Institutions: 1997–1998

Field of Study	Associate degrees	Bachelor's degrees	Master's degrees
Agriculture/natural resources	6,673	23,284	4,475
Architecture/related programs	265	7,652	4,347
Area, ethnic, and cultural studies	104	6,153	1,617
Biological/life sciences	2,113	65,868	6,261
Business	104,659	233,119	102,171
Communications	2,368	49,385	5,611
Communications technologies	1,602	729	564
Computer and information sciences	13,870	26,852	11,246
Construction trades	2,172	182	16
Education	9,278	105,968	114,691
Engineering	2,149	59,910	25,936
Engineering technologies	32,748	13,727	1,136
English language/literature	1,609	49,708	7,795
Foreign languages/literatures	543	14,451	2,927
Health professions/related programs	92,031	84,379	39,260
Home economics	8,292	17,296	2,914
Law and legal studies	7,797	2,017	3,228
Liberal arts/humanities/general studies	186,248	33,202	2,801
Library science	96	73	4,871
Mathematics	844	12,328	3,643
Mechanics/repair	10,616	91	0
Multi/interdisciplinary studies	9,401	26,163	2,677
Parks/recreation studies	895	16,781	2,024
Philosophy and religion	94	8,207	1,307
Physical sciences and science technologies	2,286	19,416	5,361
Precision production	11,085	407	15
Protective services	19,002	25,076	2,000
Psychology	1,765	73,972	13,747
Public administration	4,156	20,408	25,144
ROTC/military technologies	22	3	0
Social sciences and history	4,196	125,040	14,938
Theological studies/religious vocations	570	5,903	4,692
Transportation/material moving	1,009	3,206	736
Visual and performing arts	14,980	52,077	11,145
Not classified by field of study	3,017	1,373	868
Total	558,555	1,184,406	430,164

SOURCE: Snyder (2001, p. 306).

FIELDS OF STUDY

Table 1-8 shows that certain fields of study predominate at the three most common degree levels (associate, bachelor's, and master's).[9]

---

[9]Because of their relatively low frequency, first professional and doctoral degrees are not discussed in the remainder of this section.

At the associate degree level, the two predominant degrees are liberal arts/humanities/general studies and business; these two fields represent half of all associate degrees awarded in 1997-1998. At the bachelor's degree level, three disciplines predominate: business, the catch-all category of social sciences and history, and education. These three areas include almost 40 percent of all bachelor's degrees. At the master's degree level, business and education predominate, accounting for half of all master's degrees. Most notable in these figures is the predominance of business degrees. Business is by far the most common degree awarded at the bachelor's level and is the second most common degree at the associate and master's levels.

The different roles of public and private institutions are reflected in the level and types of degrees each awards. As noted above, public institutions granted 81 percent of the associate degrees awarded in 1997-1998. This relatively high proportion indicates the strong role played by community colleges at this degree level. Their role as a transfer institution is also reflected in the field of study for their degree awards. Fully 95 percent of the associate degrees awarded in liberal arts/humanities/general studies in 1997–1998 were awarded by public institutions; this field of study accounted for almost 40 percent of all the associate degrees awarded by public institutions (Snyder, 2001).

Also of note is the relatively greater emphasis on education and lesser emphasis on business in public rather than private institutions. While public institutions awarded 81 percent of all associate degrees, they awarded 86 percent of associate degrees in education and 69 percent of associate degrees in business. Likewise, while public institutions awarded 66 percent of all bachelor's degrees, they awarded 74 percent of bachelor's degrees in education and 59 percent of bachelor's degrees in business. Finally, while public institutions awarded 55 percent of all master's degrees, they awarded 62 percent of education degrees at this level and 39 percent of business degrees. This difference in orientation is important because, as discussed below, the trend in the past few decades has been a shift away from education degrees toward business degrees.

Trends in Fields of Study

Historical data on fields of study are not available for associate degrees[10] and are only available for selected bachelor's and master's degree disciplines. Even these limited data, however, provide an interesting view of how college majors are changing over time.

From 1970–1971 to 1997–1998, increases in the number of bachelor's and master's degrees were driven in good measure by the large and fast-growing field of business (Table 1-9). Bachelor's degrees awarded

---

[10]The NCES classification system for associate degrees has changed over time, so associate degree fields are not comparable across years.

TABLE 1-9 Number of Bachelor's and Master's Degrees Awarded in Selected Fields of Study: 1970–1971 and 1997–1998

Field of study	Number of bachelor's degrees in:		% change	Number of master's degrees in:		% change
	1970-1971	1997-1998		1970-1971	1997-1998	
Computer/information sciences	2,388	26,852	1,024	1,588	11,246	608
Communications	10,802	50,114	364	1,770	5,611	217
Public administration	5,466	20,408	273	7,785	25,144	223
Health professions	25,226	84,379	234	5,749	39,260	583
Business	114,729	233,119	103	25,977	102,171	293
Psychology	38,187	73,972	94	5,717	13,747	140
Agriculture/natural resources	12,672	23,284	84	2,457	4,475	82
Biological/life sciences	35,743	65,868	84	5,728	6,261	9
Visual/performing arts	30,394	52,077	71	6,675	11,145	67
Engineering	50,046	73,910	48	16,309	25,936	59
Architecture/related programs	5,570	7,652	37	1,705	4,347	155
Physical sciences/science technologies	21,412	19,416	−9	6,367	5,361	−16
Social sciences/history	155,324	125,040	−20	16,539	14,938	−10
English language/literature	64,342	49,708	−23	10,686	7,795	−27
Foreign languages	19,055	12,769	−33	5,217	2,927	−44
Education	176,307	105,968	−40	87,666	114,691	31
Mathematics	24,937	12,328	−51	5,695	3,643	−36
Total number of degrees	839,730	1,184,40	41	230,509	430,164	87

SOURCE: Snyder (2001, pp. 295-296).

in business more than doubled, increasing by over 100,000. At the master's degree level, the number of business degrees almost quadrupled, increasing by over 75,000. Nonetheless, a broad range of fields increased at a faster-than-average rate over this time period, including (in addition to business) computer/information sciences, communications, public administration, health professions, and psychology.

Even during this period of overall growth, several degree fields declined in number. These declining fields of study include physical sciences/science technology, social sciences/history, English language/literature, foreign languages, mathematics, and education (at the bachelor's level only). In general, the shift in the past three decades appears to be away from the humanities and hard sciences toward business, technical, and health fields. This shift in degree awards is consistent with the view that the economy is shifting toward an information services economy and with recent growth in the management, technical, and health care sectors of the labor market (see, e.g., Bureau of Labor Statistics [BLS], 2000 and "The Labor Force" section of this chapter). This shift also could be interpreted as signaling a growing vocationalism in postsecondary education.

THE ROLE OF TECHNOLOGY

New information technologies have the potential to change postsecondary education through three main avenues: virtual universities (universities that offer courses exclusively through the Internet), distance education (courses delivered to remote locations via audio, video, or computer technologies), and new instructional practices offered within traditional settings (see Bransford, Vye, and Bateman, Chapter 6 of this volume for examples). Virtual universities and new instructional practices are not well covered or well identified in current federal data collection systems; other chapters in this publication examine these issues in more detail. NCES has, however, initiated a series of regular data collections on distance education. Currently, two special-focus surveys have been done on this topic, and a third survey is underway. The results of the first two surveys are briefly summarized here.

NCES' first survey on distance education examined the nature and prevalence of distance education among higher education institutions in 1994–1995; the second examined distance education among all two-year and four-year postsecondary institutions in 1997–1998.[11] The more recent survey revealed that about one-third of all postsecondary institutions offered at least one distance education course in 1997–1998, and that many of the institutions that did not planned to do so in the near future. However, half of the institutions stated that they did not offer any distance education programs and did not plan to within the next three years (Lewis, Snow, Farris, and Levin, 1999).

Public institutions were more likely than private institutions to offer distance education courses; about 80 percent of all distance education courses in 1997–1998 were offered by public institutions. Smaller institutions were also less likely than larger institutions to offer distance education courses. Since private institutions are smaller on average than public institutions,[12] private institutions may be less likely to offer distance education because their smaller size makes them less likely to have the institutional capacity to support this type of instruction—or perhaps their smaller size indicates a greater emphasis on a personal approach to education that is inconsistent with the use of distance education.

From 1994–1995 to 1997–1998, there was a significant increase in the use of distance education among higher education institutions. Over this three-year period, distance education course offerings doubled, and distance education degree and certificate programs nearly doubled. Much of this increase was among higher education institutions that had already offered distance education in 1994–1995. As a result, the

---

[11] According to the NCES definitions used in these surveys, *institutions of higher education* are a subset of *postsecondary institutions*.

[12] In fall 1997, the average enrollment at public institutions was 6,530 students; the average enrollment at private institutions was 1,343 (Snyder, 2001, pp. 202 and 286).

percentage of higher education institutions offering distance education courses increased by one-third, and there was no increase in the number of institutions offering distance education programs.

TRENDS IN POSTSECONDARY COSTS AND STUDENT FINANCIAL AID

Extensive analyses have been conducted on college costs and student financial aid (e.g., Berkner, 1998; McPherson and Schapiro, 1998). This chapter merely notes some of the key trends in these financial measures over time and some indicators of their potential effect on postsecondary students. This section focuses on the federal financial aid system, which provides about 70 percent of all student financial aid. (Private foundations, postsecondary education institutions, and state governments are the other main providers of student aid.)

Concerns about the effects of college costs on postsecondary access and completion have grown in recent years, as costs escalated during the 1980s and 1990s (Table 1-10), outpacing both family income and increases in federal financial aid programs (College Board, 2000a, 2000b).

Rising college costs not only increase the need for student financial aid programs, they also raise the costs of these programs, particularly when the demand for postsecondary education also increases—as has been the case in the past two decades. One way the federal government has dealt with these rising program costs has been to shift from a grant-based system to a less costly loan-based system. This trend was exacerbated in 1992, when federal legislation increased the ceiling on federal loan amounts and loosened the needs assessment requirements for loan eligibility. Thus, as Figure 1-14 shows, in the 1980s, average grant aid and loan aid per (full-time equivalent) student were

TABLE 1-10 Average Undergraduate Tuition and Required Fees Paid by Full-Time Equivalent Students in Degree-Granting Institutions, by Type of Institution: Selected Years from 1976–1977 to 1999–2000

Year	Public institutions		Private institutions	
	Two-year	Four-year	Two-year	Four-year
1976–1977	$ 829	$1,807	$4,662	$ 7,420
1980–1981	792	1,628	4,886	7,324
1985–1986	991	2,039	5,679	9,467
1990–1991	1,052	2,410	7,111	11,596
1995–1996	1,355	3,114	7,756	13,386
1999–2000	1,336	3,351	8,107	14,690

SOURCE: Snyder (2001, pp. 344-345).
NOTE: Tuition amounts have been adjusted to constant 1999 dollars.

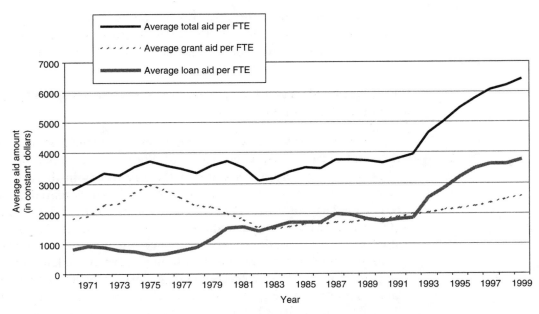

FIGURE 1-14 Average aid per full-time equivalent (FTE) student in constant dollars, overall and by type of aid: 1970-1999.

SOURCE: Data from College Board (2000a) and Snyder (2001, p. 230).

about equal, but since 1992 average loan aid has increasingly out-weighed grant aid.

So while the percentage of students who receive financial aid and the average amount of aid per student have increased (Snyder, 2001; College Board, 2000a), more aid has been awarded in the form of loans than grants. In the mid-1970s, about 20 percent of student aid dollars were distributed as loans, but by 1999, about 60 percent was in the form of loans (College Board, 2000a). In addition, real-dollar funding for the major federal need-based *grant* program (Pell grants) has declined so that the maximum Pell grant in 1999–2000 had a lower purchasing power than it had two decades earlier (College Board, 2000a).

As noted by McPherson and Schapiro (1998), this shift from grants to loans has the net effect of shifting federal aid from support directed to low-income students to support that is more broadly targeted on middle- and upper-middle-income students. This shift is also supported by the newest federal initiatives to financially support students—tuition tax credits. These forms of aid are even more "needs" neutral than student loans and thus represent a further targeting of student aid away from lower-income students toward middle- and upper-income students. These changes would be understandable if increases in college costs and declines in federal aid had negatively affected the ability of students from middle- and upper-income backgrounds to attend college—but, as explained below, there is no evidence that this occurred.

Effect on Student Access

These changes in college costs and federal financial aid have inevitably raised concern about their potential effects on students' access to college, persistence in college, and debt burden. On the surface, the evidence suggests no negative effects—college enrollments have been increasing, even as tuition has gone up and grant aid has gone down. Part of the reason for this seeming lack of effect on access may be that the middle- and upper-income families that have traditionally supplied the majority of college students have not been significantly affected by these changes. Econometric studies (e.g., McPherson and Schapiro, 1998; Kane, 1995) have found that the distribution of student aid and high tuition costs adversely affect the enrollment of low-income students but have little effect on the enrollment of middle- and upper-income students. This differential effect can be at least partially explained by differences in the degree to which cost increases have eaten into family incomes. As the incomes of families at the lowest levels have remained relatively flat, increasing attendance costs have taken a proportionately bigger "bite" out of the pockets of lower-income families. From 1971–1972 to 1998–1999, attendance costs increased from 42 percent to 62 percent of the income of families in the lowest income quintile, but increased only from 13 percent to 16 percent of the income of families in the middle income quintile, and remained at a fairly steady 5 to 6 percent of the income of families in the highest income quintile (College Board, 2000b).

McPherson and Schapiro also found that from 1980 to 1994 a constant proportion of entering freshmen from low-income families enrolled in public two-year colleges, while middle- and upper-income students increasingly chose to attend four-year schools. Specifically, from 1980 to 1994, the percentage of entering freshmen from all income groups who entered public two-year institutions declined from 36 percent to 31 percent, while the percentage of low-income freshmen who entered public two-year institutions remained relatively constant at 46 percent in 1980 and 47 percent in 1994. These findings suggest that trends in college costs and financial aid may be limiting the choice of institutions only among low-income students, as well as decreasing their likelihood of entering any postsecondary institution.

Another indicator of the selective effect of college costs and financial aid policies comes from data on students' immediate transition from high school to college. As seen in Figure 1-15, between 1980 and 1986, the immediate transition rate for Black and Hispanic students declined or remained constant while the rate for White students increased. As a result, the gap in immediate enrollment rates between Whites and each of these minority groups increased from the early 1970s to the late 1990s (NCES, 1999). The divergence in trends during the 1980s might reflect the combination of rising college costs, the shift in federal aid from grants to loans, *and* an American economy in recession. Periods of economic decline may make the joint effects of

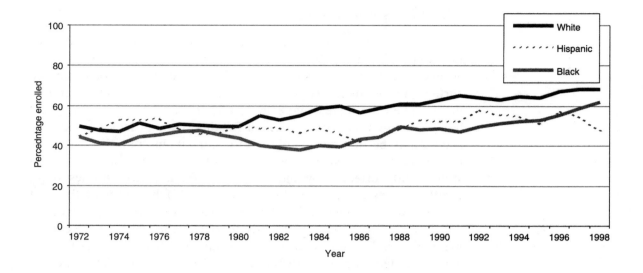

FIGURE 1-15 Percentage of high school completers aged 16–24 who were enrolled in college the October after completing high school, by student race/ethnicity: 1972–1998.

SOURCE: Data from National Center for Education Statistics (2000, p. 149).

NOTE: The 1973-1997 data for Black and Hispanic students are 3-year rolling averages.

high college costs and restricted grant availability more noticeable or widespread than they would otherwise be.

Student Debt Burden

Concerns have also been raised about the effects of student financial aid on students who can attend college only by assuming a significant amount of student loan debt. One concern is that the prospect of assuming a large amount of debt may keep some individuals from entering college or may force some students to leave college prematurely. Another concern is that the debt assumed by students may have detrimental effects on their lives after leaving school. Unfortunately, data to assess these concerns are scarce. Recent news reports suggest that the debt burden assumed by young adults is a growing problem (e.g., *USA Today*, 2001). Not all of a young adult's debt burden is attributable to college debt, of course, but anecdotal evidence suggests that for some young adults, college debt may be an important factor in their total debt burden.

How much debt do students have? Systematic data on this topic are available from a study of 1992–1993 bachelor's degree recipients (Choy and Geis, 1997). This study has two limitations that should be kept in mind. First, the focus on bachelor's degree recipients excludes (1) students who left school without completing a degree, some of whom

TABLE 1-11 Percentage Distribution of 1992–1993 Bachelor's Degree Recipients by Borrowing and Debt Status in 1994

Status as of 1994	%
Never borrowed	51
Borrowed	49
Borrowed and now owe:	
$0	8
$1–5,000	14
$5,000–9,999	13
$10,000–14,999	8
$15,000–19,999	4
$20,000 or more	3

SOURCE: Choy and Geis (1997).

may have dropped out due to excessive debt burden, and (2) individuals who have foregone college enrollment because of potential debt burden. Second, the study reflects the experiences of students who received financial aid *before* the 1992 changes in federal student aid policy that resulted in higher levels of student borrowing.

Choy and Geis (1997) found that about half of all 1992–1993 bachelor's degree recipients had borrowed money for their education, including borrowing from friends or relatives as well as through student loan programs (Table 1-11); the average amount borrowed was $10,200. In 1994, about one year after graduation, 17 percent of these student borrowers no longer owed money, leaving 41 percent of 1992–1993 bachelor's degree recipients in debt; these former students owed, on average, $9,068. The amount owed varied widely, with 14 percent of all bachelor's degree recipients owing less than $5,000, 15 percent owing more than $10,000, and 3 percent owing more than $20,000.

Choy and Geis also examined two potential effects of this debt burden on bachelor's degree recipients—effects on career choices (whether those with more debt were compelled to seek higher salary jobs) and on further postsecondary education (whether those with more debt postponed or gave up on further study). There was no evidence that bachelor's degree recipients with higher amounts of debt gave more weight to income when seeking a job than did other students. Bachelor's degree recipients with more debt, however, were less likely to apply to graduate school or to enroll in further postsecondary study within a year of receiving their bachelor's degree. In addition, 10 percent of student borrowers who had considered but not applied to graduate school stated that high amounts of student debt were a factor in their decision to delay further education.

Because student loan amounts have increased substantially since the time of the Choy and Geis study, it is likely that the amount of student debt has also increased substantially, and the effects of this debt burden may be more extensive now than they were in this study. The next NCES survey of bachelor's degree recipients, in 2001, can be used to address this issue.

A surprising feature of these relatively dramatic trends in postsecondary costs and student aid is their *lack* of dramatic effect on postsecondary enrollments in general (excluding the tentative evidence of negative effects on low-income families). For example, while tuition increases and the shift in state and federal aid from institutions to students should be making the postsecondary education market more competitive, students seem to still be attending the same types of institutions as in the past (at least within the nonprofit sector), at ever-increasing rates.

THE MILITARY OPTION

If college costs too much or is otherwise unappealing to a high school student, the military provides a potential alternative choice.[13] Even though the military "takes" a relatively small proportion of young adults each year (roughly 200,000 new recruits annually), it is an important alternative because of its interest in "high-quality" recruits, and because of the training and education benefits it provides. The military attempts to attract the types of young adults that many colleges and universities would like to enroll (thus competing with postsecondary education), but it also provides service members with a range of education benefits that may encourage their participation in postsecondary education. In fact, military surveys have found that over one-third of 16–21 year olds rate "pay for education" as the single most important reason to consider joining the military.

For the most part, however, the military serves primarily as an alternative to entering the labor market, rather than as an alternative to college attendance. As is true for recruitment into any sector of the labor market, the ease of military recruitment depends on the state of the economy. When the economy is strong and jobs are plentiful, as has been the case in recent years, recruitment is more difficult; conversely, when the economy is in recession and jobs are scarce, recruitment is relatively easy.

Military Recruitment

Military enlistment requirements include an age requirement (generally ages 17–35) and education requirements. The education requirements differ for enlisted personnel (who constitute 85 percent of the military) and for officers (who constitute the remaining 15 percent). With few

---

[13]In this chapter, *military* refers to active-duty personnel in the Air Force, Army, Navy, and Marines. Members of the Reserve Forces and the Coast Guard (which is operated by the Department of Transportation in peacetime and by the Department of Defense in wartime) are not counted here as military.

exceptions, enlisted personnel must have completed high school. Interestingly, this education requirement does not exist to ensure that enlisted recruits have a minimal aptitude (separate aptitude testing requirements exist for this) but to minimize attrition. Military studies have shown that recruits who have not completed high school have a relatively high attrition rate; thus, high school dropouts are not viewed as a cost-effective military investment (Office of the Assistant Secretary of Defense, 2000b).

Military officers typically must have a four-year college degree. Prospective officers can receive their college education through military academies, but few do so. In 1999, for example, only 17 percent of officer accessions, or 2,859 new recruits, entered the services from military academies (Office of the Assistant Secretary of Defense, 2000a). The majority of officer accessions come from ROTC programs at participating colleges and universities or from other postbaccalaureate routes. Thus, although military academies can serve as an alternative college provider for prospective officers, the academies' relatively small size and limited training capabilities (e.g., they do not train military doctors or lawyers) mean that they are a "small-time" competitor for traditional postsecondary institutions. Nonetheless, military academies do tend to be highly selective, attracting students that many other colleges would also like to enroll.

The military strives to enlist personnel who perform well both in training and on the job. To ensure that this goal is met, every potential new recruit into the military takes the Armed Services Vocational Aptitude Battery (ASVAB). One component of the ASVAB, the Armed Forces Qualification Test (AFQT), assesses math and verbal skills. The military uses the AFQT to predict trainability and job performance; it serves as the screening device to ensure that new recruits meet the military's targets for "high-quality" enlistments. In 1981, about 20 percent of new recruits came from the lowest allowable training level (of five levels) on the AFQT. Since that time, regulations have been put into place to ensure that few new recruits are at this low level; as a result, fewer than 2 percent of new recruits in 1999 were at the lowest allowable training level. The percentage of new recruits at the middle two AFQT levels increased from 49 percent in 1981 to 61 percent in 1999, and the percentage of new recruits in the highest two AFQT levels increased from 30 percent to 37 percent.

Partly because of its stringent enlistment requirements, the military does not draw its recruits predominantly from the lower social classes or lower ability levels, as some might believe. For example, in 1999, almost all active duty enlisted accessions had a high school diploma or equivalent, and 93 percent of these accessions held a regular high school diploma (compared to 77 percent of 18-24 year olds in general) (Office of the Assistant Secretary for Defense, 2000a). In addition, the percentage of recruits who score in the below-average category on the AFQT is lower than the percentage among their civilian counterparts.

The military does, however, attract relatively high proportions of Blacks and other non-Hispanic minorities. For example, in 1999, 22 percent of enlisted personnel and 8 percent of officers were Black, compared to 13 percent of civilians aged 18–44. Hispanics, on the other hand, are underrepresented in the military, comprising only 9 percent of the enlisted force and 4 percent of officers, compared to 13 percent of civilians aged 18–44. Women also continue to be underrepresented in the military, although their representation has increased from 2 percent of all enlisted personnel in 1973 to 14 percent in 1999. (All data are from Office of the Assistant Secretary for Defense, 2000a.) This increase in female participation in the military parallels increases in female participation in postsecondary education and (as discussed below) in the civilian labor force.

Over time, the size and composition of the military are largely affected by defense policy, which in turn is sensitive to both political changes (such as the breakup of the Soviet Union) and changes in job demands within the military (e.g., as equipment becomes more technologically complex). From 1973, the year in which the all-volunteer force began, the size of the military was relatively stable until the drawdown of the 1990s. From 1989 to 1999, the active-duty military declined in size from about 1.8 million to 1.1 million (Office of the Assistant Secretary of Defense, 2000a). In the foreseeable future, the size of the military is expected to remain stable at around 1.3–1.4 million, although its "quality" may continue to change in response to a growing reliance on new technologies.

Military Training and the Montgomery GI Bill[14]

The U.S. military is one of the largest training institutions in the world. Virtually every member of the military receives extensive job training upon entry to the service, as well as periodically during his or her service tenure. Formal training, in addition to on-the-job training, is often an important consideration for military promotions. To meet these training needs, the military provides training opportunities at its own "school houses." In addition, the military offers a number of education benefits. Tuition assistance programs are common, and opportunities for paid, full-time college study are provided on a selective basis. For purposes of this chapter, however, the most important education benefit the military provides is the Montgomery GI Bill (MGIB).

Since the end of World War II, the military has offered a "GI Bill" that provides education benefits, including college financial aid, for separating service members. The original purpose of these benefits was to compensate service members for educational opportunities lost while in the conscripted service and to ease their transition to civilian

---

[14]Information in this section of the chapter is drawn from Office of the Assistant Secretary of Defense (2000b).

life. Since the initiation of the all-volunteer force in 1973, the provision of education benefits has served a somewhat different purpose. First implemented in 1984, today's Montgomery GI Bill is intended to ease the transition to civilian life and to serve as a *recruitment* and *retention* incentive. The MGIB provides military personnel with an education fund (to which the service member contributes $1,200) that can be used to pay for college costs at any time from initial separation up to 10 years after separation from the military. In year 2000, the benefit for those who enlisted for at least three years was $536 per month for up to 36 months, or $6,432 per year, for a total potential benefit of $19,296.[15] (In comparison, the 1999 average Pell grant per recipient was $1,923 and the average federal student loan per recipient was $4,667 [College Board, 2000a].)

New military recruits are automatically enrolled in the MGIB program unless they specifically request withdrawal from the program. This policy results in a high enrollment rate, currently around 96 percent. Not all participants use their benefits though. In 1999, 56 percent of eligible veterans had used at least some of their MGIB benefits. This translates to about 650,000 students attending college on an MGIB benefit between 1992 and 1999. Since benefits can be used over a 10-year period and all MGIB-eligible veterans are still within that 10-year timeframe, this usage rate is expected to increase over time.

From an educational perspective, two important effects of the MGIB are not known. One is the extent to which the program increases college enrollments. It is not known how many of the veterans who use the MGIB would have entered postsecondary education without the benefit and how many are enrolling in school primarily because of the availability of the benefit. Second, the college completion rate of veterans who use the MGIB is as yet unknown. Nonetheless, the 56 percent usage rate does suggest that the MGIB is easing the transition to college for many adults. Largely because of the MGIB, today's military may function for some young adults not as an alternative to college but as an alternative entry route to college.

From the military's perspective, the MGIB is a highly successful and valuable program. To ensure that the program continues to function as an effective recruitment and retention incentive, a number of modifications have been proposed by Congress and/or the administration to enhance the MGIB program. These proposals include the following:

• Allowing MGIB benefits to be used by any member of the service member's immediate family;

---

[15]In most branches of the military, additional college funds are available to those who enlist in selected critical or hard-to-fill occupations. These additional funds can increase the total MGIB benefit to $50,000.

• Expanding the program to include coverage of the costs of licensing or certification;

• Expanding the program to cover the costs of "high-tech/short-term" programs offered by business, such as Novell Network Engineer certification courses; and

• Increasing the monthly stipend to cover the average costs of tuition and expenses at public postsecondary institutions and indexing the stipend to changes in education costs.

It is worth noting that these proposed changes suggest a strong interest in expanding the MGIB program to include coverage of education and training programs that are often provided by agencies or institutions other than the colleges or universities.

THE LABOR FORCE

Like the military, the civilian labor force serves as an alternative pursuit to college enrollment for students leaving high school. As is also true of the military, the labor market often provides incentives for college study by requiring initial or further skill development that can be obtained through postsecondary education (e.g., continuing education requirements for doctors), by offering raises or promotions for those who obtain further education, and through the provision of employer financial support for workers who go to college.

Labor Force Composition and Trends

In 1999, about 139.4 million adults aged 16 and older were in the U.S. civilian labor force. In comparison, 68.4 million adults were out of the labor force (U.S. Census Bureau, 2000). Among adults aged 16 and older, this represents a labor force participation rate of 67 percent. Among those in the prime working years, aged 25–64, the labor force participation rate is 80 percent. The labor force participation rate is related to education level, as those with higher levels of education participate at higher rates than those with lower levels of education. For example, in 1999, 63 percent of adults aged 25–64 with no high school diploma participated in the labor force, as did 78 percent of those with only a high school diploma, 83 percent of those with only some college, and 88 percent of college graduates (U.S. Census Bureau, 2000).

Over the decades, the labor force participation rate has been rising, primarily because of women's increased participation. From 1950 (the earliest year of published data) to 2000, women's participation rate has increased while men's participation rate has decreased. Since 1965, women's participation rate has increased faster than the rate for men has decreased, resulting in a steady increase in the rate of overall labor force participation, from 59 percent in 1965 to 67 percent in

2000.[16] The declining participation rate for men appears to be due to changing policies concerning social security, disability benefits, and pension benefits, which have made it easier for men, particularly older men, to leave the labor market (Fullerton, 1999).

The Labor Force in Postsecondary Education

Some adults who are in the labor force are also enrolled in postsecondary education, either because they are students who need to work to pay for their schooling or because they are workers who have decided to return to school. In 1995–1996, about 13.3 million of the 19.5 million students who were enrolled in postsecondary education (68 percent) were also in the labor force. This suggests that in 1995 about 10 percent of the total labor force was enrolled in college. About 3.9 million of these working students (20 percent of all students, and 3 percent of the labor force) defined themselves primarily as employees who were going to school ("student employees"), a group that is in many ways distinct from other students.

Among undergraduates, student employees tend to be concentrated in public two-year institutions, suggesting that workers seeking further education and training are particularly likely to attend public two-year institutions (which are primarily community colleges). In 1995–1996, 67 percent of undergraduate student employees were enrolled in public two-year institutions, 17 percent in public four-year institutions, 5 percent in private for-profit institutions, and most of the remaining 11 percent in private four-year institutions (Lee and Clery, 1999).

The Demand for Skills

Historically, skill demands in the labor market have increased over time, and the recent past is no exception. For example, a 1994 national survey of employers found that 57 percent reported that skill demands were increasing for jobs in their companies while only 2 percent reported a decline in skill demands (National Center on the Educational Quality of the Workforce, 1995). Nonetheless, the majority of all current labor market jobs do not require education beyond the high school level. In 1998, 72 percent of all occupations required only work experience or on-the-job training. In comparison, 7 percent of all occupations required an associate degree or vocational training, and 22 percent required a bachelor's degree or higher (BLS, 2000). Because these requirements are based primarily on the education composition of labor market participants, they closely match the education level of the population. In 1998, 7 percent of adults age 25 or

---

[16]From 1965 to 2000, women's participation rate rose from 35 percent to 60 percent, while men's participation rate dropped from 81 percent to 75 percent. (These labor force participation data are from the Bureau of Labor Statistics Web site http://stats.bls.gov.)

older had an associate degree, and 24 percent had a bachelor's degree or higher (Snyder, 2000).

Occupational projections suggest that the largest *number* of new jobs in the coming decade will be in occupations that require only short-term on-the-job training, mainly because that is the education requirement for most of today's existing jobs (BLS, 2000). Job *growth*, however, is more concentrated in jobs that require postsecondary education. Projections of employment growth from 1998 to 2008 show that 57 percent of new jobs will be in occupations that do not require postsecondary education, 11 percent will be in occupations that require an associate degree or vocational training, and 33 percent will be in occupations that require a bachelor's degree or higher (BLS, 2000). The faster-than-average growth among jobs that require postsecondary education is expected to result mainly from increases in health and computer-related occupations. For example, among occupations at the associate degree/vocational training level, the fastest-growing occupations are registered nurses, computer support specialists, and licensed practical nurses. At the bachelor's degree level, the fastest-growing occupations are computer systems analysts, general managers/executives, and computer engineers. These projections reflect where growth has occurred in the recent past—and, as seen above, are largely consistent with recent trends in degree fields of study, where growth has been most pronounced in business, technical, and health fields.

Skill demands in the labor market appear to be increasing both because of the changing nature of the labor market as a whole (i.e., the shift to higher skill jobs) and because the skills required for specific jobs are also increasing. This increase in skill demands is reflected in increasing proportions of workers participating in work-related education activities (including college enrollment). These increases are particularly notable among workers in the trades occupations and in sales and service occupations, as opposed to professional occupations (Creighton and Hudson, 2002).

Employer Financial Support

Employers often provide support for the further education of their employees, including participation in postsecondary education. For example, in a 1995 survey of business enterprises with at least 50 employees, the BLS found that 61 percent of these employers offered tuition reimbursement programs in 1994 (Frazis, Gittleman, Horrigan, and Joyce, 1997). This training practice was second only to the financing of off-site training (including conference attendance) among the education and training benefits provided by employers.

Another perspective on the role of employers in supporting postsecondary education comes from surveys of college students. This perspective shows that while many employers offer tuition assistance, relatively few college students receive it. Using the NCES National Postsecondary Student Aid Study, Lee and Clery (1999) found that

6 percent of all undergraduates in 1995–1996 (about 700,000 undergraduates) received financial aid from their employers. However, among undergraduates who consider themselves to be primarily employees who are going to school, a much higher percentage—25 percent—received employer aid. Employer financial aid is also more common among graduate students than among undergraduates; among graduate students who considered themselves primarily employees, 42 percent received employer aid.

Lee and Clery (1999) also found that students in some fields of study were more likely than those in others to receive employer aid. At the undergraduate level, over one-third of students enrolled in business, engineering, and computer/information science programs received employer aid, compared to one-quarter of those in health programs and no more than one-fifth of those in other program areas. At the graduate level, students in business programs were more likely to receive employer aid than were students in all other program areas (14 percent versus no more than 6 percent). These findings suggest that recent growth in business and computer-related degrees may be partially the result of employer support for workers to obtain these degrees.

Yet another perspective on employer support for postsecondary education comes from surveys of adults. Lee and Clery (1999) also used NCES' Adult Education Survey to examine the extent to which adults received employer support for their participation in "credential programs." Because of ambiguity in the definition of this term, credential programs may include vocational training programs and noncredit courses taken to receive continuing education requirements or other formal credentials, in addition to for-credit college enrollments. Among adults in these programs, 24 percent received employer financial support, and 33 percent received some other form of employer support (such as time off from work). About half of adults in credential programs (53 percent) received one or the other type of employer assistance.

The likelihood of receiving employer financial aid for a credential program varied depending on one's occupation, with workers in occupations that have higher skill demands (and workers with higher incomes) being more likely to receive employer financial support than those in occupations with lower skill demands (and lower incomes). For example, in 1995, one-half of executives, administrators, and managers who enrolled in credential programs received financial assistance from their employers. This figure compares to 10 percent of those employed in marketing and sales and 4 percent of those who were handlers, cleaners, helpers, or laborers (Lee and Clery, 1999). These findings suggest that employer support for college education may increase in the future, as the labor market (slowly) shifts to the management and technical jobs that employers most often support.

The findings summarized above demonstrate one important difference between federal student financial aid and employer aid. While the federal government provides financial support for postsecondary education for the benefit of society, employers provide this support primarily for the benefit of their company. This goal means that employers tend to financially support those workers who are most likely to increase company productivity or profitability as a result of their education—i.e., managers, skilled technical workers, and other high-skill, high-demand workers who cannot be easily hired with the requisite skills or who cannot continue to function effectively without further education. Thus, while employer aid can and does support postsecondary education, it tends to do so in a way that further exacerbates differences between the educational "haves" and "have nots."

One reason so many employers provide tuition assistance is that federal policy provides incentives to employers to do so through "Section 127" benefits. This legislation allows employers to provide their employees (as of 2000) up to $5,250 tax-free to pay for undergraduate tuition. Employers have the additional incentive of not having to pay their share of the FICA contribution on this funding (i.e., the aid does not count as earnings). Current Section 127 legislation had been scheduled to expire in December 2001, but the Economic Growth and Tax Relief Act of 2001 recently made these benefits permanent, which means that this policy will be in place for at least the next 10 years (when the new Act expires). The 2001 Act also extended these benefits to cover graduate school tuition. Both the long-term provision of this benefit and its extension to graduate school may further encourage employer support for postsecondary education, and thus may further encourage the participation in postsecondary education of working adults.

Postsecondary Institutions as a Provider of Worker Training

In addition to postsecondary education, workers often receive other types of education and training, much of it provided by their employer. The 1995 BLS survey of employers found that 93 percent of enterprises that have at least 50 employees provided some type of formal training for their workers and that 70 percent of workers in these enterprises received formal employer-provided training over a one-year period (Frazis et al., 1997). Postsecondary institutions are a source for some of this employer-provided training but not the bulk of it. According to the BLS survey, only 17 percent of employers used postsecondary institutions as a training source for employer-provided training (BLS, 1996).

Another perspective on the role of postsecondary education as a provider of adult education and training comes from the 1995 NCES Adult Education Survey. This survey shows that among all adults who took courses that were *not* part of a credential program, postsecondary institutions were the instructional provider for 31 percent of these adult learners, second only to business and industry (36 percent) (Hudson, 1999).

The Adult Education Survey also found that, although half of adults enrolled in postsecondary institutions were taking courses leading to a credential, half were not. This implies that adults are as likely to use postsecondary institutions for noncredential purposes as for credential purposes. This finding is inconsistent with NCES student surveys showing that most students are enrolled in degree programs.[17] This inconsistency suggests that a significant amount of continuing education and other noncredit course taking is occurring within postsecondary institutions that is not captured by NCES' regular student surveys. This limitation, in turn, implies that the student enrollment data discussed earlier in this chapter show how postsecondary institutions are used by only about half of those who receive instruction from these institutions.

One type of college course taking that is missing from NCES surveys is course taking designed to lead to an industry or company credential only. Not much is yet known about these activities. Adelman (2000) has recently examined credentialing in the information technology (IT) industry, the largest sector of the industry credentialing movement. His data show that while IT credentials were virtually unheard of a decade ago, as of January 2000, 1.7 million credentials had been awarded by the IT industry. It would appear that the credentialing "movement" is well underway in the IT industry. A less advanced, but broader effort to encourage industry credentialing is being advanced by the National Skill Standards Board (NSSB), an organization initiated by the National Skill Standards Act of 1994. The NSSB is a coalition of leaders from business, labor, employee, education, and community organizations who are working to build "a voluntary national system of skill standards, assessments, and certification systems" to enhance workforce development. The NSSB proposes to develop skill standards in 15 industry sectors. At present, standards have been developed in the manufacturing and the sales and service industries; standards are under development in the education and training and the hospitality and tourism industries. It is not yet clear how the work of the NSSB will link to postsecondary education, but the general goal seems to be to develop a credentialing system that is industry-based, portable, and ultimately international in scope—much like the existing IT credentialing system.

These initiatives raise questions about the trade-off between a broad, formal education and a more narrow credentialing of skills. Most educators would argue that the acquisition of narrow skills *instead of* a broad education is a bad choice for individuals, reducing their labor market flexibility (as well as their general intellectual foundation). But as occupations become increasingly specialized and technical, the credentialing of skills instead of or *in addition to* general educa-

---

[17]For example, the 1995–1996 National Postsecondary Student Aid Study found that only 3 percent of beginning postsecondary students were *not* enrolled in a degree or certificate program (Kojaku and Nunez, 1998).

tional credentialing is likely to grow in popularity. It remains to be seen what role postsecondary institutions should and will play in this credentialing movement.

SUMMARY

From the national data, postsecondary education appears to be doing quite well. Enrollment levels, enrollment rates, and degree completions have been increasing, in decades when the size of the college-age cohort was shrinking, costs were rising, and student aid was uneven at best. Further, since one of the key predictors of college attendance is whether one's parents went to college (see, e.g., Kane, 1994), postsecondary education is also reinforced through a self-perpetuating process: The more adults there are who have a college education, the more children there will be in the next generation who also seek a college education. In turn, the more highly educated workers there are in society, the more high-skill jobs the economy can support, further increasing education and skill demands. Given these trends, plus projections of a growing cohort of college-age adults in the next few decades, postsecondary education would seem to be in a good position overall.

But the national data also hint at some potential problems. Increasing college costs may be limiting access for some students, student loan programs may lead to undesirable debt burdens, and business and industry appear to be pushing for credentialing processes that could operate independently of the postsecondary education system. Surveys of employers and adults also show that the majority of adult course taking occurs outside of postsecondary education. Taken together, these findings suggest that the combination of a cost-restricted postsecondary education system on the supply side and a growing interest in further education on the demand side may be setting the stage for the growth of alternative education systems and providers.

As the other chapters in this volume demonstrate, postsecondary institutions *are* increasingly adopting new missions, new education programs, and new instructional delivery strategies, while new providers (e.g., virtual universities, corporate universities, industry credentialing agencies) are offering a wider range of alternative learning routes. Unfortunately, these alternative strategies and systems are not well covered in national data systems, so they do not appear in the portrait of postsecondary education created by these data.

It is reasonable to ask why these alternative systems are so difficult to assess within a national data collection. The basic problem is that alternative and emerging systems often do not meet the criteria necessary for cost-effective collection of systematic, reliable data. First, a national data collection depends on a clear and consistent definition of all the entities from which one intends to draw a survey sample. Thus, before one can survey postsecondary institutions, one must operationally define them and then be able to identify all institutions that meet the definition. This task becomes more difficult when new institutions open and close at a rapid rate or when institutions or systems emerge that do not fit existing definitions. Data collections also rely on the willingness of survey participants to share information and on their capacity to provide information. Both of these respondent characteristics are often compromised in new and emerging systems. For-profit postsecondary education institutions, for example, are sometimes unwilling to respond to surveys for fear that their competitors will learn too much about them. Finally, new alternatives are by definition different from the norm, so that existing survey instruments and procedures may simply be unable to capture or describe them.

In short, it is always difficult for national surveys to accurately capture an emerging system or a system in flux. So national data collections are probably not the best source for finding out what is happening "at the margins." This is not to say that the current data collection system for postsecondary education cannot or should not be improved. There are a number of ways in which the current system could be adapted to better capture the full breadth of education alternatives facing adults. Three proposals are suggested here.

First, until better methods are devised for capturing information directly from alternative providers, the best source of information on these providers is the adults who enroll in education programs. The NCES Adult Education Survey is our best source of information on adults, but its sample size is typically too small to allow analysis of participation in activities that may be relatively new and small scale. A larger sample of adults is needed. Second, it would be useful to regularly survey employers about existing policies and practices that may influence workers' participation in traditional postsecondary education and other forms of learning. Previous employer surveys have been conducted (but discontinued) by the Department of Labor and the Department of Education; perhaps a joint Labor-Education survey effort should be attempted. Finally, more focused surveys, such as the NCES surveys on distance education, are needed to monitor emerging delivery systems that cannot be captured in existing surveys. Potential topics for these focused surveys include customized training, continuing education, the use of new technologies in traditional classrooms, and institutions' role in industry certification.

To end on a positive note, existing federal data sources provide a wealth of information about the traditional postsecondary education system, only a small part of which could be included in this chapter. We know much more about postsecondary education today than we ever have in the past and—even with a moving target—our knowledge is sure to improve in the future.

REFERENCES

Adelman, C. (2000). A parallel universe. *Change*, *32*(3), May/June, 20–29.
Berkner, L. (1998). *Student financing of undergraduate education: 1995–96* (NCES 98-076). Washington, DC: U.S. Department of Education, National Center for Education Statistics.

Berkner, L. (2000). *Trends in undergraduate borrowing: Federal student loans in 1989–90, 1992–93, and 1995–96* (NCES 2000-151). Washington, DC: U.S. Department of Education, National Center for Education Statistics.

Berktold, J., Geis, S., and Kaufman, P. (1998). *Subsequent educational attainment of high school dropouts* (NCES 98-085). Washington, DC: U.S. Department of Education, National Center for Education Statistics.

Boesel, D., Alsalam, N., and Smith, T.M. (1998). *Educational and labor market performance of GED recipients*. Washington, DC: U.S. Department of Education, Office of Educational Research and Improvement, National Library of Education.

Bureau of Labor Statistics. (1996). *BLS reports on the amount of formal and informal training received by employees*. BLS news release, December 16, 1996. Available: http://stats.bls.gov/news.release/sept.nws.htm [October 25, 2001].

Bureau of Labor Statistics. (2000). Charting the projections: 1998–2008. *Occupational Outlook Quarterly, 43*(4) Winter 1999–2000, 8–38.

Choy, S.P., and Geis, S. (1997). *Early labor force experiences and debt burden* (NCES 91-286). Washington, DC: U.S. Department of Education, National Center for Education Statistics.

College Board. (2000a). *Trends in student aid*. New York: College Entrance Examination Board.

College Board. (2000b). *Trends in college pricing*. New York: College Entrance Examination Board.

College Board. (2000c). *1996–2000 profiles of college-bound seniors, SAT national profile reports*. Available: http://www.collegeboard.org/sat/cbsenior/yr1997/nat/cbs1997.html; http://www.collegeboard.org/sat/cbsenior/yr1998/nat/cbs1998.html; http://www.collegeboard.org/sat/cbsenior/yr1999/NAT/cbs1999.html; http://www.collegeboard.org/sat/cbsenior/yr2000/nat/cbs2000.html. [December 10, 2001]

Creighton, S., and Hudson, L. (2002). *Participation trends and patterns in adult education: 1991 to 1999* (NCES 2002-119). Washington, DC: U.S. Department of Education, National Center for Education Statistics.

Frazis, H., Gittleman, M., Horrigan, M., and Joyce, M. (1997). Formal and informal training: Evidence from a matched employee-employer survey. *Advances in the Study of Entrepreneurship, Innovation, and Economic Growth, 9*, 47–82.

Frazis, H., Gittleman, M., Horrigan, M., and Joyce, M. (1998). Results from the 1995 survey of employer-provided training. *Monthly Labor Review, 121*(6), 3–13.

Fullerton, H.N., Jr. (1999). Labor force participation: 75 years of change, 1950–98 and 1998–2025. *Monthly Labor Review, 122*(12), 3–12.

Guzmán, B. (2001). *Census 2000 brief: The Hispanic population*. Washington, DC: U.S. Department of Commerce, U.S. Census Bureau.

Horn, L.J., and Berktold, J. (1998). *Profile of undergraduates in U.S. postsecondary education institutions: 1995–96* (NCES 98-084). Washington, DC: U.S. Department of Education, National Center for Education Statistics.

Hudson, L. (1999). Adult participation in lifelong learning: An examination of noncredential coursetaking. Paper presented at the annual meeting of the Association for Institutional Research, Seattle, WA, May.

Kane, T.J. (1994). College entry by blacks since 1970: The role of college costs, family background, and the returns to education. *Journal of Political Economy, 102*(5), 878–911.

Kane, T.J. (1995). *Rising public college tuition and college entry: How well do public subsidies promote access to college?* NBER Working Paper No. 5164, July. Cambridge, MA: National Bureau of Economic Research.

Kaufman, P., Kwon, J.Y., Klein, S., and Chapman, C.D. (2000). *Dropout rates in the United States: 1999* (NCES 2001-022). Washington, DC: U.S. Department of Education, National Center for Education Statistics.

Kojaku, L.K., and Nunez, A. (1998). *Descriptive summary of 1995–96 beginning postsecondary students* (NCES 1999-030). Washington, DC: U.S. Department of Education, National Center for Education Statistics.

Lee, J.B., and Clery, S.B. (1999). *Employer aid for postsecondary education* (NCES 1999-181). Washington, DC: U.S. Department of Education, National Center for Education Statistics.

Levesque, K., Lauen, D., Teitelbaum, P., Alt, M., and Librera, S. (2000). *Vocational education in the United States: Toward the year 2000* (NCES 2000-029). Washington, DC: U.S. Department of Education, National Center for Education Statistics.

Lewis, L., Snow, K., Farris, E., and Levin, D. (1999). *Distance education at postsecondary education institutions: 1997–98* (NCES 2000-013). Washington, DC: U.S. Department of Education, National Center for Education Statistics.

McPherson, M.S., and Schapiro, M.O. (1998). *The student aid game*. Princeton, NJ: Princeton University Press.

Mortenson, T.G. (1999). Where are the boys? The growing gender gap in higher education. *The College Board Review, 188*, August, 8–17.

National Center for Education Statistics. (1997). *Indicator of the month, subbaccalaureate persistence and attainment*. Washington, DC: U.S. Department of Education.

National Center for Education Statistics. (1999). *The condition of education 1999* (NCES 1999-022). Washington, DC: U.S. Department of Education.

National Center for Education Statistics. (2000). *The condition of education 2000* (NCES 2000-062). Washington, DC: U.S. Department of Education.

National Center for Public Policy and Higher Education. (n.d.). *Measuring up 2000: The state-by-state report card for higher education*. San Jose, CA: Author.

National Center on the Educational Quality of the Workforce. (1995). *First findings from the EQW national employer survey*. Philadelphia: University of Pennsylvania.

Office of the Assistant Secretary of Defense (Force Management Policy). (2000a). *Population representation in the military services: Fiscal year 1999*. Arlington, VA: U.S. Department of Defense, Defense Manpower Data Center.

Office of the Assistant Secretary of Defense (Force Management Policy). (2000b). *Biennial report to Congress on the Montgomery GI Bill education benefits program*. Arlington, VA: U.S. Department of Defense, Defense Manpower Data Center.

Smith, T.M. (1996). *The condition of education 1996* (NCES 96-304). Washington, DC: U.S. Department of Education, National Center for Education Statistics.

Snyder, T.D. (2000). *Digest of education statistics 1999* (NCES 2000-031). Washington, DC: U.S. Department of Education, National Center for Education Statistics.

Snyder, T.D. (2001). *Digest of education statistics 2000* (NCES 2001-034). Washington, DC: U.S. Department of Education, National Center for Education Statistics.

Snyder, T.D. and Hoffman, C.M. (1991). *Digest of education statistics 1991* (NCES 91-697). Washington, DC: U.S. Department of Education, National Center for Education Statistics.

USA Today (2001). Debt smothers young Americans, Feb. 13, pp. 1–2.

U.S. Census Bureau. (1992). *Statistical abstract of the United States: 1992*. Washington, DC: U.S. Government Printing Office.

U.S. Census Bureau. (1996). *Statistical abstract of the United States: 1996*. Washington, DC: U.S. Government Printing Office.

U.S. Census Bureau. (2000). *Statistical abstract of the United States: 2000*. Washington, DC: U.S. Government Printing Office.

2

Community Colleges in the 21st Century: Challenges and Opportunities

Thomas Bailey*

Community colleges account for a substantial share of American higher education. Nearly one-half of all undergraduates in postsecondary institutions in fall 1997 were enrolled in community colleges (NCES, 2000d), and over the span of any given year, more for-credit under-graduate students enroll in community colleges than in baccalaureate-granting institutions. Although data on noncredit education are unreliable, community colleges have large and growing enrollments in noncredit courses. In many community colleges, more students enroll in the noncredit offerings than credit-bearing courses. Moreover, the types of students who enroll in community colleges are precisely those who are of most concern to scholars and policy makers. Indeed, minorities and immigrants are overrepresented in two-year schools. Community colleges are also much more likely than four-year schools to enroll first-generation postsecondary students or students from low socioeconomic backgrounds (NCES, 2000f).

But after several decades of growth, community colleges now face a particularly challenging environment. Changes in pedagogic and production technology; state funding policy; the expectations of students, parents, and policy makers; demographic trends; and the growth of new types of educational institutions and providers are threatening established patterns of community college activities and potentially altering the role of the colleges within the wider land-scape of higher education. In this chapter, I first describe some of the challenges facing community colleges and then articulate the positive

*Thomas Bailey is director of the Institute on Education and the Economy and the Community College Research Center at Teachers College, Columbia University. This chapter is based on research funded by the Alfred P. Sloan Foundation.

trends that may increase the demand for the services of community colleges and possibly lead to growing enrollments. The subsequent section describes how community colleges are responding to the challenges they face. One of the most important responses to those challenges has been a strategy in which the colleges seek new enrollments, revenues, and activities. The next section discusses the controversy about this missions-expansion strategy and identifies the reasons why this is attractive for community colleges. The chapter ends with some assessment of the balance of positive and negative trends with suggestions for policy and research.

CHALLENGES

Throughout the 1960s, 1970s, and part of the 1980s, community colleges enjoyed strong enrollment growth. But in contrast to the previous decades, community college enrollments declined slightly during the 1990s. Total fall enrollments peaked in 1992 at 5.7 million students, but stood at about 5.4 million in 1998 (NCES, 2000d). For the first time, colleges in many states faced declining enrollments, although in some states they turned back up by the end of the decade.

Moreover, during the 1990s, state funding priorities shifted away from higher education as prisons and health care accounted for larger shares of state budgets. Thus the share of state budgets going to higher education shrank from 12.2 percent in 1990 to 10.1 percent in 2000 (National Association of States Budget Officers [NASBO], 2000).

California is a good example. Like many state systems, the California public higher education system went through a severe budget crisis early in the decade. While the economic recovery brought some improvements to state universities and colleges, that improvement did not keep pace with overall economic growth. And as the economy faltered in the first years of the new century, higher education budgets again came under pressure. As a *New York Times* article from September 11, 2001, stated, "State Colleges, Feeling Pinch, Cut Costs and Raise Tuitions."

Moreover, within the public state systems, community colleges must provide an education with fewer resources than their four-year counterparts. For example, in the 1995–1996 school year, instructional expenditures for public community colleges stood at $3,420 per full-time equivalent student, compared to $5,486 for public colleges and $6,946 for public universities (NCES, 2000e).

Changing expectations about educational attainment will also influence community college enrollments. Increasingly, students state that they expect to earn a bachelor's degree. In 1980, 57 percent of all high school seniors stated that they either probably or definitely would graduate from a four-year college program. By 1997 that share had risen to over 77 percent (NCES, 2000f). Baccalaureate aspirations had risen even among students enrolled in community colleges. In the early 1980s, about 45 percent of such students stated that their objective was to earn a bachelor's degree, while in the early 1990s, 70 percent had that goal (Schneider and Stevenson, 1999). As students focus more on earning four-year degrees, we would expect to see enrollments shift towards four-year colleges. Indeed, total enrollments in these institutions did rise between 1995 and 1998 while community college enrollments were stable. And the NCES projects that four-year enrollments will grow faster over the next decade than two-year enrollments (NCES, 2000e).

To be sure, community colleges transfer programs are designed to provide access to four-year programs, but policy makers and researchers continue to criticize low transfer rates. Of those first-time college students who started at a community college in 1989, about 22 percent had transferred to a four-year school five years later (NCES, 2000a) and less than one-tenth of students who begin in two-year colleges ever complete a bachelor's degree (Schneider and Stevenson, 1999). On the other hand, many students start two-year programs without a clear intention of transferring; therefore, it is difficult to evaluate any given transfer level. Nevertheless, as the number of students who do want a four-year degree grows, there will be more pressure to increase transfer rates.

While policy makers pressure colleges to increase their transfer rates, they are also introducing measures that will increase the number of poorly prepared students who are attending these colleges. Developmental courses already absorb resources, and many students in regular college courses continue to need extra help. There are certainly some success stories (Hebel, 1999; Roueche and Roueche, 2001). Developmental education is a central component of the colleges' mission to provide access; however, large numbers of poorly prepared students complicate college efforts to improve transfer and graduation rates.

Over the last two decades, the colleges' social and economic environment has changed. Other institutions—including public and non-profit four-year colleges, community-based organizations, for-profit companies, in-house company trainers, and even other community colleges—compete with community colleges in every function that they carry out. Many public four-year colleges have expanded their continuing education offerings, sometimes even offering full degrees, in an attempt to reach the type of adult and part-time student who have traditionally been served by community colleges. For-profit companies are offering short-term training, preparation for technical certifications, and full degrees at several levels. In the last few years, for-profit educational institutions such as the University of Phoenix and the DeVry Institutes have attracted significant attention as potential competitors. These institutions appear to have been able to attract adult students with strong occupational objectives. In the past, community colleges have prided themselves on being able to service precisely these types of students.

The potential effect of computer-based distance education is perhaps the greatest unknown concerning the nature of the competitive landscape. Certainly to the extent that distance education reduces the need for students to be at a particular place at a particular time and does so at a reasonable cost, the educational market will be a free-for-all. In general, research suggests that distance education is as effective at teaching substance as traditional classroom formats, although the students have to be motivated and organized. Community college professors argue that many of their students need the structure provided by the personal contact in the classroom. But whatever the problems and potentials, distance education is growing rapidly. According to data collected by the NCES, between 1995 and 1997, the share of community colleges offering distance education course grew from 58 to 72 percent. The equivalent shares for public four-year institutions were 62 and 79 percent. Most of the rest of these colleges (two- and four-year) said that they planned to offer courses through a distance education format within three years. (By 1997, private colleges were far behind.) And during those two years, distance education enrollments more than doubled to 1.6 million, although the number of students involved was smaller since these figures represent duplicated headcounts (NCES, 1999a).

Although the continued growth of computer-based distance education seems certain, many questions remain about the impact of those developments on different types of institutions. At this point, most of the students who participate in computer-based distance education also take regular courses at the same institution. So far, students whose only contact with an institution is through an online course are more rare. But what can be said is that the growth and potential of distance education have created tremendous uncertainty in higher education. And community colleges may be at a disadvantage in the online educational race, since they have much more restricted budgets than four-year public schools and lack the for-profits' access to capital markets.

POSITIVE TRENDS

While the colleges certainly face difficult challenges, several current developments are likely to increase the demand for a community college education over the next several years. First, the number of students in the typical college-going age is projected to increase sharply over the next decade. The children of baby boomers (the baby boom echo) are moving through their college years and are expected to expand college enrollments. The NCES projects that two-year college enrollments, which stood at roughly 5.7 million for fall 1999, will grow by 11 to 16 percent over the next decade (Gerald and Hussar, 2000).

In addition, the growing foreign-born population in the United States will also create an increasing demand for community college education. Immigration has already had an impact on college enrollments in California. The City University of New York (CUNY), New York City's public higher education system, was already almost 50 percent foreign born in the fall of 1997 while the population of the city as a whole was about 41 percent foreign born. And within the CUNY system, recent immigrants were overrepresented in the two-year programs (Bailey and Weininger, 2001).

The patterns of postsecondary enrollments have changed over the last two decades, and these trends may also benefit community colleges. Much of the policy and research about college enrollment has often been dominated by a traditional conceptualization in which students attend college full-time immediately after high school and continue their enrollment uninterrupted until they graduate. But this view is increasingly misleading. If we define a traditional student as one who attends college full-time and full-year until they graduate, then only 17 percent of those who started college for the first time in 1989 were traditional students enrolled in four-year institutions. Another 17 percent were traditional students who started in two-year institutions. The remaining 66 percent of all first-time college students could be considered nontraditional students because either they attended part-time, interrupted their studies, or changed institutions. Furthermore, this share of nontraditional students would rise further if we counted students who delayed their first-time entry into college.[1] And data from the High School and Beyond survey, which includes students who should have graduated from high school in the early 1980s, suggest that the number of nontraditional students grew significantly during the 1980s. For example, the percentage of undergraduates who attended more than one institution increased from 40 percent to 54 percent during the 1970s and 1980s, and data from the 1990s suggest that this share will have increased to over 60 percent during the first years of the new decade (Adelman, 1999; NCES, 2000b).

The growth of the importance of these diverse pathways through postsecondary education may favor community colleges, which are more oriented towards nontraditional students than four-year schools. For example, community college students are much more likely to enroll part-time and tend to be older than four-year college students (and therefore delayed or interrupted their enrollment). In 1998, 57 percent of part-time undergraduates were enrolled in community colleges. And 60 percent of four-year college students were 18–24 years old, while 48 percent of all two-year college students were in that prime college-going age (NCES, 2000c).

Developments in technology and its effects on skill requirements will also continue to create a demand for community college education. Projections of the growth of employment in different occupations and trends in the earnings of workers with various levels of education

---

[1]These numbers are based on calculations by the author using data from the Beginning Postsecondary Students (BPS:89/94) survey. This data set, collected by the National Center for Education Statistics, includes a sample of students who entered post-secondary educational institutions for the first time in 1989. It collects data on those students through the 1993–1994 school year.

show that at least some education beyond high school will be necessary to have access to jobs with earnings that might allow an individual to support a family. While college graduates do earn more than those with an associate degree, the value of one year of community college education is more or less equivalent to the value of a year of education at a four-year college. The same can be said for the economic value of credits earned at the two types of institutions (Grubb, 1999a; Kane and Rouse, 1995). Between 1973 and 1998, the share of prime-age workers with some education beyond high school but no bachelor's degree more than doubled from 12 to 27 percent, while the share of the workforce that had a bachelor's degree increased from 16 to 30 percent (Carnevale and Desrochers, 2001). While the role of associate degrees relative to bachelor's degrees remains in flux, these trends indicate that a growing number of jobs in the economy can be effectively held by workers with postsecondary education short of a bachelor's degree.

Weak high school preparation will also continue to create a role for community colleges, essentially giving students a second chance to prepare for college-level work. NCES judged that even among families with incomes above $75,000 a year, less than 60 percent of high school graduates were either highly or very highly qualified for admission to a four-year college. Another 30 percent were either somewhat or minimally qualified. But the levels of preparation for high school graduates from families earning less than $25,000 a year were much worse. Forty-seven percent were not even minimally qualified and only 21 percent were either highly or very highly qualified for admissions to a four-year college (NCES, 2000f). And 40 percent of students at four-year colleges and 63 percent of community college students take at least one remedial course (NCES, 2000b). Moreover, several states, including New York and Georgia, and universities, such as California State University, are now trying to limit access to four-year institutions of students who need remedial help. In the case of CUNY, remedial education is concentrated at community colleges and is being phased out of the 11 four-year colleges. Thus all of these trends indicate that the role of community colleges providing developmental education will continue and probably increase.

In the increasingly competitive postsecondary market, low tuition continues to be one of the community colleges' most important assets. This provides an important buffer against competition in states like California where full-year tuition at a community college in 1997 was less than $500. In contrast, community college tuition in New York State was over $2500 in that year (American Association of Community Colleges [AACC], 2001).

Trends over the last 20 years suggest that the community college tuition advantage over public four-year colleges has grown. In the 1971–1972 school year, four-year college tuition exceeded two-year tuition by $530 (2001 dollars). That gap grew steadily over the subsequent three decades to $2016 for the 2001–2002 school year (College Board, 2001)

THE COMMUNITY COLLEGE RESPONSE

Community colleges therefore continue to enjoy many advantages. These include low tuition, local political support, and favorable demographic and educational trends, at least for the next few years, which will increase the potential supply of students at community colleges. The growing emphasis on noncredit education and on delayed, interrupted, multiple-institutional, and part-time college enrollment favors the more nontraditional history and emphasis of community colleges, at least when compared to public and nonprofit four-year institutions. But increasingly competitive markets, evolving student expectations, and significant changes in funding systems and pedagogic technologies have created a much more volatile and uncertain environment. How have community colleges responded to these developments?

Community college administrators and faculty realize that their students and the public that funds them continue to expect the colleges to provide opportunities to transfer to four-year colleges. Many states are implementing a variety of policies designed to facilitate transfer from both academic majors (the traditional transfer-oriented majors) and occupational majors that have traditionally been viewed as terminal community college programs (AACC, 2001). These policies include common course content and numbering systems that guarantee that credit earned at a community college will be accepted in that state's four-year schools.

Indeed, over the last two decades, many researchers and college administrators and faculty have argued that the fundamental role of the community college is to provide more or less open access to lower division collegiate education. From this point of view, providing transferable liberal arts education is the core function of the colleges. It is through this function that community colleges realize their mission as the nation's primary site of equal access to higher education (Eaton, 1994; Cohen and Brawer, 1996; Brint and Karabel, 1989).

As Eaton (1994) observed:

> The collegiate community college is an extraordinary way for a democratic society to provide the best of higher education to as many people as can reasonably benefit. It is a profound statement of the unique value this country assigns to the individual and of its faith in the future. As a collegiate institution, the community college is unparalleled in providing, sustaining, and expanding educational opportunity and accomplishment within the society. (p. 5)

Although state agencies and college faculty and staff have worked hard to promote transfer, this has not been the primary or most prominent community college response to the financial and political challenges that they have faced over the last decade. Much of the energy and enthusiasm at the college level is focused on other activities. All presidents will articulate their commitment to transfer education, but raising the transfer rate is rarely a college's first priority.

During the last half of the 1990s, many community college staff turned their attention to pedagogic issues. This reform movement seeks to establish and strengthen the "Learning College." Improving the quality of teaching may be one approach to engaging young people and addressing the criticisms that the colleges do a poor job of retaining their students. While this has generated a great deal of useful discussion about teaching, according to Grubb (1999b), so far colleges have not introduced, on a widespread basis, the types of institutional changes necessary to bring about a significant change in teaching.

Thus, many colleges, as a strategy to improve their position and do a better job of serving their constituencies, have tried to reform their current operations. But as a widespread response to budgetary pressure, many community colleges have sought new markets, new students, and new sources of revenues. One indication of this is the dramatic shift in the sources of community college funds. In the past, community colleges have depended primarily on state appropriations. In 1980, 53 percent of all college revenues were accounted for by this source. But by 1996, the state share of revenues had dropped to 34 percent (Merisotis and Wolanin, 2000). The share of local revenues also fell slightly from 17.3 to 15.6 percent. In contrast, the revenue share accounted for by state and federal grants and contracts grew dramatically from 1 percent in 1980 to 18 percent by 1996.

In any case, almost every community college is aggressively developing its noncredit and continuing education programs. The continuing education catalog of a community college will show a wide array of courses, although various types of computer-related training, including preparation for IT certification exams, are increasingly common. At least in terms of the number of students (not FTEs), noncredit enrollments often surpass credit enrollments. These courses outside of the traditional degree streams have many advantages for the colleges. They can be developed with fewer constraints associated with accreditation, state regulation, and faculty prerogatives. In many cases, they can generate surpluses (although in most cases, the accounting does not take account of the costs of space and college administrative overhead). Some noncredit enrollments are generated through customized training contracts with companies. In these cases, specific firms contract with a college (often the resources come from state economic development funds rather than directly from the company) to provide specific training, frequently at the company site (Dougherty and Bakia, 1999). While such contracts represent a minority of noncredit enrollments, they often have a high profile and carry political significance disproportionate to their size, since they solidify partnerships with influential local businesses.

While community colleges have broadened their missions by seeking out new types of postsecondary students, they have also sought to expand their roles vertically—providing education to high school students and in some cases postassociate degree students.[2] The growth of dual enrollment programs for high school students has been one of the most talked-about trends in community colleges over the last year or two. Many colleges have enrolled hundreds of high school students, and, in some cases, those enrollments have increased dramatically in just a few years. College administrators, especially financial officers, are very enthusiastic about these efforts. Most of the offerings are in the social sciences and humanities and therefore do not need expensive equipment. Often, the courses are taught at the high schools and do not require additional space. And the instructors are usually adjuncts or high school teachers who are certified (essentially through their educational credentials) to teach college-level courses. The colleges therefore incur extremely low costs and are often reimbursed at the regular FTE rate. The students can usually earn *both* high school and college credit. So far, little is known about what happens to these students, but it is likely that many of them go on to four-year rather than two-year colleges. They therefore represent a new market for the community colleges. Alternatively, the involvement in the high school may increase the likelihood that the high school students will choose that particular community college. Therefore the dual enrollment programs have both financial and marketing benefits for the colleges.[3]

In another trend towards vertical expansion, community colleges in some states are also exploring the possibility of offering applied bachelor's degrees. Although this strategy has its proponents, it remains controversial and perhaps the preponderance of community college officials are skeptical. Some presidents argue that if community colleges start offering four-year degrees, their commitment to open access may be weakened. The differences in the conditions of employment of faculty at two- and four-year colleges may also pose a problem to this vertical expansion of the community college mission. Will community college faculty working in four-year programs still be willing to teach the typically much higher community college load? Although the applied baccalaureate is definitely controversial, the movement does seem to be gaining some momentum.

As they search for new functions and markets, the colleges try to find opportunities to exploit the skills and staff they already have. For example, a strong computer science department would give a college an advantage in offering noncredit programs to prepare students for information technology certifications. Nevertheless, in many cases, there is very little coordination among programs that are substantively related. This is particularly true with regard to the coordi-

---

[2]See Smith-Morest (2001) for a full discussion of horizontal and vertical mission expansion.

[3]Other institutions are beginning to take notice of this market. Administrators at one college said that the community college, the local four-year public university, and two private nonprofit colleges were all offering courses in one local high school.

nation between credit and related noncredit programs. Often the extension or adult education functions are housed in separate buildings, use different faculty, and are managed by different administrators. Credit and noncredit programs in similar areas may actually be in competition for students or perhaps for relationships and partnerships with local businesses that could hire graduates and provide equipment.

In many cases, the developmental education function is poorly coordinated with the core substantive programs. Some educators have argued that there are important pedagogic benefits to the coordination of academic and vocational education, and this does appear to be a strategy to reduce the potential conflict between transfer-oriented academic programs and more applied occupational terminal degrees (Grubb, 1999b). Nevertheless, while many community college faculty members and administrators favor the integration of academic and vocational instruction, it is difficult to find well-developed programs that actually put the approach into practice (Perin, 1998).

Thus, community colleges have responded to the challenges that they face by building out and by seeking new markets and functions, more than by focusing on more intensive efforts to improve what they are already doing. The result is that most community colleges are now institutions with multiple missions directed at addressing the needs and interests of a wide variety of constituencies. The list of missions includes transfer to a bachelor's program, terminal occupational education, developmental education, adult basic education, English as a second language, education and training for welfare recipients and others facing serious barriers to employment, customized training to specific companies, preparation of students for industry certification exams, noncredit instruction in a plethora of areas (including purely avocational courses), small business development, and even economic forecasting.

THE DEBATE ABOUT MULTIPLE MISSIONS

This comprehensive strategy is not without its critics. Advocates of the primacy of the transfer function have been among the most vocal opponents of this broader strategy. These critics argue that the growing emphasis on occupational education, as opposed to academic-oriented transfer programs, has a negative effect on transfer rates. According to this view, an accent on vocationalism draws students into programs that largely do not encourage transfer. At the same time, vocationalism demoralizes the academic programs that encourage transfer (Dougherty, 1994). Brint and Karabel (1989) think that this function has changed the entire mission of community colleges and turned them into vocational schools for low- and middle-class occupations, thus limiting students' opportunities for advancement. An institution established to "level up" disadvantaged segments of society has leveled down the critical literacy skills required for the degree programs. Clark (1961), in his classic work on community colleges, suggested that the colleges played a functional role in adjusting (down) the expectations of students so that they would be consistent with the realities of the labor market. As the mission of community colleges evolved to meet a broader range of needs, the earlier emphasis on liberal education and on the transfer function appeared to take a back seat to the newer demands: vocational mission "eclipsed" the emphasis on transfer and liberal education (Wechsler, 1968; Katsinas, 1994).

While these critics oppose mission expansion because it weakens the academic transfer function, others object to the comprehensive model because it detracts from what they believe should be the core function of the community college—vocational education (Blocker, Plummer, and Richardson, 1965; Grubb, 1996). A growing number of policy makers and business leaders look to occupational education at the community college as a key site for building the work force for the next century (Hebel, 1999). Indeed, Leitzel and Clowes (1991) consider vocationalism to be the most important distinctive niche of community colleges within the system of higher education. Clowes and Levine (1989) argue that career education is the only viable core function for most community colleges. According to Grubb (1996), the colleges and their role in society are not served well by the continued criticism of the vocational function and a strong emphasis on transfer and academics: "One implication for community colleges is that they need to take their broadly defined occupational purposes more seriously. . . . They are not academic institutions . . . even when many of their students hope to transfer to four-year colleges" (p. 83). He argues that (1) the emphasis on academic education implies that there is only one valued postsecondary institution, defined by the research university; (2) community colleges cannot win the academic battle because they are not selective; and (3) community colleges mostly fail in large transfer numbers, therefore their clientele is left with outcomes of uncertain academic value.

Another argument against a comprehensive strategy is more general—community colleges simply cannot do everything well and therefore must choose a more limited set of objectives on which to focus. As Cross (1985) asked, "Can any college perform all of those functions with excellence—or even adequately in today's climate of scarce resources and heavy competition for students?" After predicting growing fiscal pressures on the colleges, Breneman and Nelson (1980) made a similar argument, stating that the "most fundamental choice facing community colleges is whether to emphasize the community-based learning center concept, with an emphasis on adult and continuing education and community services, or to emphasize transfer programs, sacrificing elsewhere if necessary. . . . It may no longer be possible to have it both ways" (p. 114). This perspective probably owes something to the argument that businesses must focus on their core competencies, and indeed, the successful for-profit institutions of higher education have tended to pursue a much more focused strategy. For example, the University of Phoenix concentrates on educating adult working students and does not try to serve the 18-year-old "traditional" college population. The DeVry Institutes specialize in a small number of technical degrees and simply do not expect to enroll students interested in majoring in the humanities, the social sciences, or many of the sciences.

Despite these calls for more focus, community colleges and indeed whole state systems have continued to move towards comprehensive models. Even states such as Wisconsin, which has maintained a technical college system with a primary mission of providing occupational education, have developed programs to facilitate the eventual transfer of their students to four-year programs. Few new colleges are being built, but one recent example clearly shows the appeal of the comprehensive model. The college planners used several approaches to survey the needs of the community and found an interest in a wide variety of transfer and occupational courses. The college then planned to try to respond to almost all of these interests.

Why have community colleges rejected a more focused approach in favor of a comprehensive strategy? Why has their response to financial pressures been to seek new markets and sources of revenue rather than to concentrate primarily on their core functions?

First, political factors, on the one hand, make presidents very reluctant to shed programs and, on the other, create incentives to take on new ones. New programs have the potential to create new constituencies that in turn generate state- and local-level political support at the needed level to maintain the flow of tax revenues. Thus, even if a new program outside of the college's traditional activities loses money in an immediate sense, it may create a political environment that leads to additional reimbursements from the state, county, or local government for its core activities.[4]

Second, sometimes new programs are believed to generate surpluses. If the institution has any excess capacity (which many did have in the 1990s after a period of stable or falling enrollments), then the programs can be mounted at a low marginal cost. Even small surpluses from programs can provide presidents with discretionary funds when most of the revenues from the core credit programs are tied up in faculty salaries and other fixed costs. As state funding becomes more uncertain, these alternative sources of revenue appear more attractive. This development can be seen in the dramatic growth of the share of college budgets accounted for by state and federal grants.

Moreover, it is not surprising that in search of new revenues, institutions will seek new markets rather than try to increase their market share in their old activities. For example, attracting more transfer students with bachelor's degree aspirations would require the

---

[4]For example, one of the reasons that a community college I visited in 2001 had introduced a dual enrollment program with local high schools was to build political support among taxpayers for additional local revenues.

college to convince students who previously did not enroll despite the presence of the transfer program. This might seem particularly difficult, especially as four-year colleges are trying to attract the same students. Exploiting unserved markets seems to be easier than increasing market share in mature markets.

Third, college administrators are not convinced that additional missions will weaken current activities. Even if they were convinced, they would not know which activities on their own could provide a strong financial and political foundation. One of the fundamental tenets of the view that the community colleges are failed transfer institutions is that all of the new activities, particularly the growing importance of occupational education, have weakened the traditional transfer functions. Most community college administrators reject this notion. Moreover, most colleges do not keep data or records in such a way that they could evaluate the extent of cross-subsidies or the negative (or positive) effects that one program or function has on others. While it is easy to count new revenues as students enroll in new programs, it is much more difficult to measure the costs, especially the strain on infrastructure and the attention of administrators, of those new programs. Furthermore, despite the logic of the argument that one institution cannot do many things well, there is no definitive empirical evidence for this negative effect.

Fourth, some community college experts have argued that a wide variety of program offerings under one roof is exactly what community college students need. According to this view, these students often have ambiguous or unrealistic education goals. If properly guided, these students can take advantage of the varied offerings as their interests change and as they converge on goals that better match their interests and skills. In these conceptualizations, it is argued that community colleges should further develop their comprehensive missions so that students have whatever support they need in order to move into gainful employment, regardless of whether that support involves general education, skills training, or student support services (Baker, 1999; Gleazer, 1980; Vaughan, 1985).

Thus, it is not surprising that colleges have continued to move towards a more comprehensive strategy. Shedding programs risks losing visible enrollments and political support in favor of an abstract goal of focused organizational efficiency, which, though logical, lacks definitive empirical measurement and evidence.

OUTLOOK AND RECOMMENDATIONS

Community colleges have many strengths: demographic and technological development, the growing importance of nontraditional pathways through college, commitment to access and open admissions, and a continued supply of students whose weak high school preparation creates a need for community college remedial services. The for-profit competitors that have attracted so much attention have only succeeded in garnering a market share in the two-year sector in the low single digits. Moreover, according to the latest available data, at least through the middle years of the 1990s, that market share did not grow (Bailey, Badway, and Gumport, in press). Although the for-profits may offer formidable competition to community colleges for some types of students, it is unlikely that they will threaten a significant part of the community college market in the foreseeable future.[5] Moreover, public and private/nonprofit four-year institutions may represent a more significant threat to community colleges than for-profit institutions.

But as long as the gap between community college tuition and the tuition charged by other postsecondary institutions remains as large as it is, community colleges will have a strong buffer against competition. And that gap continues to grow.

Nevertheless, while the colleges will continue to attract enrollments, complacency is hardly in order. State and local legislators will continue to put financial pressure on the colleges both through general fiscal restraints and possibly demands for greater accountability for outcomes. But the community college response to these pressures has been to seek new markets and revenues rather than to concentrate primarily on a smaller number of core functions. As we have seen, the strongest incentives push the colleges toward a more comprehensive strategy. The danger with this strategy is that while it may generate enthusiasm and revenues about new activities, it may do so without necessarily improving the quality of the core degree-granting transfer and occupational programs.

Given that community colleges will continue to pursue a comprehensive strategy, what can administrators and state policy makers do to guarantee that colleges will be effective within the framework of comprehensiveness? The first and perhaps most obvious approach is to pay particular attention to the core functions of teaching and student services, especially student advising. Excitement about new alliances with local businesses or burgeoning noncredit classes to prepare students for industry certification exams should not detract from efforts to introduce the institutional features needed to improve teaching in the colleges or to increase and upgrade student advising services.

Second, colleges need to search for and exploit the complementarities between their different functions. Too often, the potential for cooperation and coordination is rarely realized. Such cooperation has long-run financial and substantive benefits, yet it also requires a significant commitment on the part of the institutional leadership and some investment of resources in the short run.

Finally, colleges need to be able to analyze the effectiveness of their different programs and need to have better measures of the benefits and especially the costs of those programs. As it is now, administrators

---

[5]On the other hand, community colleges may have a good deal to learn from the higher quality for-profit institutions, especially in the area of student services. For a more detailed discussion of this, see Bailey, Badway, and Gumport (2001).

in most colleges are not able to determine which programs generate surpluses and which require cross-subsidization. This vagueness about costs tends to encourage an increase in the number of programs and activities since the revenues generated by the new enrollments are easier to count than the direct and, especially, the indirect costs associated with those programs. This is not to say that colleges would never want to continue, or even to expand, programs that require cross-subsidization. Nevertheless, whatever the objectives, better information will help them achieve those objectives. In the end, there may be many sound economic and social reasons for the multifunction college, but those reasons have yet to be measured systematically.

Community colleges make up a large and fundamentally important sector in higher education. While they face some significant challenges, they continue to have significant potential for the next several years. Strong incentives have encouraged them to take on an increasing number of missions and functions. As a result, they have evolved into extremely complex institutions, carrying out a large variety of activities that serve a diverse set of constituencies. Colleges need to continue to focus on improving the services that they already provide and to do a better job of finding and exploiting complementarities among missions so that they can realize the potential benefits that coordinated activities can bring.

REFERENCES

Adelman, C. (1999). *Answers in the tool box: Academic intensity, attendance patterns, and bachelor's degree attainment*. Washington, DC: U.S. Department of Education.

American Association of Community Colleges. (2001). *State-by-state profile of community colleges, 2000*. Washington, DC: Community College Press.

Bailey, T.R., and Averianova, I.E. (1998). *Multiple missions of community colleges: Conflicting complementary*. New York: Columbia University,Teachers College, Community College Research Center.

Bailey, T.R., Badway, N., and Gumport, P. (in press). *For-profit higher education and community colleges*. Palo Alto, CA: Stanford University, National Center for Post Secondary Improvement.

Bailey, T.R., and Weininger, E. (2001). *Performance, graduation, and transfer of immigrants and natives in CUNY community colleges*. New York: Columbia University, Teachers College, Community College Research Center.

Baker, G. (1999, February/March).Building the comprehensive community college. *Community College Journal*, 3–19.

Blocker, C.E., Plummer, W., and Richardson, R.C., Jr. (1965). *The two-year college: A social synthesis*. Englewood Cliffs, NJ: Prentice-Hall.

Breneman, D.W., and Nelson, S.C. (1980). The community college mission and patterns of funding. In D.W. Breneman and S.C. Nelson (Eds.), *New directions for community colleges* (pp. 73–81). San Francisco: Jossey-Bass.

Brint, S., and Karabel, J. (1989). *The diverted dream: Community colleges and the promise of educational opportunity in America, 1900–1985*. New York: Oxford University Press.

Carnevale, A.P., and Desrochers, D.M. (2001). *Help wanted...credentials required*. Princeton, NJ: Educational Testing Service.

Clark, B. (1961). The "cooling out" function in higher education. In H.A. Halsey et al. (Eds.), *Education, economy, and society* (pp. 513–521). New York: Free Press.

Cohen, A.M., and Brawer, F.B. (1996). *The American community college* (3rd ed.). San Francisco: Jossey-Bass.

Clowes, D.A., and Levine, B.H. (1989). Community, technical, and junior colleges: Are they leaving higher education? *Journal of Higher Education, 60,* 349–356.

College Board. (2001). *Trends in college pricing 2001.* Washington, DC: Author.

Cross, K.P. (1985). Determining missions and priorities for the fifth generation. In W. Degan and D. Tillery (Eds.), *Renewing the American community college: Priorities and strategies for effective leadership* (pp. 34–52). San Francisco: Jossey-Bass.

Cross, K.P. (1993). Improving the quality of instruction. In A. Levin (Ed.), *Higher learning in America* (pp. 287–308). Baltimore: Johns Hopkins University Press.

Dougherty, K.J. (1994). *The contradictory college: The conflicting origins, impacts, and futures of the community college.* Albany, NY: State University of New York Press.

Dougherty, K.J., and Bakia, M.F. (1999). *The new economic development role of community colleges.* New York: Columbia University, Teachers College, Community College Research Center.

Eaton, J.S. (Ed.). (1994). *Colleges of choice: The enabling impact of the community college.* New York: American Council on Education.

Gerald, D.E., and Hussar, W.J. (2000). *Projections of education statistics to 2010.* Washington, DC: U.S. Government Printing Office.

Gleazer, E.J. (1980). *The community college: Values, vision, vitality.* Washington, DC: American Association of Community and Junior Colleges.

Grubb, W.N. (1996). *Working in the middle.* San Francisco: Jossey-Bass.

Grubb, W.N. (1999a). *Honored but invisible: An inside look at teaching in community colleges.* New York: Routledge.

Grubb, W.N. (1999b). *Learning and earning in the middle: The economic benefits of sub-baccalaureate education.* New York: Columbia University, Teachers College, Community College Research Center.

Hebel, S. (1999). Community College of Denver wins fans with ability to tackle tough issues. *Chronicle of Higher Education,* May 7, 45.

Kane, T.J., and Rouse, C.E. (1995). Labor-market returns to two- and four-year college. *American Economic Review, 85,* 600–614.

Katsinas, S.G. (1994). Is the open door closing? The democratizing role of the community college in the post-Cold War era. *Community College Journal, 64*(5), 24–28.

Leitzel, T.C., and Clowes, D.A. (1991). The diverted dream revisited. *Community Services Catalyst, 24*(1), 21–25.

Merisotis, J.P., and Wolanin, T.R. (2000). *Community college financing: Strategies and challenges.* Washington, DC: Community College Press.

National Association of State Budget Officers. (2000). *State expenditure report.* Washington, DC: Author.

National Center for Education Statistics. (1999a). *Distance education at postsecondary education institutions, 1997–98* (NCES 2000-013). Washington, DC: U.S. Department of Education.

National Center for Education Statistics. (1999b). *Participation in adult education in the United States, 1998–99.* Washington, DC: U.S. Department of Education.

National Center for Education Statistics. (2000a). Beginning Postsecondary Students Longitudinal Study, 1989–94 (BPS:1989-94) datafile.

National Center for Education Statistics. (2000b). High school & beyond longitudinal study of 1980 postsecondary education transcript study (HS&B:So PETS) datafile.

National Center for Education Statistics. (2000c). Integrated Postsecondary Education Data System (IPEDS), "Completions" survey datafile.

National Center for Education Statistics. (2000d). Integrated Postsecondary Education Data System (IPEDS), "Fall Enrollment" survey datafile.

National Center for Education Statistics. (2000e). *Projections of educational statistics,* Washington, DC: U.S. Department of Education.

National Center for Education Statistics. (2000f). *The condition of education 2000.* Washington, DC: U.S. Department of Education.

Nora, A. (2000). *Reexamining the community college mission.* Washington, DC: Community College Press.

Perin, D. (1998). *Curriculum and pedagogy to integrate occupational and academic instruction in the community college: Implications for faculty development.* New York: Columbia University, Teachers College, Community College Research Center.

Roueche, J.E., and Roueche, S.D. (2001). *In pursuit of excellence: The Community College of Denver.* Washington, DC: Community College Press.

Schneider, B., and Stevenson, D. (1999). *The ambitious generation: America's teenagers motivated but directionless.* New Haven, CT: Yale University Press.

Smith-Morest, V. (2001). Integrating multiple missions of today's community colleges. Paper presented at the American Education Research Association meeting, Seattle, WA, April.

Vaughan, G.B. (1985). Maintaining open access and comprehensiveness. In D.E. Puyear and G.B. Vaughan (Eds.), *Maintaining institutional integrity* (pp. 17–28). San Francisco: Jossey-Bass.

Wechsler, H. (1968). *The transfer challenge: Removing barriers, maintaining commitment.* Washington, DC: Association of American Colleges.

3

The Impact of the Changing Economy on Four-Year Institutions of Higher Education: The Importance of the Internet

*Carol A. Twigg**

Society's higher education requirements are undergoing a fundamental transformation. A rapidly growing student population is becoming older and increasingly diverse. In addition, the new economy requires a workforce capable of handling an exploding knowledge base, and industries are looking to educational institutions to provide the necessary education and training. There is financial pressure, too: colleges and universities must control and even reduce costs, as well as manage new competitive dynamics, while responding to growing demands. On their own, each of these factors is significant; collectively, they challenge fundamental higher education strategies and practices as we cross the threshold to the 21st century.

At the same time, emerging digital technology, especially the Internet, is having a significant impact on society in general and on institutions of higher education in particular. Eli Noam (1995) has pointed out that the three major functions of scholarly activity—the creation of information and knowledge, the preservation of information and knowledge, and the transmission of information and knowledge to others—are based on a set of technologies and economics. Together with history and politics, they give rise to a set of institutions. Change the technology and economics and the institutions must change eventually. Noam and others believe that the traditional model of higher education is in the process of breaking down. The reason is not primarily technological; technology simply enables change to occur. The fundamental reason is that today's production and distribution of information and knowledge are undermining traditional information flows and, in so doing, creating alternatives to the university's structure.

*Carol A. Twigg is executive director of the Center for Academic Transformation at Rensselaer Polytechnic Institute.

The impact of computing and communications technologies is already so great that every business and organization today operates in two worlds: a physical world of resources that we can see and touch and a virtual world of information. Two Harvard Business School professors, Jeffrey Rayport and John Sviokla (1994, 1995), have coined the term *marketspace* to distinguish the virtual world of information from the physical world of the marketplace. A few examples illustrate the distinction. When consumers use answering machines to store their phone messages, they are using objects made and sold in the physical world. When they purchase electronic answering services from their local phone companies, they are utilizing the marketspace—a virtual realm where products and services exist as digital information and are delivered through information-based channels. Banks provide services to customers at branch offices in the marketplace as well as electronic services to customers in the marketspace. Airlines sell passenger tickets in both the "place" and the "space."

When students arrive on campus as freshmen and move into residence halls, they enter the physical world of higher education. When they access the Web to write a research paper and communicate with their professors via e-mail, they move into the learning marketspace. Colleges and universities provide educational services to students in classrooms, and they offer online courses via the Internet. Bookstores sell learning materials in both the "place" and the "space."

Academics, consultants, and managers have commonly described the stages involved in the process of creating value in the physical world as links in a "value chain." The value chain, according to Rayport and Sviokla (1994), is a model that describes a series of value-adding activities connecting a company's supply side (raw materials, inbound logistics, and production processes) with its demand side (outbound logistics, marketing, and sales). By analyzing the stages of a value chain, companies and institutions can redesign their processes to improve efficiency and effectiveness.

Colleges and universities often have difficulty describing the traditional value chain of higher education. Most frequently, the student is viewed as the "raw material" that moves along the production line only to emerge, like Detroit's snazziest model, fully finished at the end. A more accurate description is that colleges and universities supply knowledge to those who need it; a successful transaction between teachers and students is what we call learning. Heretofore, that transaction took place almost exclusively in the physical world of the campus, surrounded by a series of ancillary services that also add value for the customer (for example, credentialing).

Although the value chain of the marketspace can mirror that of the marketplace (buyers and sellers can transfer funds over electronic networks just as they might exchange cash when face to face), the value-adding processes that organizations must employ in the information world are unique in that they are virtual. More important, the economics of the two chains differ. A conventional understanding of the economies of scale and scope does not apply to the virtual value chain as it does to the physical value chain. In many instances, products and services can be brought to market faster, better, and cheaper in the marketspace. New competitors are viable in the marketspace because of the new economics of doing business in the world of the space.

One simple example of how these differences apply to higher education is to think about how easy it is to start a university in the world of the space: no need to build classrooms, libraries, and dormitories; no need to persuade faculty and staff to live in an undesirable location; no need to recruit a football team. Today we are witnessing the creation of entirely new online institutions in less time than it takes to develop a plan for a traditional campus. Whether today's versions of the virtual university will succeed in the long run is irrelevant; if they do not, someone else will learn from these early experiences and build a better mousetrap.

Rather than focus on the creation of whole new institutions, we need instead to consider another characteristic of the virtual value chain: the ease with which its links can be disaggregated, or pulled apart. Unlike the physical value chain, which exists as a linear sequence of activities with defined points of input and output, the virtual value chain is nonlinear, a matrix of potential inputs and outputs that can be accessed and distributed through a wide variety of channels.

The links in the higher education value chain include, among others, marketing (providing information to prospective students); admissions (qualifying and selecting students); enrollment services (handling registration, billing, financial aid); presentation of instructional material (providing lectures, books, and other materials); student interaction and academic support (offering advising, tutoring, and library support); student services (helping with placement, counseling, information technology, and athletics); and evaluation and credentialing (conferring grades, degrees, certificates, and transcripts). Even today, pieces of the physical value chain are being outsourced in an effort to improve efficiency and effectiveness. Enrollment management firms, textbook publishers, testing organizations, library and administrative software suppliers, and others sell their products and services either to institutions or directly to student customers.

The world of the space escalates the opportunity to create value in new ways at each stage of the virtual value chain. Each extract from the flow of information can constitute a new product or service. The consequences for higher education are huge. Many observers are convinced that hundreds of new companies, each specializing in one link of the value chain, will emerge. These companies may supply products and services to institutions, or they may decide to bypass institutions and go directly to student consumers. Others may see as their customers the major aggregators of the demand for higher education—that is, employers. Or companies may do all three simultaneously by using different branding strategies. In any event, all institutions will be able—if they choose—to take advantage of these developments to increase and improve services for students at a lower cost.

This paper begins by discussing the major economic and technological trends affecting higher education in general and four-year institutions in particular. These trends suggest that the "space" will increasingly dominate the world of postsecondary education. The paper next discusses the major trends, issues, and challenges associated with virtual education—including new organizational structures that are emerging—and assesses how well four-year institutions are aligned with these trends. It concludes with a description of current developments in virtual education, taking note of the threats and opportunities these developments present to four-year institutions.

A few words about terminology are in order. Throughout this paper, the terms distance learning, distance education, distributed learning, virtual learning, borderless education, and online learning are used more or less interchangeably. At times, the use of distance learning seems appropriate because the issues under discussion most frequently concern off-campus (distance) versus on-campus learning. At other times, particularly when describing the new higher education environment, the phrase distributed learning more clearly expresses the changing nature (and the blending) of all forms of higher education. In any event, the reader should not draw unwarranted conclusions from a particular usage.

TRENDS AFFECTING FOUR-YEAR INSTITUTIONS

Society's higher education requirements are undergoing a fundamental transformation brought about by changes taking place in what has been called the new knowledge economy. This new economy requires a workforce capable of handling an exploding knowledge base. Some experts have estimated that the shelf life of a technical degree today is less than five years. Although many of the critical skills required in the high-performance workplace have not changed, the pace of knowledge advancement requires constant updating. Education no longer ends at graduation. Viewing a college education as the mastery of a body of knowledge or complete preparation for a lifetime career has become outmoded. Increasingly, students who already possess a degree are looking for learning opportunities that will improve job or career skills.

With these changes in business and industry, Americans today will work at several different jobs during their lifetimes, each job requiring new skills, new knowledge, and new attitudes and values. The education and training of the current labor force are key to increasing productivity over the next two decades. The American Society for Training and Development (ASTD) estimates that more than 75 percent of the nation's workforce need retraining. Consequently, adults will continuously enter and reenter higher education.

Driven by the increasing requirements of the knowledge economy and by the income premium related to postsecondary education, the demand for four-year institutions is exceeding current capacities. According to the National Center for Educational Statistics (NCES), the earnings advantage of male college graduates over male high school graduates was 50 percent in 1997, compared with 19 percent in 1980. Today, approximately 70 percent of high school graduates go on to college, up from just 56 percent in 1980. The next decade will see college enrollments by 18–22 year olds jump from 15 million to 20 million students (Green, 1997).

In addition, the number of older and employed part-time students is growing because of the need to upgrade skills and knowledge. It is predicted that in the 21st century, each individual in the workforce will need to accumulate an additional 30 credit hours every seven years (Dolence and Norris, 1995, p. 7). Today, the traditional college-age group makes up a shrinking majority of the student population. "Traditional" undergraduates—those who are 18–22 years old, attend full-time, and live on campus—constitute less than one-fourth of all students in higher education. The New Majority is over 25, attends part-time, and lives off-campus. Many of these students work or have child-rearing responsibilities; they place a premium on time management and on balancing education with other demands. In addition, an even greater number of adults would like to pursue a college education but cannot because of inconvenient class hours, campus inaccessibility, family responsibilities, business travel, or physical disabilities. While remaining a suitable option for the minority of college students who match the traditional profile, residential education alone simply cannot serve the needs of today's working adult students.

Concerns About Quality and Cost

As demand for higher education continues to grow, public concerns about the quality of traditional institutions are increasing as well. The overall trend toward external certification as a way to ensure quality indicates a lack of confidence about how well our institutions are doing. Despite having a reputation as being the best in the world, U.S. higher education suffers from serious deficiencies, as indicated by failure rates of 60 to 70 percent among college freshmen, a 28 percent dropout rate for students between freshman and sophomore years, satisfactory completion rates as low as 40 to 50 percent for basic introductory courses, graduation rates of 43 percent within six years for all but the most selective schools, and freshman- and sophomore-level classes taught mostly by graduate students or temporary instructors (Twigg, 1996).

Generally, degree acquisition, graduation, and grades are no longer viewed as adequate indicators of competency. Measures of quality are changing. Today, quality assurance agencies are moving toward an emphasis on the assessment of learning outcomes as a way to measure quality. The move toward external testing of teachers for certification represents an extension of the current practice in other professional fields such as law, engineering, nursing, and accounting, all of which already have some form of external validation. A new industry that certifies competency is emerging. In the information technology field, Java or Microsoft certifications are at least comparable to higher education degrees and are perhaps even more important (Adelman, 2000). Many states—including Washington, Colorado, and Illinois—are considering requiring exit exams at every level of higher education.

These concerns about quality are coupled with even greater concerns about the cost of attending four-year institutions. The fundamental financial problem with four-year colleges and universities is not so much their per-student costs as it is the upward trajectory of these costs: that is, the built-in inflationary engine behind higher education. A major part of this cost pressure is attributable to the absence of sustainable productivity increases from the substitution of capital for labor, as is characteristic of the majority of the economy. Since the principal cost in higher education is for labor, its unit costs tend to track wages and salaries—which, in turn, tend to reflect the real growth of the economy and thus in nonrecession years to exceed the rate of inflation.

At the same time, the revenue to meet these increased cost pressures comes from three primary sources: taxpayers, parents, and students. Each source is seriously limited. Substantial increases in either federal or state tax revenues to keep up with inflation in higher education, to cover the backlog of deferred maintenance and program restoration, and to meet the higher training and education levels required by a technologically complex society are unlikely. Similarly, parental revenues seem to have peaked, and parental revenues are of decreasing relevance due to the growing numbers of older students or students from families with virtually no discretionary income. Finally, students' revenue is not likely to increase, with student debt loads ($15,000–$30,000 for the undergraduate years and $50,000–$100,000 by the end of graduate or advanced professional education) and workloads (many students are working 20 to 40 hours a week while still carrying a "full-time" academic load) already of national concern (Johnstone, 1992).

Growing Emphasis on Market Dynamics

Higher education students today, particularly those in the New Majority, are becoming much more sophisticated, seeking both accountability and quality. They are more likely to define quality in the language of the quality improvement movement (that is, satisfaction of customer needs) than in the traditional quality measures used in higher education (that is, rich resources as represented by the size of libraries, student-faculty ratios, and the number and size of grants and contracts won by the faculty). Today's students are increasingly selecting curricula that enhance their chances of both initial and sustained employment. They also have reason to believe that increased competition among higher education providers will work to their advantage as consumers.

Students are using their purchasing power to be more selective about which institutions they attend. Colleges and universities compete fiercely for private funds and try to attract benefactors and students by establishing distinctive identities. Faculty, especially younger faculty responding to academic uncertainties and business opportunities, take a more entrepreneurial approach to their careers and are less attached to any one institution. At the same time, higher education institutions are facing competition from new educational providers—from corporations like Motorola to private organizations such as DeVry. Many higher educational bodies are fighting back by expanding their continuing and corporate education programs (Marchese, 1998).

Although many observers have noted the increasingly competitive atmosphere in which higher education operates, there are numerous reasons to believe that this is only the proverbial tip of the iceberg. Dwayne Matthews (n.d.) has noted that, even though colleges and universities believe they operate in a competitive environment, they do so only on the margins. They are protected from true competition by the geographical constraints on student mobility, the hurdle of accreditation (with its burly bodyguard, financial aid), protectionist state policies such as designated service areas, and the financial subsidy of public institutions. These barriers are falling—in some cases so rapidly that it is hard for public institutions to even know what is happening, much less develop a response. Until now, public higher education, serving 80 percent of U.S. college students, has been a regulated monopoly enterprise somewhat akin to a public utility. Today, the natural monopolies of higher education institutions are rapidly coming to an end, at least in their immediate service areas, as distance education, supported by advancing educational technology, grows in capacity. The opening of higher education markets to true competition means that state policy can shift away from controlling the behavior of higher education institutions to ensuring the effective functioning of the higher education market.

In recent years, state coordinating structures have been under considerable pressure to support more decentralized, deregulated forms of operation. A number of factors have contributed to this environment, not the least of which has been the enthusiasm to apply successful business practices to state agencies and functions. Another important factor has been the declining share of state dollars that make up higher education budgets in public institutions. At the same time, public institutions have been under pressure to demonstrate results and to report to the public on agreed-upon accountability measures. In short, state policymakers have granted greater institutional autonomy and flexibility in return for greater accountability.

In considering other financial options that might emerge during the next decade, some experts argue that public support will shift from public institutions to private and proprietary institutions. This shift would be stimulated not only by the current negative impressions of the responsiveness of public education but also as a consequence of new funding mechanisms. At the state level, student-carried vouchers may substitute for today's territorial franchises. In the virtual university environment in which there are no boundaries of geography or time, today's system of funding the institution rather than the individual will make less and less sense.

One thing is certain. Whether through direct appropriations for public institutions from state governments, through tax exemption and federal grants for private institutions, or through need-based aid for proprietary organizations, public subsidies have long been the life-blood of higher education. Any change in public support will have a dramatic impact on the decision-making process in higher education and on the ability of many institutions to survive.[1]

The Influence of Technology

The explosive growth of the Internet, signaling the convergence of computing and communications technologies, is an additional trend both driving and enabling significant changes in the economy. Many observers have noted that the Internet is literally transforming all institutions and organizations in society, resulting in a societal change that is analogous to the transition from an agrarian world to an industrial one.

This technology is maturing at a time when the traditional educational model is cracking under the strain of new societal requirements. Meeting the needs of an increasingly heterogeneous student body requires greater flexibility in access and significant improvements in quality, all accomplished in a cost-effective, affordable manner. The Internet is ideally suited to meet these new learning needs. More important, emerging networking technologies do not just respond to new learning requirements—they also help to shape them.

Through the Internet, it is now possible to offer instruction to anyone, anytime, anywhere. Almost all colleges and universities are wiring their campuses for broadband comprehensive access and are ensuring that each student has 24-hour access to a laptop computer and the Internet. The plummeting costs of networked devices will make access even more affordable and widespread. The Internet enables the creation of new teaching and learning methods that can dramatically reduce the two biggest costs of the current system: the instructional personnel and the physical plant. These technologies are extraordinarily cost-effective; virtually unlimited access to the Internet costs under $300 annually, about the equivalent of five textbooks.

Massive amounts of intellectual resources are now available on the Web, and more resources are uploaded every day. Soon, entire digital libraries of both general and specialized knowledge will be available. Students will be able to access the best resources from

---

[1]For a full discussion of the public policy implications of the interplay between the new economy and the capabilities of digital technologies, see Mingle, Heterick, and Twigg (1998).

around the world—high-quality, self-paced, customized, and world-class content and pedagogy.

The idea of customization applied to education suggests that our definition of quality will increasingly take into account individualized learning styles as we construct learning experiences for students. Howard Gardener (1993) argues that there are at least seven types of intelligence but that traditional Western pedagogy, based on lectures and textbooks, makes use of only two (verbal and logical). Engaging the other five types of intelligence—spatial, musical, kinesthetic, interpersonal, and intrapersonal—will increase student success. Digital learning applications make this possible. The Myers-Briggs personality diagnostic instrument shows substantial variation in learning and problem-solving styles among the population. We also know that there is a significant difference between the abstract, reflective learning style of most college and university professors—and the ways in which professors approach teaching—and the more concrete, active learning style typical of their students (Schroeder, 1993). Again, digital applications enable us to tailor materials to the learning styles of students.

Digital learning applications are steadily improving. Search tools that enable complex and stored queries, as well as automated updates, are developing rapidly. Web-enabled presentation software is becoming easier to use while facilitating the communication of ideas and information in ever more powerful ways. Hybrid CD-ROMs provide the multimedia richness of CD-ROMs and the up-to-date capabilities of Web sites. Real-time audio and streaming video can now be delivered through standard 56 kbs. Virtual reality applications will offer additional enriching tools. Interactive databases, spreadsheets, and Java applications engage users with customized exercises, demonstrations, simulations, and tests.

Collaborative applications enable students to interact with each other and with teachers. Features include topic threading and real-time chat tools. Web-based audio and video conferencing are now stable applications. Faculty can make presentations using audio or video with synchronized html/presentation software; demonstrate concepts using shared electronic whiteboards; and test students, including using surprise pop-up quizzes, asking questions of individual students and providing individual feedback. Students can move through live or archived materials according to their own schedule and convenience and can communicate with teachers, other instructional resources, and fellow students. Push technologies deliver software and local information (news, announcements, and other time-sensitive data) and instructional content. High-performance servers will enable large volumes of students to reliably access course material while also participating in live events.

In addition, the Internet offers unprecedented opportunities to collect, organize, and analyze large, real-time sample consumer research. Sources include responses to online surveys regarding student satisfaction and perceptions; tracking of learner behavior on-site (e.g., on what learning points do students spend the most time? what is the sequence and pattern of interest? what questions do students ask?); transactional data on student registrations, dropouts, and completions; and interaction and outcome data generated from base-line assessments, exercises, and exams. Students, instructors, institutions, accreditors, and consumer agencies all have access to these data, enabling benchmarking and competency assessment. Because of the feedback available, digital products and services can be fine-tuned and product development accelerated.

The key challenge is to integrate these technologies into a coherent electronic learning environment. Virtual classroom applications are already emerging, but given the exponential pace of Internet-based innovation, educational applications will become even more powerful in the next few years.

A New Higher Education System

What is emerging is a new higher education system—what some have called a "global learning infrastructure," a student-centric, virtual, global web of educational services—as the foundation for achieving the learning goals of society today (Twigg and Miloff, 1998). This vision contrasts with the current brick-and-mortar, campus-centric college or university; it even goes beyond the paradigm of the virtual university, which remains modeled on individual institutions.

The Internet enables the functions that are currently "bundled" by individual colleges and universities to be disaggregated, disintermediated, globalized, and carried out more efficiently by separate specialized entities. Due to its sheer size, the four-year educational sector will drive some Internet innovation, and some individual institutions will undoubtedly exploit these technologies to advance their programs. But even larger publishing, workplace training, and other knowledge management applications will drive the majority of innovation.

The global learning infrastructure will encompass a flourishing marketplace of educational services, a marketplace in which millions of students will interact with a vast array of individual and institutional educational suppliers. With its emphasis on creativity and competition, this infrastructure enables a wide range of players—colleges and universities, media, publishers, content specialists, and technology companies—to market, sell, and deliver educational services online. The global learning infrastructure draws its capabilities from digital technology and the Internet. It is being developed in phases but will ultimately cross all institutional, state, and national borders. It could not have existed five years ago—but it will be pervasive five years from now.

CURRENT TRENDS IN VIRTUAL EDUCATION

As noted above, a new system of higher education is being developed in phases. A number of current trends in the place and space of higher education illustrate this development.

Distributed Learning: The Convergence of Face-to-Face and Distance Education

Many people in higher education view "distance education" as something disconnected from the core academic program. Others counter that this idea derives from how distance education was conducted in the past and that today's distance learning programs are becoming fully integrated into campus life. As an example, the University of Illinois at Urbana-Champaign (UIUC) now views distance learning as part of its central mission to serve the people of the state of Illinois, as part of the core values of the institution. UIUC's master's degree program in library science is offered online as a "scheduling option." This program is the same as the one offered on campus: students meet the same entrance requirements; the same faculty teach on campus and online; and students are evaluated in the same way. Illinois has moved from the idea that "distance education is of poor quality" to a conviction that "distance education is mainstream."

UIUC is not an exception. On those campuses seriously engaged in online learning—versus those merely talking about it—the integration exemplified by UIUC is typical. The term *distributed learning* has evolved specifically to describe this integration and to move away from the perceived distinction between on- and off-campus use of technology in academic programs. Distributed learning encompasses both on- and off-campus online teaching and learning. The term had its origins in the networking community, where experts talk about distributed intelligence on the network, for example, in contrast to the central intelligence of the mainframe computer. The term suggests that learning is being distributed throughout the network. Consequently, the kind of either/or (on-/off-campus) distinction that the term *distance learning* suggests is no longer appropriate.

Increase in the Virtual Delivery of Services

During the past five years, an explosion has occurred in the delivery of services via the Web—in commerce, in government, in health care, in the not-for-profit sector, and of course, in higher education—radically increasing access to information and timely response times in providing service. Campuses are moving toward offering every kind of traditional student service via the Web, including admissions, registration, billing, financial aid, advising, tutoring, library, placement, counseling, information technology, grades, degree audits, and transcripts. Without exception, new institutional providers begin with the assumption that most, if not all, of these services will be delivered via a kind of "one-stop shopping" approach. In providing such services, these organizations have an advantage over traditional campuses since they are not faced with legacy systems that must be maintained during the transition to more up-to-date approaches.

New companies are specializing in one aspect of student service provision, retaining multiple institutions as clients. For example, SMARTHINKING is a new Internet company that provides human, real-time, online academic support for core courses in higher education. A significant area of student need—and one that institutions have difficulty meeting effectively—is for tutoring help in basic courses. Through chat technology, virtual whiteboards, and personalized feedback, SMARTHINKING offers students one-on-one tutoring and homework help, online writing labs, and an extensive library of self-help resources. By drawing from a large pool of teaching assistants—a pool larger than what any single institution can attract—SMARTHINKING can ensure the highest quality TAs at affordable prices for client institutions. Whether students take classes on-site or at a distance, whether they need help at 2:00 p.m. or 2:00 a.m., qualified help is only a click away.

Simultaneously, other new Web-based services for students (and prospective students) will do more than replicate traditional services online. Some examples of what to expect in the near future include the following: consumer services that will advise students (and their parents) and help them evaluate the myriad of online educational offerings; academic credit banks that will function as trusted intermediaries, enabling students to deposit credits from any source and, when certain requirements have been met, to earn an accredited degree; and brokering services that will allow the numerous educational suppliers to exchange information and products and to work together.

Changes in Students' Expectations

Just as students are beginning to expect "better, cheaper, faster" delivery of student services, so, too, are they beginning to want their academic experiences to have some of the same characteristics. Adult students, with their primary emphasis on professional advancement, want learning that is as close to "just-in-time" as they can get. Yet almost all four-year institutions still follow a traditional term-based calendar, even for their online courses. This type of calendar offers little or no flexibility.

A very small number of institutions have begun to respond to students' desire for greater flexibility. For example, Rio Salado College in Phoenix, Arizona, has revolutionized the college calendar by starting each of its online courses every two weeks. This means that no student who wants to take a course ever has to wait more than two weeks to start. The University of Phoenix uses a cohort model in which a course begins whenever between 8 and 13 students are ready to start. Students at New York's Excelsior College (formerly Regents College) and SUNY's Empire State College combine on-campus courses, online courses, test preparation, and independent study to individualize the time and place of study. It is not coincidental that each of these institutions was created explicitly to serve working adults.

Students also seek the ability to "mix and match" courses leading to a degree. The transfer process in higher education has become more varied and pervasive. In addition to vertical transfer (movement from a two-year college to a four-year college), students now pursue horizontal transfer as they move from one institution to another. Many students now attend more than one institution at a time; for example, the majority of 1996 baccalaureate graduates attended at least two colleges and universities. Many students taking online courses are enrolled in another different institution as well. Students attending corporate universities and other unaccredited institutions are seeking to transfer their coursework to accredited institutions. Globalization leads to increasing numbers of students enrolling in foreign institutions and seeking to transfer credits to U.S. colleges and universities (Council for Higher Education Association [CHEA], 2000).

End of the "Cottage Industry" Approach to Course Development

U.S. higher education remains what Bill Massy and Bob Zemsky have called a "handicraft" industry in which the vast majority of courses are developed and delivered as "one-ofs" by individual professors. In most cases, it is difficult to speak of a "course" offered by an institution other than at the advanced level. The predominance of the multiple-section model means that whole courses are treated differently depending on who happens to be teaching the particular class, be they full-time, tenured faculty, or adjunct appointees. This model produces varied approaches to subject matter, resulting in uneven quality and a lack of correspondence between student "input" (ability) and "output" (result as measured by common assessment instruments). To be sure, excellence may be a by-product of a subset of these offerings, but it seldom characterizes the whole.

In most four-year institutions, this repetitive, labor-intensive approach has been transferred to online education as well. With some technical support, professors are encouraged, more or less, to do their own thing. It is not surprising that most studies of distance education produce "no significant difference." Since individual professors replicate traditional approaches in the online environment, why should we be surprised at the result? In contrast, new providers—ranging from the British Open University to traditional commercial publishers and newly created software companies—have moved to a production model of course development and delivery. Courses are collaboratively developed, taking advantage of subject matter experts, learning theorists, and assessment practitioners, in addition to a panoply of information technology and graphic artist professionals, with the goal of making radical improvements in quality.

Potential for "Cherry Picking" Programs and Courses

In the virtual environment, major investments of time and resources will likely be made where the payoff is high, creating the material for institutions and companies to "cherry pick" the most attractive options. Developing online master's degree programs, for example, is more attractive than trying to replicate the full baccalaureate degree program. The tremendous growth in online MBAs, from both traditional providers and new entrants, is indicative of this trend.

Another category ripe for cherry picking is that of high-demand fields such as information technology, a field requiring specialized knowledge that is growing in unprecedented directions. Adelman (2000) has described the exploding phenomenon of certification in the information technology industry and the certification training that is occurring outside the boundaries of traditional higher education. In 1999, third-party examiners administered an estimated 3 million assessments at 5,000 sites in 140 countries. And as of January 2000, 1.7 million certifications had been awarded. Adelman notes that in the information technology field coursework may be recommended but is usually not required because of the amount that can be learned by experience and self-study. A 1997 Microsoft survey of its certificate holders, for example, found that 98 percent indicated self-study as their preparation method, with 91 percent using books as their primary learning route.

A third target area for cherry picking are those courses with high enrollment and a relatively standardized curriculum; such courses are the primary target for college textbooks as well, for much the same reasons. Studies have shown that undergraduate enrollments are concentrated in relatively few academic areas. At the community college level, about 50 percent of student enrollment is concentrated in just 25 courses. The course titles include introductory studies in English, mathematics, psychology, sociology, economics, accounting, biology, and chemistry. Those same 25 courses generate about 35 percent of the enrollment at the baccalaureate level. Courses developed and offered in those areas that demonstrated improved quality of learning and/or reduced cost of instruction have a potentially enormous student audience.

Conclusion

The world of virtual education brings with it the dissolution of geographical boundaries in the postsecondary education industry. At the same time, we are witnessing a more profound dissolution of other boundaries, reflecting the influence of the changing economy. Educational values in society at large are widening, in contrast with the values of traditional higher education providers. The distinction between education and training begins to blur when the predominant educational requirements of both students and employers are learning outcomes that are relevant to the workplace. The distinction between "high-quality" education, as represented by a four-year university or college, and nonsponsored study begins to blur in the information technology field, where independent certification attests to learning achievement regardless of the source. The distinction between nonprofit and for-profit institutions begins to blur when for-profit organizations produce higher-quality educational products and services than their nonprofit competitors. Four-year institutions no longer have a monopoly on quality.

ISSUES AND CHALLENGES POSED BY VIRTUAL EDUCATION

The emerging world of virtual education poses tough challenges for those organizations—be they traditional institutions or new entrants—who aspire to be players in the new educational marketplace. Among those challenges are questions about academic quality, the opportunities and threats posed by new systems of organization, and how to establish a new market position in a rapidly changing environment.

Questions About Academic Quality

Licensing authorities and accrediting agencies have long assumed that institutions that have certain attributes (e.g., president, board, full-time faculty) will be able to carry out various degree-granting educational missions. Current quality reviews are based primarily on an examination of institutional "inputs": the capacity and resources of institutions and programs. In many ways, accreditation has historically been based on an act of faith. That is, if certain capacity and resource conditions are present, student learning will take place. The unbundling of services, an implicit attribute of distributed learning, poses new challenges for determining which capacity and resource factors are essential. Educators who emphasize input measures become nervous when distance learning programs appear to eliminate many of the capacity and resource conditions of higher education (e.g., full-time faculty and physical campuses).[2]

Despite the existence of literally hundreds of research studies demonstrating that distance education is as effective as—and in some cases more effective than—face-to-face education,[3] traditional educators and others continue to have questions about quality. Those who do

---

[2]For a full discussion of the quality assurance issues related to distributed learning, see Twigg (2001).

[3]Russell (n.d.) has compiled a comprehensive research bibliography on the "no significant difference" phenomenon as reported in 355 research reports, summaries, and papers. See also Clark (1983).

not want to believe the research seem to be missing a rather central and obvious point about the teaching of distance and online courses. Just as they do in face-to-face teaching environments, college and university faculty members are the ones making judgments about whether or not students are learning in distance education. Every student who receives college credit for a course—whether taken online or on campus—does so because the faculty member teaching the course (who has been appointed and reviewed by his or her colleagues and institution) has evaluated what and how well the student has learned. Are we to believe that college faculty suddenly lose all ability to evaluate students' performance simply because the students are not in a physical classroom?

Nevertheless, electronic education is still in its infancy. All involved agree that there is much to learn about how to motivate, support, guide, teach, and evaluate students in these new virtual environments. Advocates of online education suggest that technology-mediated education has the potential to enable an active learning process, to support extensive interaction among students and between instructor and students, and to build community among students, professors, and other partners. Rather than covering old ground to produce yet another "no significant difference" result, research on new pedagogies that take advantage of the electronic environment is needed to determine which approaches are most effective and why.

New Systems of Organization

The virtual environment makes possible—indeed, drives toward—new systems of organization. Traditional business models—those that are vertically integrated and self-sufficient—are becoming obsolete. New business models are more strategic. They identify and focus on a small number of core competencies, on the two or three things that the organization does better than any other organization in the world, and they outsource noncore competencies to a flexible network of service providers. Thus, modern organizations are composed of a small set of core competencies combined with sophisticated processes and skills aimed at integrating the services of outside organizations into the work of the core organization.

An organization's core competencies are those services, products, or other deliverables that create value and that differentiate it from its competition. In higher education, core competencies are teaching, research, and public service. No one would contend that food service, housekeeping, and bookstore management are core competencies. These functions are commonly outsourced, and some institutions are beginning to outsource facilities management and information technology functions as well. Colleges and universities may well follow the example of business and also consider outsourcing "customer contact" activities, including registration and financial aid services. Why, for example, does every institution in a multicampus state system need its own staff for these services?

Institutions, either alone or in partnership, need to develop new business competencies in order to effectively build and participate in the virtual environment. These competencies include how to spot and assess opportunities, evaluate new and fluid sources of competition and collaboration, determine the relative merits of various partnering strategies, and make the appropriate investments under what are still highly uncertain conditions; how to operationalize business models that appropriately allocate costs and revenues among business processes and partners; how to integrate physical and virtual brand and promotional activities; and how to manage issues of knowledge access, competition, and exclusivity among partners and users.

Establishing Market Position

New systems of organization and concerns about quality lead to the necessity of identifying an institution's competitively sustainable areas of greatest strength. What role does an institution want to play— or, equally important, want not to play—in the new virtual environment? Does it want to concentrate on developing content or on organizing the delivery of content produced by others?

- Elitist markets: competing with or exceeding Harvard and MIT in specialized areas
- Mass markets: appealing to large numbers of students in areas of broad appeal
- Niche markets: concentrating on particular academic or professional subject areas
- Educational brokers: bringing together consumers and suppliers and integrating particular aspects of the educational process
- B2B vs. B2C: marketing to companies and organizations (business to business, or B2B) or to individual consumers (business to consumers, or B2C).

Branding becomes increasingly important. Some educational leaders believe that traditional branding is key, that "medallion" institutions will have a competitive edge in this new marketplace. Others say that new brands will emerge—such as occurred with the online company Amazon.com—and that brands created by institutions like the University of Phoenix are more aligned with the needs of the new economy.

How will local four-year institutions compete with multimillion-dollar interactive courses that feature the world's leading content experts, instructors, designers, and programmers? All entrants into the learning marketspace need to recognize that whereas their opportunities may be global, they will also face competitors unrestricted by traditional geographical boundaries.

CURRENT ORGANIZATIONAL DEVELOPMENTS IN VIRTUAL EDUCATION

To assess the significance of the challenges that virtual education poses to traditional four-year institutions, we must cut through the hype. A recent report, *The Business of Borderless Education: UK Perspectives,* notes: "Documenting current activity in borderless higher education is not easy. In a world of 'spin' it is in the interests of new providers to emphasize potential and to massage reality . . . [but] obtaining data on actual student enrolments is difficult" (CVCP and HEFCE, 2000, p. 4). We must avoid the dangers of overgeneralizing about the impact of virtual education on the basis of what are currently only limited developments in very specific subject areas.

At the same time, there has clearly been an explosion of activity in online delivery and tremendous interest in creating virtual colleges and universities. In most cases, traditional institutions are extending their campuses into the space by replicating the processes of the place, seeking to compete primarily on brand recognition. Let us now turn to a brief examination of how both traditional four-year institutions and newly emerging organizations and configurations are responding to the trends and issues discussed above.

Traditional Institutions

Most of the traditional providers of higher education are not meeting the challenges of the knowledge economy. Many four-year institutions continue to focus on 18- to 22-year-old students and, consequently, have no interest in serving the New Majority. Despite a growing interest in online learning among these institutions, the vast majority of teaching and learning activity remains limited to the classroom. Most of these institutions are content to stick with traditional academic values. For example, they see nothing wrong with professors who have no "real-world" experience. Consequently, most classroom activity, by design, lacks an applied-knowledge focus. In addition, the extent to which significant virtual education activities can be undertaken within existing college and university structures is open to question. Potential difficulties include the following:

- *Lack of leadership.* The attitudes, values, skills, and knowledge of executive leaders and decision makers in higher education differ entirely from those required to respond to the new economy.
- *Time-consuming decision-making processes.* Current decision-making structures—or the lack of them—on campus form an obstacle to developing large-scale responses.
- *Conflicts with "mainstream" activities.* It is difficult to emphasize traditional on-campus activities while simultaneously launching new kinds of activities.
- *Finance issues.* Traditional educators may not have the ability to raise capital to infuse the development of virtual activities. They

have little experience with developing business plans or successfully developing products. Without the expectation of profit, private investors and entrepreneurs will not make the investments—and take the risks—that are needed to create and market a new technology.

• *Staffing issues.* Academics generally lack the skills and abilities necessary to meet the challenges of virtual education. This is one of the reasons why "support" and "faculty development" loom so large on the higher education agenda.

Even though information technology and distance education are high on the agenda of every four-year institution—at least at the executive level—there is a wide gap between that interest and the development of serious, large-scale responses to the trends discussed above. First, despite an explosion in online activity, most of today's online course activity consists of current students who are engaged in an alternative option to classroom learning. Although there is nothing wrong with providing such alternatives, this is a long way from serving the burgeoning needs of the knowledge economy. Second, most online activity is confined to disparate courses rather than making up full degree or certificate programs. To be sure, a small number of institutions have done heroic work in this arena, but most four-year institutions are nowhere near offering the number of full programs or workplace-oriented courses that are required by the new economy. Third, almost all of the newly announced virtual efforts on traditional campuses are developing exceedingly slowly. Timing is generally set by the institution, not by the needs of the customer.

Virtual University Consortia

Almost every state in the United States is engaged in some kind of virtual university consortium effort. In some cases, the consortium involves only public institutions: the State University of New York (SUNY) Learning Network, UMass Online, Georgia G.L.O.B.E., the University of Texas Telecampus, and the recently announced Tennessee Virtual University. In other states, the effort involves both public and private institutions such as the Kentucky Virtual University (KYVU), the Michigan Virtual University, the Illinois Virtual Campus, and the Ohio Learning Network.

Once again, the changing economy is the driver behind these efforts. This excerpt from the KYVU homepage typifies these efforts:

Various kinds of foci are possible:

The mission of the KYVU is to be a student-centered, technology-based system for coordinating the delivery of postsecondary education that meets the needs of citizens and employers across the Commonwealth. . . . Consistent with the statewide strategic agenda for post-secondary education, the primary purposes of the KYVU are to:

- Enhance and expand educational access and increase educational attainment across Kentucky.
- Upgrade workforce skills and expand professional development through basic and continuing education.
- Increase collaboration and foster efficiency and effectiveness in delivering courses and programs.
- Enhance educational quality.
- Increase global competitiveness of Kentucky's educational resources (Kentucky Virtual University [KYVU], 1998).

What else do these state consortium efforts have in common? All operate a "portal"—a Web site that lists participating institutions and courses and, in some cases, degree programs offered online. Their primary operational activity is as a referral service, since none of the consortia are degree-granting and none offer their own courses but rather list those of the participating campuses. Students must choose a "home" campus in which to enroll. Because each of the campuses has its own residency requirements and transfer policies, students inevitably have limited opportunities for study beyond what a particular campus traditionally offers. As a consequence, the majority of students taking courses in these virtual university endeavors are simply on-campus students studying online at their home campuses.

It is questionable how far these efforts, as currently constructed, can go toward meeting their primary goal of economic development, since despite the hype, students must still follow traditional practices at a home campus. These consortia are generating demand for higher education because of the publicity surrounding their creation, but they are also generating frustration on the part of students because of anti-quated residency and transfer policies. The result is that those institutions with more flexible degree completion policies will benefit.

Independent Nonprofit Institutions

Another category of participants in the virtual education space is independent nonprofit institutions. Some of these—like the Western Governors' University (WGU), the United States Open University (USOU), and Jones International University—have been recently formed. Others—like the National Technological University (NTU) and Excelsior College (formerly Regents College)—have been around for years.

Founded in 1984, the National Technological University was established to deliver academic courses directly into corporation training facilities, via satellite, for engineering professionals. Today NTU awards master's degrees in 18 engineering, technical, and business areas and offers more than 1,300 academic courses, all supplied by 52 leading U.S. universities, including about half of the top 25 engineering schools. Courses today are delivered via satellite, the Internet, videotape, and CD-ROM.

The Western Governors' University opened its doors in 1998. Like NTU, WGU does not teach its own courses but instead has partnerships with other institutions all over the United States to provide instruction through distance education. WGU awards degrees by assessing students' knowledge through a set of competency-based exams. WGU has achieved candidate status for accreditation through a consortium of four regional accrediting agencies.

In 1999, Britain's Open University (BOU) announced plans to begin offering an Americanized version of its distinctive distance education program through a U.S.-based sister institution, the United States Open University. Currently in a pilot stage, the USOU faces a number of serious challenges, including adapting BOU's course structures to U.S. students and finding the right students to enroll.

Each of these institutions targets working adults. Demand is high in professional areas—business and management, health care, education, and information technology. Because these institutions grant degrees and enable students to study according to the demands of their busy lives, the independent nonprofits are closely aligned to the needs of the changing economy.

Partnerships and Subsidiaries

A number of four-year institutions are creating partnerships with private companies. For example, several leading universities—including Columbia University, Stanford University, the University of Chicago, and the London School of Economics and Political Science—have established partnerships with UNEXT.com, a start-up Internet company. NYU Online is a partnership between New York University and click2learn.com. Other institutions are creating for-profit and nonprofit subsidiaries. Examples include the University of Maryland University College (UMUC), eCornell, Duke University's Duke Corporate Education Inc., and NTU. Most of these efforts result from the need for institutions to find a way to offer both credit and noncredit courses to individuals and corporate universities—that is, a way to respond to the demands of the changing economy.

Traditional institutions choose to form partnerships or subsidiaries for several reasons. The first reason is to create an opportunity to secure capital in order to finance the institution's expansion. Traditional institutions are funded on an operating basis, primarily by tuition and/or state allocations. Neither of these sources can generate enough capital to invest in expansion. The second reason, closely related to the first, is to enable the development, marketing, and delivery of online courses. For example, NTU and UMUC are each a way for their parent institutions to retain core academic functions (establishing admission standards, degree program requirements, and faculty qualifications and awarding degrees) while moving noncore functions (evaluating demand, marketing services, recruiting students, developing products like courseware, and handling back-office functions) to the for-profit subsidiary. Accreditors and states see this as a way to raise capital without compromising academic integrity (Goldstein, 2000).

A third reason is that the new entity can take on risks, thus protecting the parent from unnecessary risk. The fourth reason is to gain flexibility in staffing policies and practices such as hiring and compensation (e.g., share of profits). Duke's Fuqua School of Business had been successfully offering programs to top management for a price tag of $80,000 in tuition, but Duke also found a large demand for training at lower levels. Since the Duke faculty had little interest in meeting this demand and since Duke's personnel policies made it difficult to respond flexibly to the market, Duke created Duke Corporate Education Inc. Ownership is 60 percent Duke University, 20 percent employees of the new entity, and 20 percent other investors. Five full-time faculty and 30 part-time faculty will transfer from Duke to the new entity, which will also initially hire about 60 to 70 new employees.

What is the prognosis for these new entities? Many institutions will form partnerships and subsidiaries because they are resolving the real friction between institutional structures and the demands of the new economy. Even though many of the current efforts are simply reinvestments by the parent (Duke, Cornell), the need for flexibility is a clear driver. In essence, what Cornell and Duke are doing is creating a continuing education operation. Although they may gain needed flexibility, a key question remains: Can they attract external capital? Meanwhile, both NTU and UMUC believe they have an excellent product that has been held back due to lack of public knowledge. If that is indeed the case, these new subsidiaries will be very effective in "growing" these institutions. If not, capital will flow to more profitable ventures.

Corporate Universities

Corporate universities exist predominantly in the United States. According to Corporate University Exchange, their number rose from 400 in 1988 to 2,000 in 2001 (Meister, 2001). The significant increase in the number of corporate universities could be a sign that companies no longer consider continuing education and training as a cost that should be cut but rather as an investment that can attract and retain the best workforce. Companies may realize that they must prepare employees to compete in the global economy, to meet and exceed service expectations, to adjust to changing roles and new technologies, and to respond to current and future global pressures.

Despite the large numbers of "corporate universities," in most instances these organizations represent a "rebranding" of their company's human resources and training functions. Little has changed except the name. The majority are focused on improving the competitive edge of their own companies through improved group and individual performance, and most show few signs of activity at the higher education level. Despite the adoption of a lot of the language of higher education in corporate training circles, few if any companies are, in fact, trying to compete with traditional institutions. Their offerings are primarily noncredit, nondegree courses; 82 percent are used primarily to convey corporate culture to the company employees. Even Motorola University, a frequently cited corporate university exemplar, generates only about 7 percent of its revenue externally, mostly through enrollment in courses like "How to Establish a Corporate University."

Some observers believe that corporate universities represent a potential threat to traditional institutions. Until very recently, colleges enjoyed a captive market, and corporations paid whatever institutions charged for executive education. But today, by launching their own corporate universities, companies are taking it upon themselves to educate their employees and/or to demand courses that fit their particular business needs and challenges. They are also requiring that courses be developed more quickly and at more competitive prices. In addition, corporations want their educational partners to provide many more, often time-consuming and costly services such as round-the-clock access to professors, mentors, and fellow students (Meister, 2001; CVCP and HEFCE, 2000).

For-Profit Institutions

Despite the large amount of attention recently directed at for-profit institutions of higher education, many of them have been around for a relatively long time. DeVry was founded in 1931, the Keller Graduate School of Management in 1973, and the University of Phoenix in 1976.

Two things are worth mentioning in a discussion of the impact of for-profit institutions on traditional four-year institutions. The first is that even though these institutions, like their nonprofit counterparts, are primarily site based, their greatest growth trajectories are occurring in the online market. The University of Phoenix, for example, currently enrolls 75,000 students, a 22 percent increase over 2000. Its online campus grew by 44.7 percent, to 13,779 students. The projected growth of its site-based programs is 17–18 percent; the projected growth of its online programs is 35–40 percent. In examining these trends, the authors of *The Business of Borderless Education: UK Perspectives* observed that technology is not the primary competitive issue, despite their view that in the longer term "the majority of continuing professional development is likely to become virtual." The U.K. and Australian teams agreed: "At present, virtual, corporate and for-profit institutions are not far in advance of traditional universities in exploiting the potential of technology to change their educational model" (CVCP and HEFCE, 2000, p. 5).

Rather, the biggest competitive challenge to existing institutions, particularly those that serve working adult students, lies in the more efficient way that the new private providers utilize staffing resources and in their highly professional approach to teaching and learning.

Close attention is paid to quality through mandated teacher training, rigorous evaluation of the teaching process, an emphasis on supporting all teachers including part-timers, a focus on professional expertise, and close attention to service levels for learners.

Key elements in the ability of the new providers to attract adult students include convenient locations; "24/7" full-time learner support; frequent enrollment points; short intensive study periods; the potential for "banking" and transfer of credit; and a curriculum that is taught by practicing professionals and that is of direct and immediate applicability to the workplace. *The Business of Borderless Education* correctly observes that in the professional development market "the social aspects of learning are perhaps less significant than in undergraduate education" (CVCP and HEFCE, 2000, p. 15). These providers are creating a new kind of institution—one built on inclusiveness and accessibility, much like the community college, rather than on the exclusiveness and inaccessibility that typifies medallion institutions. In the process, they are creating new "brands."

Conclusion

Three important points emerge from our brief analysis of the current organizational developments in virtual education. First, each type of institution is being driven by the demands of the changing economy and the needs of the New Majority, despite differences in strategies for development. Second, these phenomena will inevitably have different impacts on the various types of four-year institutions. Traditional four-year institutions that depend heavily on adult students are clearly more threatened by competition in this market than are those that focus on traditional undergraduates. The third point—and the most significant in my opinion—is the likely relative decline in traditional four-year institutions' influence on the world of postsecondary education and on the public dialogue. Institutions that once dominated the development of public policy may be increasingly marginalized if they fail to respond constructively to the needs of the changing economy.

IMPLICATIONS FOR THE FUTURE

A central premise of most gatherings of prominent higher education leaders today is that the "new providers" of higher education are likely to produce changes comparable to those brought about by the establishment of land grant institutions and community colleges. But some question this assumption. Can anyone, they ask, actually name six "new providers" that are up and running or will be so in the foreseeable future? Like the small boy who questioned the state of the emperor's clothing, they point out that although many proposals for new efforts are being floated, these are mostly just talk. The changes being taken for granted are hardly moving at Internet speed, if at all.

At first glance, this argument seems quite persuasive. After all, the University of Phoenix—the leading exemplar of the new providers—is really quite traditional in its operation, emulating both the form and the content of many traditional four-year institutions. Its primary distinguishing characteristic—its for-profit status—makes a lot of people in higher education uncomfortable, to be sure, especially when this for-profit status is coupled with its rapid growth rate. But other than the University of Phoenix, it's hard to name any significant players who can be called "new providers," particularly at the baccalaureate level. Despite an abundance of press releases and highly touted "alliances," the other for-profit initiatives lack one important ingredient: students. WGU's total student body, for example, is the size of one not-so-large class at a traditional university. Indeed, the vast majority of for-credit online and distance learning courses are being conducted by highly traditional colleges and universities, building on well-established academic structures and conditions for successful learning. These initiatives create greater opportunities for students, as well as greater competitive pressures among established institutions, but it's a stretch to call the Universities of Maryland, Indiana, and Wisconsin, for example, "new providers."

So perhaps our colleagues are right: perhaps the transformation we're supposed to be undergoing is just noise. Then again, perhaps those who look for examples of transformation in higher education by extrapolating from current institutional forms are missing the point. Extrapolation would suggest that transformation means moving the entire apparatus of degree-granting institutions, more or less intact, on to the Internet. To be sure, there are not many examples of this today, and there may well not be many in the future.

An alternate view suggests that the higher education transformation that is just beginning is taking a different tack. The key concept here is the disaggregation of institutional structures and processes, a disaggregation made possible largely by the capabilities of information technology—the virtual value chain. New providers of products and services are targeting pieces of the educational enterprise as the source of new businesses, pieces that can then be reaggregated under entirely new, flexible arrangements. The impact on traditional four-year institutions is and will be economic. The dispersion of the currently integrated products and services of higher education will be like pulling threads, one by one, from a piece of fabric. At first, there is little noticeable change, but as time goes on, the material begins to unravel.

Let's consider a few examples. Campuses are beginning to experience what *Converge* magazine has called "The Great College Textbook Migration" (Smith, 1999). The $3 billion college textbook market, the high overhead that is passed on to customers of college bookstores, and the 76 percent of U.S. college students who regularly use the Internet add up to a new business opportunity. Companies like VarsityBooks and BigWords, two new online efforts, can bypass the college bookstore, cut costs 25 percent to 40 percent, and eliminate the institution's share of the bookstore profits (just a "thread" in the overall campus budget), all while providing better, cheaper, and faster service to students.

How about remedial education? Companies are developing highly sophisticated instructional software that targets this segment of higher education. Most of this software is currently designed to be used in a traditional classroom or learning laboratory format. But it doesn't take too much imagination to see the possibilities for a new outsourcing business model that provides remedial educational services, an area that many institutions would gladly cede to others. What about master's degrees? Most of the serious competition from for-profit providers is at the master's level, for rather obvious reasons: the difference between 30–36 credits in a specialized area and 12–128 credits in multiple areas. Testing? Think Sylvan, Kaplan, and ETS. Placement services? Library services? Tutorial services? Specialized courses like those for information technology competencies? The list goes on. In each case, the competitive alternative is based on "better, cheaper, faster"—the watchwords of the Internet.

We are already seeing the creation of companies in each of these arenas. Some would say that these are ancillary to the main business of undergraduate education. And perhaps they are. But we are also seeing the emergence of new forms of teaching and learning that have the potential to radically improve student learning. These new approaches go far beyond education as usual on the Internet. We know, for example, that Virginia Tech has demonstrably improved the way mathematics is learned by students. Why shouldn't they (as a for-profit arm of the university, as an independent math faculty "practice," or as a new company that acquired the methodology) offer mathematics to students across the country? And why won't this example be replicated in all high-demand disciplines?

Today, few people would argue with the assertion that the Internet is transforming communications in the United States and around the world. Perhaps 20 years ago, people thought that a new communications structure would be an extrapolated replica of the old AT&T. Instead what we have is the disaggregation and reaggregation of hundreds of communications products and services in place of the monolithic structures of the past, offered by companies that didn't exist when the Internet was conceived.

Who are the new providers? In most cases, we don't yet know their names.

REFERENCES

Adelman, C. (2000). A parallel universe. *Change, 32*(3), May/June, 20–29.
Clark, R.E. (1983). Reconsidering research on learning in media. *Review of Educational Research, 53*(4), 445–459.

Committee of Vice-Chancellors and Principals of the Universities and The Higher Education Funding Council for England. (2000). *The business of borderless education: UK perspectives.* London: Authors. This report builds on an earlier study and a detailed analysis of corporate universities and educational businesses in the United States. The previous study was conducted by a team of Australian researchers: *The business of borderless education.* Available: http://www.detya.gov.au/archive/highered/eippubs/eip00_3/bbe.pdf [April 23, 2001].

Council for Higher Education Accreditation. (2000). *Transfer and the public interest.* Washington, DC: Author.

Dolence, M.G., and Norris, D.M. (1995). *Transforming higher education: A vision for learning in the 21st century.* Ann Arbor, MI: Society for College and University Planning.

Gardener, H. (1993). *Frames of mind: The theory of multiple intelligences.* New York: Basic Books.

Goldstein, M.B. (2000). To be (for-profit) or not to be: What is the question? *Change, 32*(5), September/October, 25–31.

Green, K.C. (1997). Money, technology, and distance education. *On the Horizon, 5*(6), November/December, 1, 3–7.

Johnstone, D.B. (1992). Learning productivity: *A new imperative for American higher education.* Albany, NY: State University of New York.

Kentucky Virtual University (1998). KYVU mission and purpose. Available: http://www.kyvu.org/student.nsf/ID/c41a596c1030273a8525691b00521f56 [April 23, 2001].

Marchese, T. (1998). Not-so-distant competitors: How new providers are remaking the postsecondary marketplace. *AAHE Bulletin,* May.

Matthews, D. (n.d.). The transformation of higher education through information technology: Implications for state higher education finance policy. Unpublished paper.

Meister, J.C. (2001, February). The brave new world of corporate education. *Chronicle of Higher Education, 47,*8–10.

Mingle, J.R., Heterick, R.C., Jr., and Twigg, C.A. (1998). *The public policy implications of a global learning infrastructure.* Washington, DC: Educom.

Noam, E. (1995). Electronics and the dim future of the university. *Science, 270,* 247–249.

Rayport, J., and Sviokla, J. (1994). Managing in the marketspace. *Harvard Business Review,* November-December, 141–150.

Rayport, J., and Sviokla, J. (1995). Exploiting the virtual value chain. *Harvard Business Review,* November-December, 75–85.

Russell, T.L. (n.d.). The "no significant difference phenomenon." Available: http://teleeducation.nb.ca/nosignificantdifference/ [April 23, 2001].

Schroeder, C. (1993). New students—new learning styles. *Change, 25*(5) September/October, 23–26.

Smith, B. (1999). The great college textbook migration. *Converge, 2*(9), September, 12–14.

Twigg, C.A. (1996). *Academic productivity: The case for instructional software.* Washington, DC: Educom.

Twigg, C.A. (2001). *Quality for whom? Providers and consumers in today's distributed learning environment.* Troy, NY: The Pew Learning and Technology Program.

Twigg, C.A., and Miloff, M. (1998). The global learning infrastructure. In D. Tapscott, A. Lowy, and D. Ticoll (Eds.), *Blueprint to the digital economy: Wealth creation in an e-business era* (pp. 179–201). New York: McGraw-Hill.

4

Higher Education, the Emerging Market, and the Public Good

*Brian Pusser**

> If a nation expects to be ignorant and free, in a state of civilization,
> it expects what never was and never will be.
>
> —Thomas Jefferson to Col. Charles Yancey, January 6, 1816

INTRODUCTION

One of the more remarkable aspects of contemporary research and analysis of higher education is the repeated invocation of the emergence of a market for postsecondary education and training (Ruch, 2001; Collis, 2001; Duderstadt, 1999, 2000; Munitz, 1998; Goldstein, 1999; Marchese, 1998). These accounts generally suggest that increased market competition is the inevitable result of economic and technological changes that are transforming higher education from "cottage monopoly to competitive industry" (Munitz, 2000, p. 12). They further suggest that under the market model, colleges and universities will be increasingly consumer driven (Ruch, 2001), operated like firms (Blustain, Goldstein, and Lozier, 1999; Garber, 1996), challenged by unprecedented competition (Newman and Couterier, 2001), and find their traditional forms of pedagogy and credentialing transformed by technological innovations (Newman and Scurry, 2001; Adelman, 2000).

The inherent assumptions in the presentation of an emerging market for higher education are even more striking than the ubiquity of market metaphors themselves, yet it is not clear that those assumptions are

---
*Brian Pusser is assistant professor in the Center for the Study of Higher Education at the Curry School of Education of the University of Virginia.

valid. This paper turns attention to three fundamental assumptions that shape predictions of an emerging competitive marketplace for higher education. The first is that higher education institutions operate in an environment and under conditions that can accurately be described as market competition. The second assumption is that a lack of institutional efficiency and productivity has generated demands for market solutions and that market-like behaviors on the part of postsecondary institutions will increase efficiency and productivity in higher education. Finally, there is the assumption that market approaches to the provision of higher education will produce at least the same quantity and distribution of public and private goods as are generated by the present system. While each of these assumptions has been debated in contemporary research on higher education, the argument over the case for higher education as a public good has moved to the fore over the past decade (Levine, 2001). It is a conflict that is central to contests over access, finance, and accountability in the postsecondary realm. The notion that market provision of higher education will preserve the role of higher education as a public good challenges a number of traditional beliefs about the nature of education itself. John McMurtry (1991) put it this way:

> The defining principles of education and of the market-place are fundamentally contradictory in: (1) their goals; (2) their motivations; (3) their methods; and (4) their standards of excellence. It follows, therefore, that to understand the one in terms of the principles of the other, as has increasingly occurred in the application of the market model to the public educational process, is absurd. (p. 216)

The three assumptions also engender a strong sense of inevitability in arguments for the market provision of higher education. While researchers may differ on whether a market approach is a positive development, the underlying question in contemporary accounts is not whether higher education institutions should adopt market-like behaviors, but whether they will be able to do so rapidly enough to remain competitive. As Newman and Couterier (2001) put it, "Whether policy makers and academic leaders are capable of addressing these issues in the months and years ahead or not, higher education will continue its inexorable evolution toward a market economy" (p. 9). That sense of inevitability in turn fosters demands for further adaptation of higher education systems in the United States and around the world (Clark, 1998; Tooley, 1999). It is the argument here that market approaches to higher education are less inevitable than they are ahistorical. Contemporary literature on the need to adapt to changing demands through market solutions does not sufficiently account for the evolution of the nonprofit institution as the dominant form for the provision of postsecondary education in the United States. Nor does contemporary research sufficiently explore the relative inability of market-based, consumer-driven systems to produce opportunities for universal access, leadership training, or the redress of social inequalities. In order to understand the continuing importance of nonmarket delivery of higher education in the service of the public good, we need to begin with an overview of the changing demands on the higher education system.

THE CHANGING ENVIRONMENT

Contemporary research on the contextual changes shaping higher education has focused on a number of issues, including labor market demands (Adelman, 2000; Marchese, 1998); the new demographics of postsecondary students and constituents (Carnevale and Fry, 2001; Kohl and LaPidus, 2000); the rising cost of higher education (Ehrenberg, 2000); globalization (Levin, 2001); new technologies (Mendenhall, 2001; Graves, 1999); and competition as a driver of change in postsecondary structures and processes (Levine, 2001; Marginson and Considine, 2000).

Perhaps the most influential analyses have been those focused on changes in the finance of higher education over the past two decades (Heller, 2001; McKeown-Moak, 2000; Goldstein, 1999; Kane, 1999; McPherson and Schapiro, 1998). During that period increases in enrollments have coincided with a retrenchment from state block grant support for higher education (Winston, Carbone, and Lewis, 1998). In response, institutions have rapidly increased tuition, and students and parents have taken on a significantly larger portion of the finance of higher education (Callan, 2001; Breneman, 2000). This shift in the burden of paying for higher education has revived a longstanding debate, one that encompasses considerably more than resource allocation, as it calls for rethinking the organization and delivery of higher education. In the United States and elsewhere around the world, that broader debate has recently centered on the role of market competition in the transformation of higher education and on the effect of market competition on the contributions of higher education to the public good (Altbach, 2001; Currie and Newson, 1999; Marginson and Considine, 2000; Pusser, 2000; Pusser and Doane, 2001; Tooley, 1999).

HIGHER EDUCATION AND THE PUBLIC GOOD

One of the few areas of agreement with regard to the public good is that it is a problematic concept. Even the phrase "the public good" shares space in our discourse with "the common good" and "the public interest." There are also many references to a different concept, "public goods," in concert with the ascendance of market models and economic approaches to public life. The nature of public goods is also contested, though they are commonly identified by two characteristics, nonrivalry and nonexcludability (Samuelson, 1954). Public goods are presumed to be underproduced in markets, as those two fundamental characteristics prevent individual producers from generating sufficient profit (Marginson, 1997).

Mansbridge (1998) argues that the idea of the public good is a fundamentally unsettled, contested concept, one that is at the center of broader conflicts over public action. Similarly, Calhoun (1998) suggests that the public good is a dynamic and indeterminate social and cultural construct. Reese (2000) characterizes "the elusive search for the common good" as the struggle to find common social and political understandings in a pluralistic nation. Given that we grant the concept of the public good an indeterminate status at the limit, there are a number of outcomes of education that are widely agreed upon as contributing to the public good. These include the role of education in citizenship development, building common values, and democratic participation for the national good (Cuban and Shipps, 2000), in stimulating economic growth and the diffusion of technology, as well as increases in social cohesion (Wolfe, 1995; Brighouse, 2000). Breneman (2001) notes that our ability to empirically measure the noneconomic contributions of higher education is weak and that consensus around the role of higher education in service of the public good will more likely be achieved though political and policy debate.

Acknowledgment of a public good emerging from the provision of higher education does not settle the question of how best to define or generate that public good. Since Plato pursued the meaning of "the good" and Aristotle the degree of materialism inherent in a "common good," philosophers and social theorists have contested these questions (Mansbridge, 1998). As he moved away from a medieval philosophy that set public good and private good as opposing forces, Adam Smith turned attention to the possibility that self-interest, in the aggregate, could most efficiently provide the common good. Smith's "invisible hand" has formed the foundation of contemporary neoliberal definitions of the public good as nothing more than the aggregate of private goods (Marginson, 1997).

A distinction also needs to be made between the degree to which different educational sectors contribute to the public good. There is a stronger consensus around the contributions to the public good made through the elementary-secondary system than there is for postsecondary education (Brighouse, 2000). Nonetheless, in the United States we have at various historical moments demonstrated a significant degree of consensus around creating elaborate and often costly postsecondary projects and policies in the service of the public good. The creation and expansion of higher education has been a key locus of collective commitment to the production of both public and private goods in the service of the public good. The land grant college movement, the expansion of the community college system after World War II, and the rapid increase in science and technology research programs in universities in the wake of Sputnik are oft-cited examples of promoting the public good through public investments in higher education. Over the same time frame, the nonprofit degree-granting institution in the United States has become dominant, in large measure to protect against moral hazard and underinvestment, but also to ensure that the contributions of higher education to the public good will be widely disseminated (Pusser, 2000). Market production is generally understood as for-profit production, though Hansmann (1980), Weisbrod (1998), and others offer useful models of market-like competition between organizations.

Market competition also entails production closely following demand, if that demand leads to profit. Under market production, there is little if any provision for production in the absence of demand, and the market producer is indifferent to public goods (Marginson, 1997). These latter two cases, we shall see, form a key distinction between market production and public production in general and in higher education in particular. Public nonprofit production has long been the dominant model in higher education because, unlike market production, it is oriented to public goods and the common good, as well as to private goods. Public nonprofit production is also the only vehicle for ensuring the production of educational products and services that would not justify for-profit production. Public nonprofit production, in the contemporary policy environment, is challenged by the growth of for-profit production. There are limits to public subsidies and public support for education, and those subsidies will be distributed going forward in a political economic competition between market advocates and those who argue for public provision of higher education (Pusser, 2000).

MOVING AWAY FROM COLLECTIVE SUPPORT FOR HIGHER EDUCATION

Along with rising interest in market approaches for university adaptation, a related shift is taking place in public policy and planning from the public supply to the public subsidy of higher education. This shift is accompanied by a move from collective finance to individual finance and has significant implications for higher education as a public good (Pusser, 2000). Both shifts are consistent with market approaches to the provision of higher education. An intriguing aspect of the policy debate is that the primary rationale for these changes is not the one advanced by neoclassical economists such as Gary Becker (1976), who argue that education is an investment in individual human capital and as such an appropriate investment for the individual to finance. Nor does the argument follow Howard Bowen's (1977) contention that since public subsidies have gone disproportionately to those who could matriculate without them, policy makers might appropriately shift the burden to those beneficiaries. Recent findings confirm Bowen's, as significant public subsidies continue to be available to students in middle- and upper-income brackets (Winston, 1999) and financial aid continues to shift from need-based to merit-based provision (Ehrenberg, 2000). The primary rationale supporting the shift in resource allocation strategies is that market competition driven by consumer choice is the appropriate driver of reform in higher education (Schmidt, 2001; Marginson and Considine, 2000). As a prime example, a report commissioned as part of the

National Governors Association's initiative Influencing the Future of Higher Education (2001) predicted that

> Savvy states in the twenty-first century will focus on postsecondary customers: the learner, the employer, and the public who supports educational opportunities. In competitive states, resources will increasingly flow to the learner, and state regulatory policies will ease to encourage institutional flexibility (p. 3).

This approach traces its lineage less to Becker or Bowen, although their findings are certainly influential, than to Milton Friedman. Friedman's *Capitalism and Freedom* (1962) emphasized the private benefits of higher education and called for a public retrenchment from funding. To the extent that government had a role, Friedman suggested subsidies should go to individuals, not institutions, and that competition should be increased throughout the system through the portability of financing instruments.

Despite the historical and contemporary references to the potential role of the market in postsecondary education, to date, empirical, discipline-based and theoretical research that addresses the nature or impact of market models for higher education has received less attention than a quite different literature. The most visible accounts of the emerging market, new competitors, entrepreneurial forms of finance, and the like come from the popular press, and more specifically, those periodicals that cover business and the business of higher education. In part this imbalance is due to an apparent preference in the press for reporting on economic, market-based, or profit-generating topics rather than academic ones. Add to the mix the rise of attention-garnering, publicly traded companies like the University of Phoenix, DeVry, and Strayer, and the recent partnerships between universities like Cornell and New York University with private venture capital funds, and an irresistible journalistic soup begins to emerge. Stir in a dollop of the dot-com revolution through virtual delivery of degrees and linkages between for-profit portal providers and higher education institutions, then add some business superstars like Glenn Jones (Jones International University) and Michael Milkin (UNEXT) as the pot begins to boil. Add a growing chorus of protests over the rising costs of higher education, with a pinch of critiques of the higher education bureaucracy reminiscent of those leveled earlier at the elementary-secondary system by Chubb and Moe (1990), and familiar aromas will fill the metaphorical kitchen. Stoke the fire with research provided by groups relatively new to higher education: stock analysts (Block and Dobell, 1999; Soffen, 1998) and the presidents and administrative leaders of for-profit universities (Ruch, 2001; Sperling, 1989, 2000), and there may soon be considerably more heat than light shed on the subject.

THE APPEAL OF THE MARKET

It is not difficult to understand the appeal of market discourse and ideology. One can safely hypothesize that rapid changes are taking place and that higher education institutions may not be able to respond with business as usual. One could also confidently postulate that policy makers and many others believe that much of public higher education is priced too high, that it requires too much direct state funding, and that its fundamental organization is inefficient. It is also safe to say that the idea of putting the free market to work has considerable appeal to policy makers and legislators (Marginson and Considine, 2000). Faith in the market and its potential role in reforming the provision of higher education is based in a fundamental tenet of market ideology, that competition creates efficiencies, productivity gains, and cost savings. The problems appear to be precisely the ones that the market purports to remedy (Marginson, 1997).

This is, however, a tricky terrain for researchers to navigate. Even the premise that higher education is too expensive is difficult to address without an agreed-upon metric for comparison (Ehrenberg, 2000). Too expensive compared to 30 years ago? One can't begin to make that comparison without a way to control for the vast changes in the product over that time. In which institutions is higher education too costly? The most expensive institutions, both public and private, are in many cases facing annual demand that considerably exceeds supply, a situation that in most market models would lead to further price increases (Breneman, 2001; Winston, 1997). Yet the political and popular appeal of a commonly held perspective on a phenomenon is not to be lightly dismissed. One of the contentions of this paper is that the belief in market effectiveness, market efficiencies, and market gains drives the current policy fascination with markets and market competition in higher education, despite the paucity of empirical tests. It is also the case that the policy community does not necessarily wait for research results before taking action. A number of key policy actors are currently proposing significant shifts in the funding and production of higher education using market rhetoric and market models in their justifications (NGA, 2001; Burd, 2001). In the most dramatic example, Governor Rick Perry of Texas in 2001 suggested transforming the majority of state block grant appropriations for institutions into scholarship funds sent directly to students (Schmidt, 2001).

It has been suggested in prior research that using market models or market discourse to develop policy, where the conditions are inappropriate for market analysis, may lead to flawed assumptions and misguided policies (Leslie and Johnson, 1974). To fully understand the changes taking place in higher education today, and to formulate appropriate policies based on those changes, requires an evaluation of whether the contemporary context is appropriately defined as an emerging market environment and whether the market model is useful in this case.

Markets and Higher Education

The history of theorizing on markets and market influences on higher education goes at least as far back as Adam Smith, who speculated in the 18th century on efficiencies that might be generated by linking faculty salaries to productivity (Ortmann, 1997). In a more contemporary realm, Milton Friedman's work on choice and education (1962, 1980) and Paul Samuelson's (1954) perspectives on public and private goods have done much to shape how we think about the potential for free market competition in higher education. Despite that long history, there are still a number of reasons to pause before applying a market model to an arena where some of the following conditions prevail: (1) the product is sold in the vast majority of cases for considerably less than it costs to produce; (2) some 90 percent of those seeking degrees are enrolled in nonprofit institutions; (3) of those enrollments, over 75 percent are in institutions that are nonprofit and public; (4) there are significant barriers to entry by new providers in many sectors; and (5) there are significant constraints on exit by the vast majority of providers. Before turning to these challenges in greater detail, it is also worth noting that the American higher education system is, as a production story, arguably the finest in the world (Kerr, 2001).

Changes to the Market Model

For at least three decades, economists have pointed to difficulties in attempting to apply market models to higher education (Winston, 1997; Bowen, 1977; Leslie and Johnson, 1974). One fundamental question concerns whether collective goods, like the benefits of increased levels of public education, are better generated by market or government production. Salamon (1995) suggests that collective goods are goods and services that, once produced, can be enjoyed by all, independent of whether the consumer helped pay for or produce the goods. This condition makes market production problematic, as few will pay for benefits they can enjoy without contribution (the "free rider" problem) and production will sink below optimal levels. Government, on the other hand, can use taxation as a way to ensure broader contribution to the cost of the collective good, but government production has its own shortcomings. Foremost of these is that government action is largely limited to the production of collective goods that a majority will agree merit production. Consequently, many collective goods desired by a minority of the polis will not be produced unless private nonprofit organizations are organized to produce those goods (Salamon, 1995). In innovative work produced shortly after the passage of the Higher Education Act (HEA) of 1972, Leslie and Johnson (1974) concluded:

> Upon considering collectively the major aspects of the higher education market, it becomes evident that while higher education can be generally and broadly discussed within the context of certain market terminology, the various market-related characteristics of higher education in no way approximate the sufficient conditions of the perfectly competitive market model. (p. 14)

It is no coincidence that the authors were theorizing about the nature of a market model for higher education on the heels of the passage of HEA. With provisions for portable financing through guaranteed student loans and BEOG (now Pell) grants, HEA seemed to provide the foundation of a higher education market as envisioned by Friedman. Yet what Leslie and Johnson surmised some 25 years ago, and what Gordon Winston and others have found quite recently, is that many characteristics of the production and consumption of higher education make developing a market model problematic. Those characteristics may also complicate predictions about the production of public and private goods through competitive markets in higher education.

Gordon Winston (1997) found six key factors that limit the utility of conceptualizing the contemporary provision of higher education in a free market. The first three factors, as Henry Hansmann (1980) initially pointed out, result from the fact that the higher education arena has long been dominated by nonprofit production. Nor is that dominance an anomaly or historical accident. Nonprofit institutions have held a disproportionate share of enrollments and degrees produced throughout the 20th century (Clark, 1983; Goldin and Katz, 1998).

Hansmann's three conditions also help to explain the success of the nonprofit form. First, the production of higher education is characterized by information asymmetries. That is, higher education is a difficult commodity to assess in advance and often takes considerable time to consume and evaluate. Further, producers of higher education generally have more information about the product than do the consumers. Given that the time required for a consumer to discover and redress the shortcomings of a poorly or fraudulently delivered education might be measured in years, that consumer is at considerable risk of exploitation. Second, the nondistribution constraint inherent in the nonprofit form protects the consumer from potential consequences of information asymmetry and other moral hazards, as it removes the possibility of profit serving as an incentive for producers to exploit their customers. Winston also suggests that since they operate under the nondistribution constraint, managers of nonprofits have alternative, generally more altruistic goals than managers of for-profits. Further, higher education provides benefits to society beyond the gains to the individual student. Given that it is socially useful to cultivate the maximum social benefit from higher education, the nondistribution constraint allows any public investment to go directly to production of social benefits and not to profit. When public investment is combined with direct public provision, in the case of public nonprofit production, the public has the greatest control and influence over the production of social benefits through higher education (Pusser, 2000; Goldin and Katz, 1998).

A third distinctive aspect of higher education production is that both public and independent nonprofit institutions generate revenue from a variety of sources beyond what they charge directly for admission. Because higher education institutions receive commercial revenue, tax revenue, and donations, they are appropriately characterized as "donative commercial nonprofits" (Hansmann, 1980). The mix of subsidies allows nonprofit higher education in the United States to be offered at a price far below its production cost (Winston, 1997, 1999). Winston estimated in 1996 that the average cost of a year of higher education in all schools in the United States was approximately $12,000, while the average price a student paid was just under $4,000. That average subsidy of around $8,000 was dwarfed by the subsidies offered at elite private institutions (Winston et al., 1998). These subsidies constitute a significant barrier to entry into the higher education arena.

A fourth limitation on conceptualizing the production of higher education in a market model is related to the asymmetry problem, as it has been noted that "the perfectly informed customer of economic theory is nowhere to be seen" (Winston, 1997, p. 4). Given the asymmetry problems noted earlier, this suggests that reputation and institutional history play a disproportionate role in consumer choice.

Two related factors also figure prominently here, the associative goods condition and institutional heterogeneity. Winston suggests that higher education is an associative good, and consequently one of an institution's most powerful resources is its own student body. This results in sharp competition between institutions for the most desirable students and between students wishing to attend those institutions enrolling their most highly recruited peers. What this suggests is that different institutions face quite different supply and demand conditions, and the same is true for students with differing levels of preparation and admissibility (Rothschild and White, 1993).

Marginson and Considine (2000), Ehrenberg (2000), Oster (1997), Slaughter and Leslie (1997), and others have built on the work of Winston and Hansmann to conceptualize a competitive environment of higher education composed of many different subcompetitions, based on subsidy levels, selectivity, geography, mission, and the like. Similarly, the internal allocation of resources in higher education institutions has been shaped to a large degree by organizational history, culture, and intent, as well as by competitive pressure (Marginson and Considine, 2000; Slaughter and Leslie, 1997).

This array of factors points to the complexity of developing either a production function or a theory of the firm for higher education (Masten, 1995; Winston, 1997). However, over the past two decades a quite useful body of research on the competitive responses of nonprofit institutions has emerged (Hansmann, 1980; Weisbrod, 1988; James and Rose-Ackerman, 1986; Salamon, 1995) and is quite helpful in understanding the contemporary higher education arena.

The Nonprofit Form in Higher Education

For over 200 years, there have been publicly funded, publicly regulated, degree-granting postsecondary institutions in the United States. Perhaps more importantly, over the same period, there have also been publicly incorporated institutions that have been publicly funded and regulated, and they have become by far the dominant site of postsecondary enrollment and the provision of postsecondary degrees. The public—through the establishment of state nonprofit public universities, the provision of public funds to nonprofit public and independent institutions, and the establishment of accreditation and oversight functions—has long served as provider, subsidizer, and regulator of American higher education.

Over time the provider role has been most significant, as at present some 80 percent of those enrolled in degree-granting programs are enrolled in public colleges and universities (Goldin and Katz, 1998; Hansmann, 1999). Given that approximately 85 percent of postsecondary enrollments are in public and independent nonprofit institutions, it is clear that public and independent nonprofit provision is the defining quality of the current system.

Public provision and finance of higher education, while not the original model, has long been the norm. Expanding the capacity of higher education has been a fundamental public project in the United States for two centuries. While hardly a linear expansion, growth of nonprofit higher education has been more steady than often suggested, albeit punctuated by rapid expansion around the Morrill Act, the GI Bill, and the Great Society reforms (Veysey, 1965; Hansen, 1991; Kerr, 1994; Breneman, 1992; Cohen and Brawer, 1996). The reasons for the continued development of the nonprofit form in higher education, despite the growth of market provision in many sectors of American life over the past two centuries, goes well beyond the issues of information asymmetry and nondistribution cited earlier. There are significant advantages and public benefits that can arguably only be generated by nonprofit provision. Powell and Clemens (1998) suggest that as a unique model of association within the public sphere, the nonprofit form itself is increasingly seen as a public good.

Nonprofit Provision and Finance

An analysis of the implications of demands for increased competition and market-like forms in higher education turns attention to earlier research on nonprofit competition (Hansmann, 1980, 1999; James and Rose-Ackerman, 1986; Weisbrod, 1988, 1998; Oster, 1997). In research on the role of the state in European higher education, Henry Hansmann (1999) has drawn a useful distinction between "public subsidy" and "public supply" of higher education and between "supply side" subsidies and "demand" subsidies for the support of higher education (p. 4). These distinctions are useful for understanding the changing provision of contemporary higher education.

PUBLIC SUPPLY AND PUBLIC SUBSIDY

Public supply refers to the provision of higher education in public nonprofit institutions. Public subsidy refers to the allocation of public funds to public or private, for-profit or nonprofit institutions. Public subsidies may either be provided by state or federal entities to an institution as direct institutional grants (supply side subsidies) or to students in the form of grants, loans, tax credits, and the like (demand side subsidies) that the student may use at any accredited institution. Of course, public subsidies are most often used by students at public institutions. Hansmann (1999), Oster (1997), and James (1998) point to various trade-offs between public supply and public subsidy.

Benefits of Public Supply

The fundamental arguments for public supply are that it offers the most direct utilization of public subsidies and that it is the organizational type best suited to the rapid expansion of higher education (Pusser, 2000; Hansmann, 1999). The argument for the benefit of public provision coupled with public subsidy is twofold. First, where education is provided in public institutions with public funds, the public has the greatest influence over the institution and its activities. Given the nonprofit status of public institutions, there is no diversion of the public subsidy to profit; hence, more of the subsidy goes to the production of preferred goods. Second, public higher education institutions can be rapidly built or expanded with public capital, while independent nonprofit institutions more often lack incentives and financing for such expansion (Oster, 1997). A salient example of public expansion is found in the history of public community colleges. The number of U.S. community colleges doubled from 1920 to 1950 and doubled again from 1950 to 1980. From a total of 8 community colleges at the turn of the 20th century, by 1998 there were nearly 1,600 community colleges (Phillippe, 1999). The funding, authorization, coordination, and control of this capacity building all required collaborative public effort (Cohen and Brawer, 1996). Public supply also provides the most direct mechanism for the production of public goods and benefits that would not be produced if consumer demand were insufficient to generate private nonprofit or for-profit provision or if private provision led to an undersupply of those goods and benefits. An example of this would be federal initiatives to integrate public higher education in the 1960s. Many of those initiatives were implemented through direct government intervention in public institutions where direct consumer demand had long been insufficient to effect change (Gaston, 2001).

Benefits of Public Subsidy

A primary argument for public subsidies to students for the purchase of higher education is that such subsidies may reduce underinvestment by reducing market constraints that prevent individuals from obtaining financing for higher education (Weisbrod, 1998; James, 1998). Public subsidies also serve to minimize the possibility that students will underconsume those forms of higher education that, while they might be socially desirable, entail uncertain individual returns (Hansmann, 1999).

The primary policy appeal of public subsidy is the belief that the portability of financial aid increases consumer choice and institutional efficiency (Friedman, 1962; Moe, 1996). Using portable public subsidies, students as consumers may spend state and federal grant and loan funds at a variety of locations, including public and independent nonprofits, as well as for-profit institutions. While public subsidies do give legislators and other funders leverage over institutions, subsidy is not as effective as direct supply for generating specific outputs. Portability dates to the Serviceman's Readjustment Act (GI Bill), which financed entrance into higher education for 2 million returning World War II veterans (Bound and Turner, 1999). GI Bill grants for tuition and living expenses were awarded to individuals rather than institutions and served as a forerunner to the subsequent creation of Guaranteed Student Loans and portable Pell grants in the Higher Education Act of 1965 and subsequent amendments. It is not often noted in contemporary higher education literature on market models and choice that portability of public subsidies originated some 60 years ago and was extended fairly universally nearly 40 years ago. It is also worth noting that the contemporary degree of enrollment choice and competition in American higher education is unprecedented in global higher education (Aronowitz, 2000). However, there is little empirical research to indicate that the choice provided by public subsidies has increased efficiency and productivity or led to lower costs of production. Given the increasing shift away from public supply, it is useful to also consider the implications of that shift for the creation of public and private goods.

THE PUBLIC INTEREST AND PUBLIC GOODS IN HIGHER EDUCATION

Higher education produces both collective (public) goods and private goods (Marginson, 1997; Bowen, 1977). Since the founding of the colleges in colonial times, the public has had an interest in, and contributed to, the production of public and private goods and services through higher education. The Institute for Higher Education Policy has refined an effective framework for delineating the various forms of public and private goods generated by increased levels of higher education. That framework sorts the outputs of higher education into four categories: public economic benefits, private economic benefits, public social benefits, and private social benefits (Institute for Higher Education Policy [IHEP], 1998).

A number of public economic benefits are generated as individuals acquire higher levels of education. These include greater levels of productivity, higher rates of consumer spending, increased tax revenues, enhanced workforce preparation, and decreased public expenditures for social services.

The list of private economic benefits that accrue to those with higher levels of educational attainment includes generally higher rates of employment and wages, increased levels of savings, increased labor market mobility, and enhanced working conditions.

The public social benefits generated by increased education are manifest in greater civic engagement, higher rates of voting, increased charitable giving and community involvement, and lower public health care costs. Bowen and Bok (1998) cite the production of a diverse cohort of leaders as a key public social benefit, while Howard Bowen points to the contributions of university basic research and public service, the preservation of the cultural heritage of society, and the reduction of inequality as central public benefits. He notes, "Education has an advantage over other avenues toward equality—such as graduated taxes and public assistance—because it can reduce the inequality of what people are and what they can contribute, not merely of what they get" (Bowen, 1978, p. 12).

Private social benefits that accrue to those with greater levels of education include better health and greater longevity, increased leisure time, and personal status, as well as access to better information for personal decision making (IHEP, 1998).

There are also significant interactions among these four categories. Higher individual income is a private benefit that also creates a public benefit—higher tax revenues. A higher level of civic engagement, a public benefit, in turn generates private benefits, as it enables individuals to live in more collegial communities.

Labaree has characterized the aggregate quality of public and private benefits on the basis of three defining goals: democratic equality, social efficiency, and social mobility. These three goals are readily apparent in the contemporary higher education system. In the pursuit of cultivating democratic equality, the higher education system contributes to the production of such public social benefits as citizenship development and increased equality. Social efficiency suggests that collective investment is the way to reduce underinvestment in higher education and produce a workforce appropriate for the contemporary labor market. Labaree's third goal, social mobility, is the fundamental driver of the production of private economic benefits. It suggests that education is a private good that enables individuals to succeed in social and economic competition. Labaree suggests that all three goals are political goals and that production of public and private benefits is mediated by political processes. In public policy discussions and institutional analyses, it is increasingly the case that all three of these goals are subsumed under the overarching mission of "economic development." While higher education institutions have contributed to economic production to some degree since the founding of the colonial colleges, today nearly all aspects of university mission are in some way linked to local, state, and federal economic development (Marginson and Considine, 2000; Slaughter and Leslie, 1997; University of California, Office of the President [UCOP], 1996).

The Market, Choice, and the Public Good

As evidenced by the quote from Thomas Jefferson at the beginning of this chapter, the public good and the public benefits of higher education have been discussed from nearly the founding of the country. As policy makers face pressure to increase competition and adopt market models for the organization and finance of higher education, the emerging question is quite basic: What is the public role, and what are the potential impacts of market approaches, on the contributions of higher education to the public good? Given the current organization of the higher education system, attention must also be directed to the future of the nonprofit form in higher education in the United States.

The gains to higher education that market advocates foresee are attributed to increased efficiency, driven by wider consumer choice. Yet 30 years of consumer choice supported by the portability of financial aid has done little to contain costs or limit tuition prices in higher education. Nor is it clear that the intention of postwar public policy has been to contain prices; rather, the effort seems to have been to increase capacity and choice and preserve quality. Further reductions in state block grant allocations will likely result in significant tuition increases (Callan, 2001). Although this may to some degree "level the playing field" between public, independent, and for-profit institutions, it may well also level up the price structure (Ehrenberg, 2000). While tuition at nonprofit independent institutions varies widely, for-profit institutions on average are significantly more expensive than public nonprofit institutions.

A number of researchers have predicted that increases in net cost will reduce access to higher education by lower income and traditionally underserved populations, as will a continuing shift from student grants to student loans (Callan, 2001; McPherson and Schapiro, 1998). Price sensitivity and loan sensitivity are a dual-edged sword that we do not yet have an effective grip on (Heller, 2001; Winston, Carbone, and Lewis, 1998). To the extent that market competition reduces public subsidies and levels prices, that competition may well increase stratification in the higher education system. The attention to the market also obscures the importance of the retreat from existing subsidies. While much has been written about the competition for public resources and the inevitability of state funding declines, there has been little speculation about what sort of education can be provided without the subsidies.

As state direct support declines, remedial education and other programs targeted to underprepared students may need to be funded from tuition increases, essentially a tax on better prepared students. Many other programs that are currently covered by state funds will also need to be funded through tuition increases. This sort of redistribution is increasingly unpopular at the state and federal levels, and there is little reason to assume it will be any more appealing in the long run at the institutional level. The decline in state support, the increasing use of tax credits as part of federal support for higher education, and the tilt from need-based to merit-based aid (Breneman, 2001) will likely further the divide in college-going between those from higher and lower income strata.

There is also a great deal of uncertainty over how competition affects educational quality. While there is a growing literature on the educational outputs of contemporary degree-granting, for-profit institutions (Ruch, 2001; Raphael and Tobias, 1997), these institutions constitute a very small fraction of the enrollments in postsecondary education and many have focused on adult enrollment. The success stories in this arena, the University of Phoenix and DeVry, offer fewer majors and courses of study than many public four-year colleges and universities. As one of the fastest growing institutional sectors in postsecondary education, the for-profits' targeted approach may have significant implications for public institutions attempting to compete in an era of declining state support. Over time, the range of curricular choices may well decrease, as prices increase.

A decline in access and affordability is also likely to reduce the production of public and private social and economic benefits from higher education. Reduced levels of overall college attainment will lead to decreased civic engagement, charitable giving, and community service. It predicts for increased rates of unemployment, incarceration, and public health costs. While those who attain more years of postsecondary education and those who attend more prestigious institutions will enjoy greater social benefits and increased personal status, they may also be required to navigate an increasingly polarized and problematic society, as reduction in state support reduces social benefits and increases social costs.

The Future of Nonprofit Postsecondary Education

Calls for market approaches to higher education do not necessarily portend the end of the nonprofit form of provision. It is possible to imagine, at the very least, the elite nonprofit institutions continuing as a dominant form. In an environment of relatively equal funding for nonprofit and for-profit providers, it is conceivable that the nondistribution constraint may lead to higher quality education in the nonprofits and continued demand for nonprofit institutions. It is also the case that the divide between nonprofit and for-profit structure and process in higher education is narrowing. Such entrepreneurial commercial activities in nonprofit institutions as the provision of courses and degrees through continuing education, the growth of auxiliary enterprises, and the creation of partnerships with corporations and venture capitalists are increasing in every sector of the nonprofit education arena (Pusser, 2000). A number of researchers in higher education have suggested potential negative consequences to the growth in commercial enterprises (Slaughter and Leslie, 1997; Marginson and Considine, 2000). As one example, it has been speculated that an increase in commercial enterprises may draw organizational attention away from core mission activities and require a "commercialization" of the managerial cohort. This in turn may decrease expertise in the nonprofits' core mission functions (Oster, 1997; Weisbrod, 1998).

Another significant issue is what the educational and social implications might be of an expansion of the for-profit form. Is there anything unique about the 21st century that has reduced the information asymmetries and moral hazards that have historically constrained for-profit expansion? It may be that better access to information through emerging technologies will increase consumer protection against exploitation in both nonprofit and for-profit institutions, but those who are most vulnerable to that exploitation also have the least access to information technology (Gladieux and Swail, 1999).

Preserving Higher Education's Contributions to the Public Good

Perhaps the most salient question is how higher education's contributions to the public good can be ensured if nonprofit public production gives way to a for-profit market. The fundamental mission of for-profit market production is to create private benefits for the producers and their customers. The historical mission of nonprofit production has been to create both public and private benefits. Public and private nonprofit higher education institutions have been key sites of access to leadership positions and greater civic involvement for their graduates (Bowen and Bok, 1998). Nonprofit institutions have been centers of public social and political efforts to achieve integration and the equalization of access to education. It is not at all clear that those goals can be realized through for-profit production. Public goals for the creation of public goods have been most effectively realized through direct public production of those goods.

The challenge before state, federal, and institutional leaders in higher education is to respond to a turbulent political economic environment while preserving the role of nonprofit and nonmarket provision of higher education in the service of the public good. The niche market success of the new wave of for-profit providers and the shifts to increasingly private funding of social welfare functions offer a tempting course of action: increase market competition in higher education. It may also be tempting to assume that competitive success at the periphery offers a guide to transforming the core, particularly in light of the plethora of calls urging that strategy. It isn't clear whether market approaches will induce effective transformations in higher education, but they are likely to be popular. The adoption of market initiatives may also produce expectations of greater choice, competition, and an increase in the public benefits from higher education. On the basis of existing research and the historical record, those expectations may well be for a state of grace that, as Mr. Jefferson suggested, never was and never will be.

REFERENCES

Adelman, C. (2000). *A parallel postsecondary universe: The certification system in information technology.* Washington, DC: U.S. Government Printing Office.

Altbach, P.G. (2001, May 11). Why higher education is not a global commodity. *Chronicle of Higher Education, 47,* B20.

Aronowitz, S. (2000). *The knowledge factory.* Boston: Beacon Press.

Becker, G.S. (1976). *The economic approach to human behavior.* Chicago: University of Chicago Press.

Block, H.M. and Dobell, B. (1999). *The e-bang theory: Volume 2.* San Francisco: Bank of America Securities Equity Research Division.

Blustain, H., Goldstein, P., and Lozier, G. (1999). Assessing the new competitive landscape. In R.N. Katz (Ed.), *Dancing with the devil* (pp. 51–71). San Francisco: Jossey-Bass.

Bound, J., and Turner, S.E. (1999). *Going to war and going to college: Did World War II and the G.I. Bill increase educational attainment for returning veterans?* Virginia Project on the Economics of Higher Education Working Paper. Charlottesville: University of Virginia. Available: http://curry.edschool.Virginia.EDU/curry/centers/vpehe/ [December 11, 2001].

Bowen, H.R. (1977*). Investments in learning: The individual and social value of American higher education.* San Francisco: Jossey-Bass.

Bowen, H.R. (1978). *The returns to investments in learning.* Occasional Paper Series #7. Charlottesville: University of Virginia, Center for the Study of Higher Education.

Bowen, W.G., and Bok, D. (1998). *The shape of the river.* Princeton, NJ: Princeton University Press.

Breneman, D.W. (1991). *Guaranteed student loans: Great success or dismal failure?* Washington, DC: United Student Aid Fund.

Breneman, D.W. (2000, February 11). A tuition freeze accents the cockeyed economics of higher education. *Chronicle of Higher Education, 46,* A64.

Breneman, D.W. (2001). The outputs of higher education. Paper presented at the Futures Forum 2001, Forum for the Future of Higher Education, Cambridge, MA.

Breneman, D.W., Pusser, B., and Turner, S.E. (2000). *The contemporary provision of for-profit higher education: Mapping the competitive market.* Working paper. Charlottesville: University of Virginia.

Brighouse, H. (2000). *School choice and social justice.* Oxford, UK: Oxford University Press.

Burd, S. (2001, February 2). Bringing market forces to student loan programs. *Chronicle of Higher Education, 47,* A26.

Callan, P.M. (2001). Reframing access and opportunity: Problematic state and federal higher education policy in the 1990s. In D.E. Heller (Ed.), *The states and public higher education policy: Affordability, access, and accountability* (pp 83–99). Baltimore: Johns Hopkins Press.

Calhoun, C. (1998). The public good as a social and cultural project. In W.W. Powell and E.S. Clemens (Eds.), *Private action and the public good* (pp. 20–35). New Haven, CT: Yale University Press.

Carnevale, A.P., and Fry, R.A. (2001). Economics, demography and the future of higher education policy. In *Higher expectations: Essays on the future of postsecondary education*. National Governors Association, March.

Chubb, J.E., and Moe, T.M. (1990). *Politics, markets, and America's schools*. Washington, DC: The Brookings Institution.

Clark, B.R. (1983). *The higher education system: Academic organization in cross-national perspective*. Berkeley: University of California Press.

Clark, B.R. (1998). *Creating entrepreneurial universities: Organizational pathways of transformation*. Oxford, UK: Pergamon Press.

Cohen, A.M., and Brawer, F. (1996). *The American community college, third edition*. San Francisco: Jossey-Bass.

Collis, D. (2001). When industries change: the future of higher education. In *Higher Education Review*, 65, 7–24.

Cuban, L., and Shipps, D. (Eds.) (2000). *Reconstructing the common good in education*. Stanford, CA: Stanford University Press.

Currie, J., and Newson, J. (1999). *Universities and globalization: Critical perspectives*. Thousand Oaks, CA: Sage.

Duderstadt, J. J. (1999). Can colleges and universities survive in the information age? In R.N. Katz (Ed.), *Dancing with the devil* (pp. 1–25). San Francisco: Jossey-Bass.

Duderstadt, J. (2000). *A university for the twenty-first century*. Ann Arbor: University of Michigan Press.

Ehrenberg, R.G. (2000). *Tuition rising: Why college costs so much*. Cambridge, MA: Harvard University Press.

Friedman, M. (1962). *Capitalism and freedom*. Chicago: University of Chicago Press.

Friedman, M., and Friedman, R. (1980). *Free to choose: A personal statement*. New York: Hartcourt Brace Jovanovich.

Garber, M.P. (1996, September). Wall Street Ph.D. *National Review*, 57–72.

Gaston, P.M. (2001). Reflections on affirmative action: Its origins, virtues, enemies, champions, and prospects. In G. Orfield and M. Kurlaender (Eds.), *Diversity challenged: Evidence on the impact of affirmative action* (pp. 277–293). Cambridge MA: The Harvard Educational Publishing Group.

Gladieux, L., and Swail, W. (1999, August). *The digital divide and educational opportunity*. The College Board Review, 28–30.

Goldin, C., and Katz, L.F. (1998). *The shaping of higher education: The formative years in the United States, 1890–1940* (WP 6537). Cambridge, MA: National Bureau of Economic Research.

Goldstein, M.B. (1999, October). Capital ideas. *University Business*, 46–53.

Graves, W.H. (1998). Developing and using technology as a strategic asset. In R.N. Katz (Ed.), *Dancing with the devil*. San Francisco: Jossey-Bass.

Hansen, J.S. (1991). *The roots of federal student aid policy*. In J.P. Merisotis (Ed.), *New directions for higher education: The changing dimensions of student aid* (No. 74, Summer). San Francisco: Jossey-Bass.

Hansmann, H. (1980). The rationale for exempting nonprofit organizations from corporate income taxation. *Yale Law Journal*, 91, 54–100.

Hansmann, H. (1999). *The state and the market in higher education*. (Draft manuscript.) Published in Italian as Proprietai e Concorrenza nellilstruzione Universitaria. *Mercato Concorrenza Regale*, 475–96.

Heller, D.E. (2001). Trends in the affordability of public colleges and universities: The contradiction of increasing prices and increasing enrollments. In D.E. Heller (Ed.), *The states and public higher education policy: Affordability, access, and accountability* (pp. 11–38). Baltimore: Johns Hopkins Press.

Institute for Higher Education Policy. (1998). *Reaping the benefits: Defining the public and private value of going to college*. The New Millennium Project on Higher Education Costs, Pricing and Productivity. Washington, DC. Available: http://www.ihep.com/publications [December 11, 2001].

James, E. (1998). Commercialism among nonprofits: Objectives, opportunities, and constraints. In B.A. Weisbrod (Ed.), *To profit or not to profit: The commercial transformation of the nonprofit sector.* Cambridge, UK: Cambridge University Press.

James, E., and Rose-Ackerman, S. (1986). *The nonprofit enterprise in market economics.* New York: Harwood Academic.

Kane, T.J. (1999). *The price of admission: Rethinking how Americans pay for college.* Washington, DC: The Brookings Institution.

Kerr, C. (1994). Expanding access and changing missions: The federal role in U.S. higher education. *Educational Record, 75,* 27–31.

Kerr, C. (2001). *The uses of the university* (5th ed.). Cambridge, MA: Harvard University Press.

Kohl, K., and LaPidus, J. (Eds.). (2000). *Postbaccalaureate futures: New markets, resources, credentials.* Phoenix, AZ: Oryx Press.

Labaree, D.F. (1997). Public goods, private goods: The American struggle over educational goals. *American Educational Research Journal, 34*(1), 39–81.

Leslie, L.L., and Johnson, G.P. (1974). The market model and higher education. *Journal of Higher Education, 45,* 1–20.

Levin, H.M. (Ed.). (2001). *Privatizing education.* Boulder, CO: Westview Press.

Levin, J.S. (2001). *Globalizing the community college: Strategies for change in the twenty-first century.* New York: Palgrave.

Levine, A. (2001). Privatization in higher education. In H.M. Levin (Ed.), *Privatizing Education.* Boulder, CO: Westview Press.

Mansbridge, J. (1998). On the contested nature of the public good. In W.W. Powell and E. S. Clemens (Eds.), *Private action and the public good* (pp. 3–19). New Haven, CT: Yale University Press.

Marchese, T. (1998). Not-so distant-competitors: How new providers are remaking the postsecondary marketplace. *AAHE Bulletin,* May/June, 3–11.

Marginson, S. (1997). *Markets in education.* Melbourne, Australia: Allen & Unwin.

Marginson, S., and Considine, M. (2000). *The enterprise university.* Cambridge, UK: Cambridge University Press.

Masten, S.E. (1995). Old school ties: Financial aid coordination and governance of higher education. *Journal of Economic Behavior and Organizations, 28,* 23–47.

McKeown-Moak, M.P. (2000). *Financing higher education in the new century: The second annual report from the states.* Denver, CO: SHEEO Finance Publications.

McMurtry, J. (1991). Education and the market model. *Journal of Philosophy of Education, 25*(2), 209–218.

McPherson, M.S., and Schapiro, O. (1998). *The student aid game.* Princeton, NJ: Princeton University Press.

Mendenhall, R. (2001). Technology: Creating new models in higher education. In National Governors Association, *Higher expectations: Essays on the future of postsecondary education* (pp. 37–44). Washington, DC: NGA.

Moe, T. (1996). *The positive theory of public bureaucracy.* New York: Cambridge University Press.

Munitz, B. (2000). Changing landscape: From cottage monopoly to competitive industry. *Education Review, 35,* January/February, 12–18.

National Governors Association. (2001). *The 21st century is upon us. Are we ready?* Washington, DC: NGA Center for Best Practices.

Newman, F., and Couterier, L.K. (2001). The new competitive arena: Market forces invade the academy. *Change, 33*(2), September/October, 10–17.

Newman, F., and Scurry, J. (2001, July 13). Online technology pushes pedagogy to the forefront. *Chronicle of Higher Education, 47,* B7.

Ortmann, A. (1997). How to survive in post-industrial environments: Adam Smith's advice for today's colleges and universities. *Journal of Higher Education, 68,* 483–501.

Oster, S. (1997). *An analytical framework for thinking about the use of for-profit structures for university services and activities.* Aspen, CO: The Forum for the Future of Higher Education.

Phillippe, K.A. (Ed.). (1999). *National profile of community colleges: Trends and statistics* (3rd ed.). Washington, DC: Community College Press.

Powell, W.W., and Clemens, E.S. (Eds.). (1998). *Private action and the public good.* New Haven, CT: Yale University Press.

Pusser, B. (2000). The role of the state in the provision of higher education in the United States. *Australian Universities Review, 43,* (1), 24–35.

Pusser, B., and Doane, D.J. (2001, September/October). Public purpose and private enterprise: The contemporary organization of postsecondary education. *Change, 33,* 18–22.

Raphael, J., and Tobias, S. (1997). Profit-making or profiteering. *Change, 29,* (6), November/December, 45–60.

Reese, W.J. (2000). Public schools and the elusive search for the common good. In L. Cuban and D. Shipps (Eds.), *Reconstructing the common good in education.* Stanford, CA: Stanford University Press.

Rothschild, M., and White, L. (1993). The university in the marketplace: Some insights and some puzzles. In C.T. Clotfelter and M. Rothschild (Eds.). *Studies of supply and demand in higher education* (pp. 11–42). Chicago: University of Chicago Press.

Ruch, R.S. (2001). *Higher ed, inc: The rise of the for-profit university.* Baltimore: Johns Hopkins University Press.

Salamon, L.M. (1995). *Partners in public service: Government-nonprofit relations in the modern welfare state.* Baltimore: Johns Hopkins University Press.

Samuelson, P. (1954). The theory of public expenditure. *Review of Economics and Statistics. 6*(4), 387–389.

Schmidt, P. (2001, January 4). Texas governor proposes radical shift in college financing. *Chronicle of Higher Education, 47,* A26.

Slaughter, S., and Leslie, L.L. (1997). *Academic capitalism.* Baltimore: Johns Hopkins University Press.

Soffen, S. (1998, September). *For-profit, postsecondary education: Profiting from a knowledge-based economy.* Equity Research Industry Analysis. Baltimore: Legg Mason Wood Walker.

Sperling, J.G. (1989). *Against all odds.* Phoenix, AZ: Apollo Press.

Sperling, J.G. (2000). *Rebel with a cause: The entrepreneur who created the University of Phoenix and the for-profit revolution in higher education.* New York: John Wiley.

Tooley, J. (1999). *The global education industry: Lessons from private education in developing countries.* London: The Institute of Economic Affairs.

University of California Office of the President. (1996). *UC means business: The economic impact of the University of California.* A Report by the University of California Office of the President. Oakland, CA: Author.

Veysey, L.R. (1965). *The emergence of the American university.* Chicago: University of Chicago Press.

Weisbrod, B.A. (1988). *The nonprofit economy.* Cambridge, MA: Harvard University Press.

Weisbrod, B.A. (1998). The nonprofit mission and its financing: Growing links between nonprofits and the rest of the economy. In B.A. Weisbrod (Ed.) *To profit or not to profit: The commercial transformation of the nonprofit sector.* Cambridge, UK: Cambridge University Press.

Winston, G. (1997). Why can't a college be more like a firm? In Joel Meyerson (Ed.), *New thinking on higher education: Creating a context for change.* Bolton, MA: Anker.

Winston, G. (1999, January/February). For-profit education: Godzilla or Chicken Little? *Change, 31,* 12–19.

Winston, G., Carbone, J.C., and Lewis, E.G. (1998). *What's been happening to higher education: A reference manual, 1986–87 to 1994–95.* The Williams Project on the Economics of Higher Education. Amherst, MA: Williams College.

Wolfe, B.L. (1995). External benefits of education. In M. Carnoy (Ed.), *International encyclopedia of economics of education, 2nd ed.*, (pp. 159–164). New York: Elsevier Science.

5

A Role for the Internet in American Education? Lessons from Cisco Networking Academies

Richard Murnane, Nancy Sharkey, and Frank Levy*

As of July 2001, Cisco Networking Academies—located in all 50 states and 130 countries—were teaching more than 160,000 students how to design, build, and maintain computer networks. The students learn from a common curriculum offered that is in nine languages and delivered over the Internet. Since the majority of Cisco Networking Academies in the United States reside in public high schools and community colleges—institutions that educate the vast majority of American youth—the team developing the Academy program confronted many of the same problems that beset American education. This paper describes how the Cisco Academies team dealt with these problems and particularly the use it made of information technology in crafting solutions.

We begin by providing a brief description of changes in the American economy that pose new educational challenges. The next section explains why we chose to study the Cisco Networking Academy Program and the methodology of our case study. We follow this with a brief history of the Cisco Networking Academies. The fourth section provides the core of the paper and describes how the Cisco Academies

*Richard Murnane is the Thompson Professor of Education and Society at Harvard University's Graduate School of Education. Nancy Sharkey is a doctoral candidate at Harvard University Graduate School of Education. Frank Levy is the Daniel Rose Professor of Urban Economics in the Department of Urban Studies and Planning at M.I.T. Financial support for the research and writing of this paper was provided by the National Research Council and the Russell Sage Foundation. We would like to thank the many people connected to the Cisco Networking Academy Program who provided information and allowed us to observe their work. We appreciate the helpful comments on an earlier draft of this paper provided by Clifford Adelman, Lisa Lynch, and Linda Roberts.

team dealt with seven challenges that face American education. The last section provides a summary of key lessons.

CHANGES IN THE AMERICAN ECONOMY

In recent decades, changes in the American economy have produced striking changes in the labor market earnings of American workers. Since 1979 the real earnings of workers with no postsecondary education, especially males, have declined markedly, both in absolute terms and relative to the earnings of workers with college degrees. Since 1970 the variation in earnings among workers with the same educational credentials has increased. Most economists believe that the changes in the distribution of earnings reflect to a significant extent an increase in the demand for skills. The logic is that the college/high school earnings differential has increased because college graduates are more likely to possess the skills employers increasingly demand, and the variation in earnings among workers with the same educational credentials has increased because the premiums employers pay to specially skilled workers has increased (see Murnane, Willett, and Levy, 1995). This "skills" explanation for the changes in the distribution of labor market earnings raises the obvious question: Which skills are increasingly valued by employers? A number of blue ribbon commissions (Secretary's Commission on Achieving Necessary Skills, 1991; National Institute for Literacy, 2000) and several research groups (Marshall and Tucker, 1991; Murnane and Levy, 1996), have produced lists. While varying in details, all lists include mathematics, reading, writing skills, problem-solving skills, computer skills, and the ability to work productively with people from different backgrounds.

Among the driving forces underlying current educational reform efforts is evidence from the National Assessment of Educational Progress (NAEP) that a great many American students leave high school without mastery of these critical skills. Of particular concern are patterns in NAEP test score data showing that children of color, the most rapidly growing groups in the U.S. student population and in the next generation's labor force, are especially likely to leave school lacking critical skills. While many factors including low family income contribute to the low average academic achievement of children of color, low-quality education plays a key role.

In response to concern about skills, almost every state in the country is engaged in standards-based educational reforms aimed at improving the skills of American students. It is too early to know how much of a difference standards-based reforms will make to the skills of American students (see Murnane and Levy, 2001). However, it is clear that the reform efforts are encountering a number of significant problems. These include:

1. Designing and implementing professional development efforts that increase teachers' effectiveness.

2. Recruiting and retaining skilled teachers, especially in subject areas that pay well outside of teaching.
3. Retaining a focus on developing critical skills for all students and avoiding the plethora of disjointed programs that compete for resources and student attention and do not add up to a coherent educational experience.
4. Improving curricula and keeping them up-to-date.
5. Designing and administering assessments that not only measure students' mastery of critical skills but also provide incentives for teachers to improve instruction.
6. Maintaining high-quality instruction in all classrooms.
7. Providing students with credentials that employers and colleges value, thereby providing incentives for students to do the hard work that skill mastery requires.

These problems are not new to American education. Yet their salience is particularly great today as schools struggle to provide all students with the critical skills they will need to earn enough to support families and to participate effectively in a changing democratic society.

Can new technology contribute to solving these difficult problems? Over the last 80 years, many innovators have thought so. In 1922 Thomas Edison stated: "I believe that the motion picture is destined to revolutionize our educational system and that in a few years it will supplant largely, if not entirely, the use of textbooks" (cited in Cuban, 1986, p. 9). In the 1930s, enthusiasts touted radio as "textbooks of the air" (p. 19). In the first decades after World War II, advocates saw instructional television as bringing the world to the classroom. More recently computers were seen by some as revolutionizing education. In 1984 the computer pioneer Seymour Papert wrote: "There won't be schools in the future. . . . I think the computer will blow up the school. That is, the school defined as something where there are classes, teachers running exams, people structured in groups by age, following a curriculum—all of that."

Contrary to these prophecies, the educational historian Larry Cuban concludes that none of these new technologies have had a major impact on how education takes place in American schools. None have replaced the teacher and his or her daily work with 15 to 40 students in a physical classroom as the core technology of American education (Cuban, 1986). The most recent attempt to improve schooling by making use of technology focuses on the Internet. Will the Internet be different from past technological innovations that did find their way into schools but did not revolutionize education? Only time will tell for sure. However, we can gain insights by examining how one group, the team that developed the Cisco Networking Academies, used the Internet to develop and implement a curriculum currently studied by more than 160,000 students around the world.

THE CISCO NETWORKING ACADEMY PROGRAM

Why Study This Program?

There were five reasons why we chose to study the Cisco Networking Academies. First, the program has grown extraordinarily rapidly, passing the market test of whether a great many high schools, community colleges, and not-for-profit organizations find it valuable. Second, the program is aimed primarily at high school students and other people who do not have a four-year college degree. As such, it is an exception to the general pattern in the United States that the most in-depth training goes to workers who have the most formal education. Third, in the United States the program is delivered primarily in public high schools and community colleges, institutions central to the effort to prepare the next generation of Americans for life in a rapidly changing society. Understanding how the Academies program achieved such rapid growth within existing institutions may provide insights about ways to improve the performance of these institutions. Fourth, materials describing the program state that it is aligned with national skills standards. This is intriguing because it suggests the possibility that the Academies program may not only prepare students to build and maintain computer networks but also might teach more generic skills useful in other occupations. Finally, students who complete the program and pass examinations administered by an independent organization receive credentials that may improve access to good jobs. The opportunity to earn a credential is interesting because an inability to signal skill mastery to potential employers may be an important reason why many American high school students do not do the hard work that skill mastery requires (see Bishop, Mane, Bishop, and Moriarty, 2001).

Until quite recently the Academy program consisted of a four-semester curriculum that prepares students to take the examination for the Cisco Certified Network Associate (CCNA) credential. Recently, new offerings have been added. First, a second four-semester sequence of courses now leads to a more advanced credential (the Cisco Certified Network Professional, or CCNP). The second new offering features partner-sponsored courses on the fundamentals of UNIX and Web design (developed by Sun Microsystems and Adobe Systems respectively, but delivered through the Cisco Networking Academy Program). We focus this paper solely on the initial four-semester sequence of courses.

We want to be clear on the limits of this case study. We do not seek to evaluate the effectiveness of the Cisco Networking Academies in providing marketable skills to students. In fact, Cisco does not collect data on students' demographic information and post-program outcomes that would be needed for a systematic evaluation of the program. We do not attempt to generalize from this case study about how education and training programs using the Internet work. We lack the resources to investigate systematically how different the Cisco Academies are from the many other information technology-related education and training programs (see Adelman, 2000, for a discussion of the dramatic growth in IT-related training programs).

Despite these limitations we believe that a description of the development of the Cisco Academies program is valuable for two reasons. First, its extraordinary rate of growth prompts questions about how the program works and why it is appealing to high schools and community colleges. Second, learning how the Academies team dealt with generic problems that hinder improvement in American education may provide ideas about how to deal with obstacles to progress.

Methodology

We began work on this case by learning as much as we could about the history and organization of the Academies program from materials available on the Internet. This made us realize the importance of interviewing instructors in Local and Regional Academies, participating students, and Cisco personnel who played key roles in the development and administration of the program. We requested and received permission from Cisco Systems to conduct such interviews. We then developed semi-structured interview protocols to guide the interviews.

We interviewed instructors and students in six Local Academies and four Regional Academies (all terms defined below) in the New England area. Approximately half of the Academies were located in high schools, including two in central city school districts. One was located in a community-based organization. The rest were located in publicly supported community colleges. We also spent several hours observing classes in each of two Academies located in urban high schools and two located in community colleges.

We spent two days at the Cisco Academies curriculum and assessment development center in Phoenix, interviewing the Cisco personnel who started the program and those currently responsible for curriculum, student assessment, and instructor training. We also conducted telephone interviews with several other Cisco employees and consultants working on the Academies program.

We sent an early draft of this paper to the Cisco employees and Academy instructors whom we interviewed, requesting comments and corrections of factual errors. We used their feedback in revising the paper.

GENESIS AND DEVELOPMENT

Cisco Systems sells routers, switches, software, and advice on building and maintaining computer networks to organizations around the world, including educational institutions. In 1993 John Morgridge, then CEO of Cisco Systems, hired George Ward to help build Cisco's market in educational institutions. Ward, a consulting engineer who had been head of World Wide Networks at Motorola, was well suited to the task. Not only did he understand networks; but he also liked talking to educators and helping them to design networks that met their schools' needs. Cisco's sales to schools increased.

With the sales growth came an increasingly serious business problem. Many schools and school districts lacked the expertise to maintain the networks. Nor did they have the funds to contract out network maintenance. In Ward's words, "I'd go in and design [networks] and build them and leave, and they would crash. There was limited support staff, and even more limited training" (Zehr, 1998). Ward's response was to develop a 40-hour training program aimed at teaching networking skills to school personnel so they could maintain their networks. The program included a PowerPoint presentation and a variety of hands-on activities. Ward spent much of the next year presenting the training program at schools around the country. He quickly learned that his training program was popular; however, he also learned that he could not meet the burgeoning demand for training. Cisco needed another approach to supporting school districts' needs for networking expertise.

An experience during Ward's year of travel provided an idea for a new approach. At some sites, schools allowed high school students to sit in on the training. Ward found that the students often grasped the critical skills more quickly than the adults. This led him to wonder whether Cisco should train students to maintain their schools' networks. To test this idea, Ward asked the principal of Thurgood Marshall High School, an inner-city public school in San Francisco, if he could offer a one-week training program to students in August 1996. The principal, always looking for new ways to engage students, asked one of his teachers, Dennis Frezzo, to make the arrangements.

Frezzo was an interesting choice. An optical and electrical engineer by background, Frezzo had decided in the early 1990s that he wanted to try teaching. He earned a master's degree in education from Stanford and started teaching at Thurgood Marshall in September 1994. Over the next two years, he developed several hands-on courses aimed at developing students' interest in science. Because Frezzo knew which Thurgood Marshall students were interested in science, the school principal asked him to recruit students for the summer program. However, with only two weeks to recruit students, Frezzo found that most of the highly motivated students he had in mind were not available. This left him to dig quite deep into the pool of motivation and academic talent to recruit a group of students for Ward's training program.

The training program, which was a mixture of Ward's PowerPoint presentation and many hands-on activities, worked well. Most surprisingly, Ward learned that some students at risk of dropping out due to a lack of interest in their academic programs were intrigued by his hands-on training program. This led him to return to Thurgood Marshall in December and propose that Frezzo and a colleague, Jai Gosine, try teaching a one-semester course for students. Frezzo and Gosine piloted the course in the spring of 1997, starting out with no curriculum and no equipment but lots of enthusiasm. The results were sufficiently positive to lead Ward to take the next steps.

Ward took the idea of training students to John Morgridge, who was deeply interested in education and believed that technology could play a key role in improving it. While the CEO had some doubts about whether high school students could master the relatively complex skills needed to trouble-shoot network problems, he was intrigued by Ward's idea and agreed to provide corporate funding for the next steps.

Now that Ward had support to develop his idea, he needed help. Recognizing that he knew little about how to develop a good educational program, he recruited Alex Belous, the director of technology education for the state of Arizona, to work with him. Belous's career history was very different from Ward's. After graduating from college in 1973, Belous started teaching first grade in Cave Creek, a rural community 40 miles from Phoenix. While teaching elementary school children in Cave Creek over the next 12 years, Belous came to appreciate the difficulty rural school districts with very limited resources faced in providing students with a high-quality education. This became even more apparent to Belous when he became the guidance counselor at Cave Creek's first high school, built in 1985.

A great many of Cave Creek's high school students were not going to college and their high school education did not prepare them to prosper in a changing economy. An entrepreneur at heart, Belous went to the Arizona State Department of Education and asked how he could get resources for his school to better serve these students. The advice was to develop a vocational education program. So Belous developed a program to teach computer-based office skills to Cave Creek high school students. This experience led him to believe that technology could play a role in improving education for rural children. From Cave Creek, Belous moved to the Arizona State Department of Education. Through this job, he met George Ward.

Alex Belous was a great find for Ward. He understood curriculum development and the types of challenges high school teachers would face in teaching technological skills to students. He also understood state education bureaucracies. Perhaps most importantly, he shared Ward's interest in using technology to improve the quality of education provided to underserved children.

Working initially as a Cisco consultant, Belous led the effort to turn Ward's 40-hour training program for adults into a curriculum for high school students. They agreed on four principles that would guide their effort:

1. The curriculum would be delivered online; there would be no printed version.
2. Well-trained instructors would teach the curriculum.
3. The curriculum would be updated frequently to keep it abreast of

changing technology and to improve it as students and instructors pointed out problems.

4.   Assessment of student skills would be done online.

Beyond these general principles, Ward and Belous had no master plan. When they began to work together, neither imagined that their ideas would develop over the next five years into an eight-semester program serving more than 160,000 students.

Encouraged by the interest Thurgood Marshall students showed in the pilot program, Ward and Belous invited interested educators (many of whom had participated in Ward's training courses) to a meeting at Cisco headquarters in San Jose in April 1997. Ward laid out to the group the idea of an educational program for high school students. To bring the idea to life, Frezzo described what he and his colleague had learned while trying out the one-semester program at Thurgood Marshall High School. Ward then sketched out the possibility of a four-semester program with an online curriculum and online assessment of student skills. He emphasized that this would be a partnership. Cisco would not just provide the curriculum. It would also provide training on how to teach the curriculum and ongoing support. In return, it would hold educators accountable for student learning. He asked the participants whether they would be interested in this partnership. While some participants were wary of the accountability concept, many expressed enthusiasm about the potential relationship.

Ward and Belous concluded from the meeting that a significant number of high schools were interested in teaching courses on designing, building, and maintaining computer networks. Thus, they went ahead in developing the curriculum and recruiting school partners.

When John Morgridge officially announced the Cisco Networking Academy Program in October 1997, 64 high schools in seven states were teaching the first semester of the Academies curriculum. Following the public announcement, the number of inquiries grew rapidly. While delighted by the interest, Ward and Belous quickly realized that they faced new questions. Who was going to train the instructors? What would be the financial arrangements of the partnerships? Over the next months, Ward and Belous and their collaborators worked out answers to these questions, while at the same time pushing ahead with the development of Semesters 2, 3, and 4 of the curriculum.

The answer to the training question was to develop a highly leveraged "train the trainer" model, as illustrated in Figure 5-1. Training would include both content and pedagogy. The first instructors Ward had trained became the heads of Cisco Academy Training Centers (CATCs). Cisco would pay them to provide training to instructors at Regional Academies, who in turn would provide training to instructors at Local Academies.

Initially Ward and Belous envisioned that the CATCs and Regional Academies, as well as the Local Academies, would all be in high schools. Soon, however, they found that community colleges were

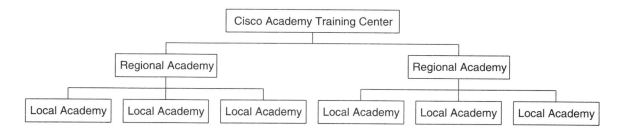

FIGURE 5-1 Cisco Networking Academies organizational structure.

interested in becoming CATCs and Regional Academies and that state governments were interested in having community colleges play this role. By 2001, half of the Regional Academies in the United States were located in community colleges. Table 5-1 provides a summary of the types of institutions in the United States in which Local Academies and Regional Academies are located. Table 5-2 provides information on the worldwide growth in the number of Cisco Academies.

TABLE 5-1   Number of Cisco Academies by Type of Academy, Type of Institution, and Location

	Within the United States		
Location	Local Academies	Regional and Local	Regional Only
High schools	2,424	67	20
Vocational programs [a]	337	23	1
Junior high schools (grades 7-9)	11	4	2
Two-year community colleges	486	211	20
Four-year colleges	101	35	7
Postsecondary technical schools	72	12	1
Nonprofit organizations	61	7	3
Military service institutions	50	0	1
Other types of organizations	82	19	22
U.S. Total	3,624	378	77
	Outside United States		
	Local Academies	Regional and Local	Regional only
Non-U.S. Total	2,197	442	174
Worldwide Total	5,821	820	251

SOURCE: Compiled in April 2001 from information available on the Academy locator portion of the Cisco Academy Web site: http://cisco.netacad.net/cnacs/pub-doc/locator.shtml

NOTE: From the available information, it is not possible to distinguish clearly between Cisco Academies in vocational high schools serving teenagers and Academies in institutions with the label of vocational education that serve adults.

TABLE 5-2 Indicators of the Growth of Cisco Networking Academies
Worldwide Academy Statistics

	Past (FY '98)	Current (FY '01)	Future (Forecast)
Local only	395	6,419	
Regional / local	61	859	
Subtotal local	396	7,278	
Regional	184	271	
CATCs	—	39	
Total locations	580	7,559	10,140
Countries	8	130	

SOURCE: Cisco Networking Academy Program (2000).

Over time the answer to the financial arrangements question emerged. Local Academies receive the online curriculum at no cost. Regional Academies may charge Local Academies for instructor training, on a cost-recovery basis. Local Academies need to buy from Cisco a rack of hardware containing five routers and two switches at a highly subsidized price of less than $10,000. Additional costs to the Local Academies may include several thousand dollars for testing equipment and disposable materials (such as cables). They are also required to purchase from Cisco the "SmartNet" service contract for approximately $1,200 per year after the first year. (The cost of SmartNet is covered in the Lab Bundle cost in the first year.) This entitles the Academies to "24/7" technical support for rapid service on their routers and switches.

Exceptions to these financial arrangements are for Academies in economic empowerment zones, which are rural and urban areas designated by the federal government as high unemployment areas, and for Academies in Native American communities. Cisco provides the package of routers and switches at no cost to the 100 Academies that are located in empowerment zones and approximately 13 Academies located in Native American communities.

Regional Academies receive one set of routers and switches from Cisco at no cost. The Cisco Learning Institute, a public charity funded and formed by Cisco, pays for CATCs to provide training to two Regional Academy instructors. In return, Regional Academies assume three responsibilities. First, they must make a "good faith effort" to recruit 10 Local Academies. Second, they provide instructor training and ongoing support to the Local Academies they recruit. Third, they monitor the quality of the Local Academy programs. Since the training, supporting, and monitoring functions use significant resources, Cisco allows Regional Academies to charge Local Academies annual support fees and fees for training sufficient to recover their costs. These fees are set by Regional Academies and range from zero to several thousand dollars per year.

THE ACADEMY PROGRAM'S EXPERIENCE WITH AMERICAN EDUCATIONAL PROBLEMS

Since most Cisco Networking Academies in the United States are located in public high schools and community colleges, the program confronts many of the challenges that face all attempts to improve the quality of education provided by these institutions. In this section we describe how the Cisco Academies program has dealt with some of these problems.

Providing High-Quality Instructor Training

Providing teachers with training (usually called professional development in education circles) that improves their effectiveness in helping students to master critical skills has been an ongoing challenge for American public education. While school districts typically devote significant resources to professional development, most of the money goes to fund one-day workshops that have little effect on how teachers teach (see Murnane and Levy, 1996, Ch. 7).

The Cisco Networking Academy Program faced a particularly difficult training challenge. It had no control over the instructors Local Academies chose to teach the Cisco networking curriculum. Many instructors chosen by the Local Academies were high school teachers or community college instructors with considerable teaching experience but no knowledge of computer networking. Others were adjunct faculty drawn from industry who understood computer networking but had no teaching experience. The challenge was to provide both the technical knowledge needed to teach the curriculum and the teaching skills needed to motivate students and explain quite difficult technical concepts.

The training program that the Academy team designed with the help of professional educators provided intensive hands-on instruction, tests of skill mastery, and ongoing support. Newly designated Local Academy instructors receive eight days of full-time instruction on the first semester's curriculum at a Regional Academy. Participants study the same curriculum that they will subsequently teach. They are expected to have read the online curriculum before coming to the training and to review the relevant chapters each night during the training.

Participants do the same hands-on labs their students will do and they take the same Internet-based end-of-chapter tests aimed at providing feedback on their skill mastery. The training guidelines specify that each participant must do a "teach-back" in each semester. The teach-back consists of preparing a lesson plan for a particular chapter and teaching the chapter to other participants and the Regional Academy instructor. In order to receive authorization to teach the first semester curriculum, participants must pass the online final examination with a score of at least 80, as well as successfully complete the teach-back. (Aspiring instructors who score below 80 may take the exam again but must score at least 85 on a second try and 90 on a third try.)

The schedule recommended by the Cisco Academies Program is that participants teach each semester's curriculum immediately after completing the appropriate training and before training to teach the subsequent semester. Instructors have 24 months to complete training for teaching all four semesters of the curriculum and to pass the CCNA examination, prepared by Cisco Systems but administered by an independent testing organization (Prometric).[1] This CCNA examination is the same examination that students who complete the four-semester Academy curriculum are encouraged to take and that adults who pay for commercially provided training take to obtain the industry-recognized CCNA credential.

After completing the training, Local Academy instructors have access to four types of support. First, they receive from Cisco an instructor's version of the online curriculum that includes detailed suggestions for how to teach each class and how to set up hands-on labs. Second, they have access to the Cisco Academies Web site, which provides answers to frequently asked questions and provides a bulletin board on which they may pose new questions. Third, as purchasers of the "SmartNet" maintenance agreement, they are entitled to help from Cisco on technical issues. Finally, they may request assistance from their Regional Academy on both technical and pedagogical issues. Regional Academy instructors told us that, at the request of Local Academy instructors, they sometimes modeled the teaching of a particularly difficult chapter, or observed an instructor teaching a chapter for the first time.

While instructor training focuses primarily on teaching the technical material in the curriculum, the design is for Regional Academy instructors to model best teaching practices. The emphasis is on minimizing lecturing and maximizing hands-on involvement. Participants also receive an online manual describing best practices. This manual begins with a description of the six levels of Bloom's taxonomy (knowledge, comprehension, application, analysis, synthesis, and evaluation), and describes ways in which teachers can reach each level of the taxonomy in the CCNA curriculum. For example, a sample of knowledge is, "Identify how many bits comprise an IT address (Semester 1)." A sample evaluation question is, "Your company has decided to use Category 6 UTP (instead of CAT 5 or 7)—support their decision." The Best Practices Manual also offers guidance on using journals, portfolios, student presentations, and group work in helping students to master critical skills. For example, the Manual states that "[t]he types of journal entries most applicable for Networking Academies'

---

[1]The CCNA examination antedates the Academy program and was originally designed by a Cisco group unconnected to the Academy program. The Academy's assessment group, headed by John Behrens, has contributed to improving the exam. The exam includes some drag-and-drop graphical items as well as multiple-choice questions.

students include: daily reflections, troubleshooting details, lab procedures and observations, equipment logs, hardware and software notes, router configurations, contacts and resources, questions, designs."

How well does the training work? While the quality of the training inevitably varies, Regional Academy instructors and people designing the training for the Cisco Academies tended to share the same opinion. The training is effective in teaching the technical skills to instructors who know how to work with students and are highly motivated. Each of the regional instructors we interviewed had stories about enthusiastic instructors with unlikely backgrounds—English teachers, culinary arts teachers—who became effective Academy instructors. This does not mean that the training is easy. One very experienced teacher at a vocational high school told us that the Academies instructor training was "the most difficult professional development I have ever done." She reported spending 17 hours each day for three weeks to complete Semester 1. The pressure to pass the end-of-semester examination makes the training intense. One member of the Cisco training team estimated that one in 10 people who start the training to become a first-semester Academy instructor either does not complete the training or do not pass the end of the semester exam.

Cisco Academy trainers reported that the training was less successful in imparting pedagogical skills to participants who tended to lecture rather than to engage participants in hands-on activities. This problem was most common among community college adjunct instructors who worked in industry. However, some high school teachers tended to spend an inordinate amount of time lecturing as well. The best practices document is very clear on the importance of engaging students in hands-on activities and on limiting the amount of time teachers spend lecturing. However, this does not happen in every Academy any more than it happens in every high school or community college science class.

How critical is technology in the Academy's professional development? The Internet plays an important role in providing support to instructors. The Cisco Academy Community Server is a valuable resource for instructors, enabling them to obtain answers to questions quickly and to access materials developed by other instructors.[2] The common online examinations provide information on the extent to which aspiring instructors have mastered critical technical skills. These are important contributions of technology to professional development. At the core, however, professional development in the Academies program depends on the quality of the Regional Academy instructors who provide the training. Technology complements the skills of the Regional Academy instructors; it is not a substitute for instructors who model best teaching practices.

---

[2]As discussed below, the community server also keeps track of students' grades on chapter tests and the semester examination, eliminating the bookkeeping activities that consume a great deal of time for most teachers.

Recruiting and Retaining High-Quality Instructors

Many public schools have difficulty finding skilled teachers in technical fields. As the economists Joseph Kershaw and Roland McKean (1962) explained 40 years ago, the problem lies in the uniform salary scale. In almost all public school districts, teachers' pay depends solely on years of experience and number of academic degrees. College graduates with training in fields such as chemistry and physics that command relatively high salaries in industry are not paid more to teach in public schools than are graduates trained in fields that provide less attractive salaries outside of teaching. The proliferation of information technology applications in the last 20 years has created a boom market for college graduates with training in computer science. When they see starting salaries typically twice those offered by public schools, few graduates with training in computer networks find public school teaching attractive. Most community colleges face the same problem created by the uniform salary scale.

One approach that the Academies program might have chosen was to attempt to "teacher-proof" the curriculum, that is, to produce a curriculum that students could learn from without the aid of skilled teachers. This would have been consistent with previous attempts to use technology to deal with the shortage of skilled teachers. However, Ward and Belous rejected this option from the outset.

The Cisco Academies solution to the shortage of technically trained instructors is to "grow its own." Since the idea for the Academy program stemmed from George Ward's realization that schools lacked the skills to maintain their computer networks, he knew that providing the technical skills needed to teach the Academy curriculum was critical to the success of the Academy program. This realization led to Cisco's investment in instructor training that is described above.

There is little question that the instructor training has been integral to the growth of the Academy program. In effect, the training and the follow-up support have increased the supply of people who understand the fundamentals of computer networking. Of course, this knowledge is useful not only in teaching the Academy curriculum, but also in a wide range of jobs in industry. As a result, many schools and community colleges find that after investing in Cisco Academy training for faculty members, they lose many of these same faculty to higher paying positions in industry.[3] Since the Academy program has no influence over the salaries schools and community colleges pay to Cisco Academy instructors, it has little leverage for solving this problem. Its only policy instruments are to make training available to new instructors and to insist that potential instructors complete the training before teaching the curriculum.

---

[3]In our interviews we heard about students in the Academy program who subsequently became instructors, so there appears to be some "grow your own" potential.

Local Academies deal with the attrition problem using the same creative ad hoc measures that schools have used for many years to retain skilled faculty. Some offer extra compensation for extra teaching or administrative work. Some seek to provide especially attractive working conditions, such as well-equipped computer laboratories. One community college that hosted a Cisco Academy provided a more direct approach. Instead of offering the Cisco classes as for-credit courses at the usual tuition of $280, this college offered them as noncredit workforce development courses for $900. Since instructors in these courses were not covered by the union contract, the college could pay Cisco Academy instructors much more than they would have received as instructors of for-credit courses.

In summary, a good training program is essential to creating a supply of instructors capable of teaching the Cisco Academy courses effectively. At the same time, it does not immunize Local and Regional Academies from the problem of retaining teachers whose skills provide them with higher paying opportunities in industry.

Retaining a Focus on Developing Critical Skills for All Students

The decade of the 1990s was a period of policy change in American education. Sparked by growing realization that a great many students leave school without mastery of basic cognitive skills and that labor market opportunities for these workers had declined markedly over the past 20 years, almost every state in the country engaged in standards-based educational reform initiatives.[4] While the plans vary across states, they have in common specification of the skills all students should master in each core subject at particular grade levels and tests to measure whether students have mastered the critical skills (Murnane and Levy, 2001). It was into this policy environment that Cisco introduced its Networking Academy Program.

From the beginning, Alex Belous saw the Academy program as contributing to educational reform. He believed passionately in the importance of education in equalizing economic opportunity. With many years of experience as a teacher in rural schools, he knew the difficulty in providing all children with rich opportunities to learn. He felt that the Internet could play an important role in equalizing educational opportunities. John Morgridge and his successor as Cisco CEO, John Chambers, shared these beliefs.

---

[4]The initial concern voiced in the 1980s in documents such as Workforce 2000 (Johnstone and Packer, 1987) was that skill deficiencies in the American workforce would hinder productivity growth. The quite rapid surge in productivity during the 1990s showed that this concern was misplaced, at least in the medium run. However, earnings data from the 1990s also showed that not all workers benefited from the growth in productivity. In particular, the earnings of workers who lacked post-secondary education and those with weak cognitive skills did not increase markedly during the 1990s and continued to be significantly below the real earnings of comparable workers in the late 1970s.

As the director of the Academy curriculum development effort, Belous led the effort to develop a curriculum that taught students to design, build, and maintain computer networks and that also taught cognitive and social skills that would be valuable to students even if they chose to pursue other occupations. In Semester 1 of the four-semester curriculum, students learn about industry standards, network topologies, IP addressing, networking components, and basic network design. Activities in semester one include learning how to convert hexadecimal numbers into binary numbers and examining building blue prints to determine where computers—and their supporting hardware—can be positioned in the building. At one high school we visited, students were also conducting a survey of all of the computers in the school. This survey included all hardware specifications as well as the types of software available to run on the machines. Students kept their records in Microsoft Access and Excel, programs they learned to use in the Academy course. Ultimately, the students' computer survey would be used to help determine the school's technology needs and capabilities.

In Semester 2, students learn about beginning router configurations and routing protocols. A sample activity from this semester is for students to work in teams to design a network topology and IP addressing scheme that includes five routers. Students then use software to create a diagram of the networks they have designed. As part of this activity, students answer a series of questions aimed at having them reflect on their work in writing. These questions range from asking students about their group experience (for example, "What did you learn from designing a topology with such a large group of people?") to what they learned about the routing process (for example, "Could you have done it any other way? If so how?").

Semester 3 of the Cisco Networking Academy Program includes advanced router configurations, local area network (LAN) switching theory and VLANS, Advanced LAN, and LAN switched design. Students also learn about Novell IPX, a protocol commonly used in the networking industry. In this semester students also participate in a "threaded case study" that involves a simulated real-world problem. For example, students create a network for a fictional school district, including a LAN at each site in the district, as well as a wide area network (WAN) connecting to more than 30 sites. This project requires students to consider everything from wiring schemes at individual schools to security for the whole system.

Semester 4 covers WAN theory, design, and technology; network troubleshooting; and, again, a threaded case study, in which students continue to improve upon the network created in Semester 3. Additionally, this semester includes reviews for the "Network+" certification exam (a vendor-neutral certification exam) as well as Cisco's own CCNA certification exam.

To date there are no systematic studies evaluating the long-term benefits to students from participating in the Cisco Networking Academy

Program and the extent to which benefits are contingent on choosing an occupation connected to computer networking. However, the curriculum does appear to offer a variety of opportunities for students to develop skills, including writing clearly and working productively in groups, that are valued in a wide range of jobs (see Murnane and Levy, 1996, for a discussion of the importance of these skills).

Our conversations with Academy students indicate significant variance in the implementation of the curriculum. Not all instructors devote significant class time to hands-on activities. Nor do all Academy instructors know how to facilitate group work effectively. Nor do all Academy instructors pay attention to the quality of the writing in students' engineering journals and work with students to improve their writing. In this respect, the Academy program illustrates a pattern replicated again and again in American education: high-quality curriculum is an essential complement to well-trained, highly motivated teachers; it is not a substitute for them.

Belous and his colleagues engage in continuous improvement of the curriculum, working to eliminate ambiguities and keep the difficulty of the text to the ninth-grade reading level. They also emphasized that since students access the curriculum online and take their tests online, the design of the courses makes it easy for students to be able to work at their own pace.

Despite the attention paid to the curriculum design, some states and school districts were reluctant to adopt the Academy program. Some of the wariness stemmed from past experiences in which corporations' contributions to school improvement had been donations of used equipment and curricula taken from commercial training programs developed for adult professionals, with no support for how to develop and teach a curriculum that made sense for high school students. Another source of caution was the perception that the Cisco Networking Academies provided a vocational curriculum that would not provide students with skills transferable to occupations other than networking computers. This matters because a large proportion of students who participate in vocational education programs do not enter the occupation for which they train, (Bishop, 1995) and a large and growing proportion of American workers change occupations over their work lives (Parrado and Wolff, 1999).

In response to these concerns, Belous contracted with research organizations to document the number of activities in the Cisco Academy curriculum that address national academic standards for science and mathematics prepared by professional organizations and critical skills described in the report prepared by the Secretary's Commission on Achieving Necessary Skills (1991), known as the SCANS report. The research groups commissioned teachers and college faculty who were familiar with both computer networking and the national standards to read the Academy curriculum and document points of alignment. The curriculum alignment document reported that Cisco Academy curriculum activities address 12 of 14 mathematics standards, either partially or fully; five of eight categories of science standards; and many of the skills listed in the SCANS report.[5] This evidence went a long way toward convincing state departments of education that students should receive credit toward high school graduation for completing Cisco Networking Academy courses. This is still an ongoing issue in some states. For example, Texas currently does not count Cisco Academy courses toward students' high school graduation requirements.

The enthusiasm of vocational educators and community colleges provided additional support. This enthusiasm was rooted in the struggles of vocational schools and community colleges to respond to the "integration" mandate expressed in the 1990 Perkins Act, the federal legislation that reauthorized federal support of vocational education. Troubled by charges that vocational education prepared students only for narrowly defined jobs—jobs that often disappeared in a changing economy—reformers called for integration of occupational and academic education in high schools and for programs that enabled students to move from career-oriented high school programs to community colleges.

The Cisco Academy Program was tailor-made for high schools and community colleges working to respond to the Perkins Act mandates. The program was attractive to students seeking preparation for relatively high-wage jobs in the growing field of computer networking. It offered instructor training, a critical need in schools trying to keep vocational offerings up-to-date. The alignment document demonstrated that the Academy curriculum taught not only technical skills relevant to networking, but it also taught math, science, and writing skills needed in a wide range of occupations. Thus, the program offered the promise of integrating occupational and academic education. Finally, because all students in Networking Academies studied the same curriculum and took the same end-of-course examinations, community colleges felt justified in offering college credit and dual enrollment to high school students who completed one or more semesters of the Academy curriculum. This was exactly the type of cooperation between high schools and community colleges that the Perkins Act and the School to Work Opportunities Act of 1994 envisioned.

In 1998 Colorado became the first state to endorse the Cisco Networking Academies. Other states soon followed. The net effect of the state endorsements was that high schools could add the four semesters of the Cisco Networking Academy program to their curriculum without fear that state education agencies would question offering these courses for credit toward graduation. In several states the endorsements meant the state department of education would pay the training and support costs associated with setting up Cisco Academies.

---

[5]As described in Cisco Networking Academy Program (2000), Educational CYBER-CONNECTIONS, Inc. was the research firm that documented the alignment between the Cisco Academy curriculum and national science and math standards; V-TECS was the research firm that documented the extent to which the Academy curriculum addressed skills described in the 1991 SCANS document (Secretary's Commission, 1991).

From our visits to five Local Academies, we have seen that the institutions teach the curriculum at very different paces (within the framework prescribed by Cisco that the four semesters must include a minimum of 180 hours of instruction, including lab time). For example, at one community college, Networking I, a three-credit course that meets for three hours a week (plus an equal amount of lab time) for 15 weeks, covers the first two semesters of the Academy curriculum. Networking II covers Semesters 3 and 4 of the curriculum. In these courses students are expected to read two chapters each week before coming to class. Class time is devoted to discussion of the concepts in the text and to hands-on activities. Students have one day after each class to complete the online chapter tests.

At the other extreme, we observed a Local Academy located in an urban high school that meets for two hours, four days a week for 15 weeks. Students spend much of the class time reading the curriculum. Students work at their own pace. They report doing little work on the course outside of class. Fewer than half of the students had completed the Semester 1 curriculum by March of the second semester.

At least part of the explanation for the radical difference in the pace of the two classes concerns differences in the students. The students in the fast-paced community college course were in their twenties, thirties, and forties; were paying their own tuitions; and were acutely aware that they needed marketable skills to improve their earnings prospects. They had also demonstrated initiative in gaining places in the oversubscribed Networking class.

In contrast, the students in the slow-paced urban high school class were teenagers whose interests seemed to focus primarily on sports and social activities. Most had no career plans. None had a computer at home. Some of the students were enthusiastic about their Cisco class and hoped it would lead to college. However, others had been assigned to it by a guidance counselor and would have preferred another program.

Cisco is developing a primer curriculum to help prepare students for the Academy curriculum. It also is developing new modules on topics such as hexadecimal and binary numbers that many students find difficult to master. This module would expand on the Semester 1 lab activity explaining how binary numbers are used in IP addresses, demonstrating how to convert numbers to binary numbers, and requiring students to make conversions.

Improving the Curriculum and Keeping It Up to Date

Providing teachers with a curriculum that focuses on the skills students are expected to master, that is accessible to students with limited reading ability,[6] and that interests a wide range of students

---

[6]We learned from Academy instructors in high schools that many students print off the online curriculum rather than read the explanations from a computer screen.

has been a constant challenge for American education. The challenge of providing up-to-date curricula is especially great when technological changes alter the critical skills that students should master.

The team that developed the Cisco Networking Academy curriculum faced a set of particularly difficult challenges. Networking technology is changing quite rapidly, necessitating frequent changes in curriculum designed to teach students to design, build, and maintain networks. The curriculum teaches technical skills and could easily become accessible only to students with very strong reading comprehension skills. Alex Belous and his colleagues were determined to keep the reading level at the ninth-grade level so as to make the curriculum accessible to as many high school students as possible. They wanted to make the curriculum available in several languages (currently nine) so that it could be used in many countries. Including many diagrams and illustrations contributed to making the curriculum comprehensible. However, the more graphics included in the online curriculum, the slower the response time for students accessing the curriculum, especially for those using less than state-of-the-art computers.

To our surprise, keeping the Networking curriculum up-to-date is a relatively straightforward matter. To keep the CCNA exam up-to-date, Cisco contracts with an outside group every two years to do a task analysis of the work involved in designing, building, and maintaining computer networks. The analysts observe the work of people holding the CCNA credential and ask them how often they carry out different tasks. The results of the task analysis are used by Cisco to remove questions from the CCNA exam that pertain to tasks that no longer are central to the work of CCNA holders and to add questions that pertain to tasks that have become more important. The changes in the CCNA exam drive changes in the Cisco Networking Academy curriculum.

The Internet plays a key role in improving the Academy curriculum. Curriculum developers use the Internet to elicit rapid feedback from members of the curriculum review committee, consisting of Academy instructors who have demonstrated an interest in curricular improvement. Instructors and students use the Internet to report problems they have encountered with the curriculum. The curriculum development team has a formal process for evaluating the feedback it receives and making changes in response to criticisms and suggestions. While this process could take place using regular mail, it would be vastly slower.

There is a trade-off in the design of a Web-based curriculum between quantity and quality of graphics and the speed with which files can be accessed. The use of more graphics makes the curriculum appealing. However, it can render the curriculum inaccessible to sites using less than state-of-the-art computers and to sites that lack resources to purchase new software. Belous and his colleagues have been sensitive to this trade-off, and have been careful not to make changes in the curriculum that would require Academies to purchase new software or hardware.

Fortunately, technological advances in displaying and transmitting graphical images have made it possible to increase markedly the number of graphical illustrations in the curriculum while also reducing the size of the curriculum files that Academies download over the Internet.[7] Including references to informative Web sites is another way that Belous and his colleagues have enriched the curriculum without increasing its size.

One important lesson Ward and Belous have learned is that there are trade-offs in the timing of curriculum revisions. Initially they made changes as often as daily. While this provided Academy sites with the most up-to-date version, the frequent changes raised havoc with instructors who would prepare lesson plans based on one version of the curriculum only to find that their students were reading a revised version that did not match their plans. Belous and Ward's response has been to make available new versions of the curriculum no more often than twice a year.

Making Assessment a Valuable Part of the Education Process

In recent years, assessments of students' skills and knowledge have come to play a critical role in standards-based educational reform efforts. In a growing number of states, students who do not score well on state-mandated assessments of core skills are not promoted to the next grade. High school students who do not pass exit examinations do not receive high school diplomas. Teachers and administrators in schools with consistently low test scores may find their jobs in jeopardy. With the increased attachment of stakes to student test score results, tests have come under increased scrutiny. One question is whether the tests assess the students' mastery of critical skills. A second is whether focusing instruction on the skills needed to do well on the tests improves or worsens the quality of instruction students receive.

From the beginning of the Academy program, Ward and Belous planned to develop online assessments of student skills. Students complete an online multiple-choice examination at the end of each of the 15 chapters that are part of each semester's curriculum. They also must complete an end-of-semester online multiple-choice exam.

As the Academy program grew, George Ward realized that it needed more expertise on assessments. This led the program to recruit John Behrens, a senior psychometrician at Arizona State University. In January 2000, Behrens became director of assessment, research, and evaluation for the Academies. Behrens has led the effort to improve assessments of students' and instructors' skills.

There are many ways that Behrens and his colleagues use technology to improve skill assessments. While all students currently

---

[7]Academy instructors download the curriculum over the Internet from the Academy central server. Then students access the curriculum on LANs.

answer the same questions at the end of each chapter and at the end of each semester, software randomly assigns the order of the questions for each test taker. Instructors value the random ordering because it increases the likelihood that student's responses reflect their own knowledge.

Student's responses to the multiple-choice questions go directly to the Cisco Academy server in Arizona and students receive back their exam grade in a minute or two. The exam grades for each student are automatically entered into a spreadsheet that the instructor can access to check on student progress and to assign final course grades. Student responses on individual test items are recorded on the Academy server and are analyzed by the assessment team to identify problematic questions. Since the exams are provided to students online from the Academy server, the assessment team can easily test new questions and replace inadequate questions with better ones.

The assessment team uses two strategies to align the assessments with curriculum goals. First, the person who prepares each exam question documents the particular curriculum goal that the question addresses. Then each item goes through a multistage quality review.

Second, the end-of-course multiple-choice exam for each semester is complemented by a hands-on practical examination. While individual instructors have discretion in designing the hands-on examinations, the instructor's guide outlines the types of tasks that should be assessed. For example, the task for the second semester is to build a network that uses five routers. The hands-on exam for the fourth semester is comprehensive in that it assesses mastery of skills taught in all four semesters. For example, students are asked to use IP addresses (Semester 1), apply a routing protocol (Semester 2), make an access list (Semester 3), and construct a wide area network (Semester 4). Students must pass the hands-on examination as well as achieve a satisfactory score (as defined by the instructor) on the end-of-course multiple-choice exam in order to receive credit for the course.

Behrens has several initiatives under way to improve the Academy assessment program and to incorporate technological advances developed by Educational Testing Service and other organizations on the frontier of test development. One initiative will overcome the current limitation that students only learn their score on each examination, not which items they answered incorrectly. In the future, feedback will not only include identification of questions answered incorrectly, but also links to the relevant sections of the curriculum and to additional resources. A second initiative is the development of multiple forms of each end-of-semester and chapter test, with comparable scoring across the different forms. This will allow instructors to use different forms of the tests for different purposes. A third initiative is the development of new online assessment formats, including microsimulations that require students to program emulated routers. A fourth is the development of adaptive testing that tailors the difficulty of the test items to the skill of the test taker. This permits more accurate assessment of the skills of individual students.

Maintaining High-Quality Instruction

A premise underlying standards-based educational reforms is that all children will receive consistently good instruction. Indeed, fulfilling this premise is necessary to justify withholding grade promotions and high school diplomas from students who do not score well on state-mandated standardized assessments. Yet a great many studies over the last 30 years have documented that the quality of teaching in American schools varies enormously.[8]

Assuring that all students enrolled in Cisco Networking Academies receive consistently good instruction has been a goal of the program since its inception. In fact, the one uneasy response to George Ward's initial presentation of the Academy concept to a group of educators in spring 1997 dealt with accountability. Educators wanted to know what Ward meant by the term and what responsibilities they would incur if they signed up to host a Local Academy.

The structural design of the Academy program makes quality assurance a particularly difficult challenge. Administration is very decentralized. CATCs are responsible for monitoring the quality of Regional Academies; in turn, the Regional Academies are responsible for monitoring the quality of Local Academies. Cisco does not select the instructors in Local and Regional Academies, nor does it pay them. The only sanction Cisco can impose on a Local Academy that does not provide consistently high-quality instruction is to work with the Regional Academy to deny program affiliation. As a result, the primary strategy for assuring instructional quality is to identify problems as quickly as possible and then to offer a variety of opportunities for improving instruction.

The Academy program makes extensive use of information collected online in identifying problems. Student's end-of-semester exam scores provide one source of information. The Academy Quality Assurance Team monitors the distribution of scores in each class, looking for classes in which a large percentage of students earn low scores. Student surveys provide a second source of information. Every student completes an online survey at the end of every semester that asks for ratings of the instructor, the curriculum, and the course assignments. Instructors can learn about their performance by accessing online the average rating their students gave on each of the 15 ques-

---

[8]Researchers from different disciplines using different methods have documented the wide variance in teaching quality in American schools. See Hanushek (1994) for a discussion of the evidence by economists. See Grossman (1990) for evidence on differences in effectiveness among English teachers and Mayer (1998) for a discussion of differences among math teachers.

tions in the survey. (See Table 5-3 for an example of feedback to an instructor from student surveys.) The single number describing the average rating students gave on the 15 survey questions is sent to the Regional Academy overseeing the particular Local Academy and to the Academy Quality Assurance team.

In addition, participants in instructor training complete online evaluations of the quality of their training. The survey asks participants to rate the class content ("The order of course topics aided my learning"), as well as the instructor's pedagogical style ("Class participation was enhanced through effective use of questions") and content knowledge ("Analogies and real-life experiences of the instructor added value to the course"). These ratings are available to the trainer, and a summary of these ratings is also transmitted to the Quality Assurance Team. The Academy team also uses the Internet to evaluate complaints about training quality. When the director of training receives an e-mail message complaining about the quality of a training program, he sends an online survey to all participants in that particular training class. The responses help him to judge whether the initial e-mail reflects a significant training problem or an isolated personality conflict.

A primary mechanism for quality assurance is the annual audit. A three-person team (including one consultant with expertise in pedagogy, a second knowledgeable about technology, and one member of the Cisco Academy team) audits each CATC. It inquires whether the CATC fulfilled its contractual obligation to conduct annual audits of the Regional Academies under it. Part of this process involves learning whether the Regional Academies conducted audits of the Local Academies under them. The auditors of CATCs also examine the student test score distributions and average student survey grades for all Regional and Local Academies under the particular CATC. The auditing team asks whether the CATC had identified patterns of low student scores or poor class ratings. It also explores whether the CATC brought the potential problem to the attention of the relevant Regional Academy and whether it followed up to see whether the Regional Academy worked with the relevant instructor to diagnose the source of the problem and develop a remediation plan.[9] Another part of each audit is to check that instructors of all Academy courses have kept their CCNA credential up-to-date, a process requiring them to pass the CCNA exam every three years. This requirement that instructors periodically demonstrate mastery of subject matter content is a bone of contention with many instructors. To date, however, the program has stuck by this requirement.

---

[9] Of course, there are several reasons students could have low scores on the end-of-course examinations, including low reading skills, inadequate facilities, and poor teaching. The Regional Academy is responsible for exploring the reason for low scores among students in a Local Academy in its jurisdiction and for suggesting improvement strategies.

TABLE 5-3 Sample of Course Feedback Results

Min	Max	Mean	Question
4	5	4.85	The instructor was adequately prepared to teach this course.
4	5	4.77	Analogies and real-life experiences of the instructor added value to this course.
3	5	4.54	Presentations were clear and easy to understand.
3	5	4.54	Answers to questions were provided in a timely manner.
3	5	4.23	Class participation was enhanced through effective use of questions.
3	5	4.69	The class was interesting and enjoyable.
3	5	4.69	"Best Practices" and good teaching strategies were modeled during the training.
4	5	4.69	Grouping strategies were utilized effectively.
4	5	4.92	Class members felt comfortable approaching the instructor with questions/ideas.
3	5	4.15	The order of course topics aided my learning.
1	5	3.85	The course schedule allowed me to complete the stated course objectives.
1	5	4.15	The activities and labs helped me achieve the stated course objectives.
3	5	4.38	The lesson assessment tools helped me evaluate my knowledge of the lesson.
3	5	4.31	Group work aided my learning.
4	5	4.62	Overall, the course materials were of high quality.

SOURCE: Cisco Academy instructor.

Quality assurance in the Cisco Academy program depends critically on the efforts of Regional Academies, the majority of which in the United States are in community colleges. While Cisco allows Regional Academies to recover the costs they incur in supporting Local Academies and training their instructors, and a few charge an annual support fee as high as $15,000, many charge little or nothing. The rationale, several Regional Academy instructors told us, is that state legislatures expect community colleges to serve as community assets. Supporting Cisco Local Academies in area high schools is one way of demonstrating that commitment. Of course, this arrangement means that the quality of support Local Academies receive and the integrity of the quality assurance plan depend critically on the good will of the community colleges and high schools that serve as Regional Academies.

Signaling Skills

Employers in the United States find it very difficult to obtain reliable information on the skills of high school graduates who apply for jobs. The high school diploma indicates only that students completed four years of high school, not that they mastered particular skills. High schools typically do not respond quickly to requests for student transcripts. A consequence of the lack of information on the skills of high school graduates is that employers typically offer the same wages and conditions of employment to high school graduates with strong skills that they offer to graduates with much weaker skills.

Bishop et al. (2001) have argued that this hiring pattern reduces high school students' incentives to do the hard work that skill mastery requires.

Graduates of the four-semester Cisco Networking Academy may obtain the Cisco Certified Networking Associate (CCNA) credential by passing the same examination that graduates of commercial training institutes take. The CCNA exam is a multiple-choice exam administered by an independent testing organization, Prometric.[10] Academy graduates may also obtain the vender-neutral Network+ credential by passing a different examination offered by an industry trade organization, CompTIA. We have no way of assessing whether the opportunity to acquire industry-recognized credentials has motivated students to enroll in Academy classes and to work hard to acquire critical skills. However, many Academy students in community colleges told us that their reason for enrolling in the Academy courses was to prepare for the CCNA exam.

Credentials that can be earned by passing examinations predate the Internet by many years. However, the online format of the CCNA exams mean that scoring is done almost instantaneously and the credential can be awarded much more quickly than if paper answer sheets were sent to a central scoring office. This may increase the attractiveness of the credential and the Academy program to potential students.

Economists have two questions about the economic value of credentials like the CCNA. The first is whether it permits the recipient to earn more than he or she otherwise would have earned. The second is whether any wage premium that is earned stems from skills the individual acquired while studying for the credential or whether the premium stems from skills that the individual already had before obtaining the credential but could not signal to employers in the absence of the credential. It has proven extremely difficult to answer these questions for most education and training credentials, and the CCNA credential is no exception in this regard. One survey reports that recipients of the CCNA credential earn approximately 10 percent more than IT workers without this credential (Gabelhouse, 2000). However, since individuals voluntarily decide whether to try to obtain the credential, it is possible that those who do obtain it differ from those workers who do not in dimensions such as motivation that affect earnings. Consequently the earnings differences could stem from differences between workers who obtain the CCNA and those who do not that are not observed by the researcher but are observed by employers. Thus, all that can be said is that the survey evidence is consistent with community college students' perception that the CCNA credential brings significant economic benefits.

---

[10]As explained by Adelman (2000), the CCNA is one of a great many IT credentials that can be obtained by passing examinations, typically administered by one of three large organizations (including Prometric). The examinations for some credentials include hands-on performance assessments.

BOX 5-1
Sample Job Announcements That Call for a Cisco Certified Network Associate (CCNA) Credential and Work Experiences

PC Technician I

SKILLS/TECHNICAL KNOWLEDGE REQUIRED:

• Education: Two-year degree or equivalent IT experience consisting of direct end user and network support and industry standard certifications (MCSE, CCNA, CompTIA, etc.)

• Experience: IT experience consisting of direct end user and network support and industry standard certifications (MCSE, CCNA, CompTIA, etc.)

JOB DUTIES: Supports, monitors, tests, and troubleshoots hardware and software problems pertaining to LAN workstations. Recommends, installs, and configures workstations. Performs repairs to desktop systems, provides end user support for LAN / LAN-based applications, proprietary computer-based manufacturing and graphics applications, and desktop hardware and operating system support. Assists in the maintenance of user network and e-mail account information, including rights, security, and systems groups. Acts as first line of support for user problem resolution, responsible for either solving end user problems or escalating issues to a higher level.

Company offers competitive compensation, bonus plans, and comprehensive benefit plans including 401K and medical insurance with prescription drug card and $15 doctor visit copay. Submit resume with salary history. Only resumes with salary history included will be considered.

Network Administrator

Network Administrator

• CCNA or B.S. in computer sciences or related field.
• 3+yrs exp. In installation, configuration, trouble-shooting and support of network routers, hubs, switches, and structured cable plants. Must possess excellent communication and documentation skills.

Source: Monster.com

To learn more about employers' treatment of the CCNA credential, we conducted a computer search for job postings that listed it as required or desired. We found many such jobs, with annual salaries ranging from $35,000 to $70,000. However, as illustrated in Box 5-1, almost all of the jobs, even those paying the lowest salaries, required a minimum of one year of experience in computer networking. Adelman (2000) has documented that this is the common pattern for IT jobs.

To help solve the experience problem, Cisco has begun a process of matching Academy students and graduates desiring work experience with employers who want help with particular projects. Students interested in jobs or internships post resumes on the Academy Web site. (If a student is under 18, he or she is identified only by ID number, not by name.) Employers who want student help post internship and job listings on a Cisco Web site (http://wpl.netacad.net). They immediately receive a list of all Academies within 50 miles. The employer then requests that the help-wanted listing be sent to all nearby Academies or to a selected subset. Academy instructors then make available to employers the resumes of those students whose skills seem to fit the job requirements. Employers may contact students at least 18 years of age directly. Academy instructors arrange interviews for students under the age of 18.

This example illustrates two points. The Internet can be a valuable resource in improving matchmaking between employers and students (Autor, 2001). By increasing students' opportunities to gain work experience that is a necessary qualification for most jobs, the Internet may improve incentives for students to do the hard work that skill mastery requires.

The second point is quite different. Considerable attention is needed to assure that the enormous search potential of the Internet does not result in violations of federal and state laws regarding the privacy of information pertaining to minors. Concern with these laws explains why Cisco collects no information on the characteristics of Academy students, not even names.

LESSONS

The Academy program differs from state standards-based reform efforts in two notable respects. First, it has a common national curriculum. While the merits of this approach can be debated, one advantage we observed is that mobile students find no difficulty in obtaining credit in one state for Cisco Academy courses completed in another state.

Another difference is that aspiring instructors must demonstrate mastery of the curriculum they will teach by passing the same end-of-semester exams that the students take and by passing the national CCNA exam every three years. While this does not guarantee that teachers know how to teach the curriculum, it does provide some assurance of subject matter mastery.

The brief history of the Cisco Networking Academies demonstrates that the Internet has the potential to be a valuable resource for improving education. For the Academies, the Internet has been important in developing and improving curriculum, in distributing an up-to-date curriculum to underserved populations, in assessing student skills, in monitoring the quality of instruction, and in providing teachers with advice on technical and pedagogical issues and with a resource for keeping track of student progress and exam grades.

At the same time, the Academies' experience shows that technology is not a substitute for highly motivated teachers with command of their subject matter and with the pedagogical skills to help students master critical skills. To the credit of George Ward and Alex Belous, they never intended that online curriculum and assessment would substitute for first-rate instructors. From the beginning they envisioned the Cisco Academies program as blending online resources with high-quality classroom instruction. The brief history of the Academies program given here shows that technology cannot insulate high schools and community colleges from the challenge of attracting and retaining talented teachers who typically are offered salaries that are considerably lower than those they could earn in other jobs.

Another lesson is that it takes time to figure out how best to make use of technology. For example, the Academies team has learned that it would be better to have students fill out the course satisfaction surveys before they receive their end-of-course exam grades rather than after. The reason is that analysis of survey responses suggests that students who do not do well on the final exam are particularly critical of the course and the instructor. The team has also learned that retaining for auditing purposes only the single number that represents the average rating students in a class give on all 15 rating questions is a mistake. While a low average grade may identify a quality problem, average responses on individual questions are needed to diagnose the source of the problem. The Academy team also learned that there is a trade-off between keeping the curriculum up-to-date and keeping it stable so that instructors can make lesson plans ahead of time. Too frequent curriculum revisions create more problems than they solve.

These examples illustrate that even with a team that included experienced professional educators and experts on information technology, figuring out how to make the most effective use of the Internet to improve education required much trial and error. The important gains do not come from simply substituting online resources for books. They come from developing new teaching and learning roles. For example, in the Academy program the most effective instructors are not lecturers who spend most class time talking while students take notes. They are coaches who engage students in learning from each other and in developing the confidence to assume responsibility for their learning and for commenting constructively on the quality of instruction. For many teachers and students, these are new roles that are not easy to assume. Figuring out how to bring about these cultural changes and how to use the Internet to facilitate these changes is a slow process.

A final question to consider is whether the Internet is different from the many technological innovations—radio, instructional films,

TV—formerly seen as transforming education. In perhaps the most critical respect, the Internet is not different in that it is not a substitute for effective interaction of teachers with students. In other respects, the Internet is somewhat different from previous generations of instructional technologies. The Internet facilitates two-way communication. Not only can Local Academy students and teachers receive exams and new versions of the curriculum over the Internet but also they can send back to the central Academy team information critical to evaluating the quality of the exams and the curriculum.

A second difference is that the Internet markedly increases the ability of teachers and students to search for information that can be useful in solving problems and constructing arguments. In so doing, it reduces the importance of memorizing facts that can be quickly retrieved from online sources. It also dramatically increases the importance of learning to search efficiently, to sort through the vast amount of information the Web can make available, and to synthesize and make sense of an abundance of information (NRC, 1999).

It is too early to tell exactly how the Internet will alter the demand for particular skills or the capacity of human societies to teach the critical skills. However, the experience of the Cisco Networking Academies suggests that it is a mistake to see technology as substituting for effective teachers in helping students to learn. Instead, the appropriate perspective is that technology will be most valuable in complementing the skills of highly motivated teachers who know their subject matter well and know how to engage students in learning.

REFERENCES

Adelman, C. (2000). *A parallel postsecondary universe: The certification system in information technology.* Washington, DC: U.S. Department of Education, Office of Educational Research and Improvement.

Autor, D.H. (2001). Wiring the labor market. *Journal of Economic Perspectives, 15,* 35–50.

Bishop, J.H. (1995). *Expertise and excellence.* Ithaca, NY: Cornell University, School of Industrial Relations, Center for Advanced Human Resource Studies.

Bishop, J.H., Mane, F., Bishop, M., and Moriarty, J. (2001). The role of end-of-course exams and minimal competency exams in standards-based reforms. In D. Ravitch (Ed.), *Brookings papers in education policy 2001.* Washington, DC: The Brookings Institution.

Cisco Networking Academy Program. (2000). *Curriculum alignment document.* San Jose, CA: Cisco Systems.

Cuban, L. (1986). *Teachers and machines: The classroom use of technology since 1920.* New York: Teachers College Press.

Gabelhouse, G. (2000, December). CertMag's salary survey. *Certification Magazine.* Available: http://www.certmag.com/issues/dec00 [December 12, 2000].

Grossman, P.L. (1990). *The making of a teacher: Teacher knowledge and teacher education.* New York: Teachers College Press.

Hanushek, E.A. (1994). *Making schools work: Improving performance and controlling costs.* Washington, DC: The Brookings Institution.

Johnstone, W.B., and Packer, A.E. (1987). *Workforce 2000: Work and workers for the twenty-first century.* Indianapolis, IN: Hudson Institute.

Kershaw, J.A., and McKean, R.N. (1962). *Teacher shortages and salary schedules.* New York: McGraw-Hill.

Marshall, R., and Tucker, M. (1991). *Thinking for a living: Education and the wealth of nations.* New York: Basic Books.

Mayer, D.P. (1998). Do teaching standards undermine performance on old tests? *Educational Evaluation and Policy Analysis, 20,* 53.

Murnane, R.J., and Levy, F. (1996). *Teaching the new basic skills.* New York: Free Press.

Murnane, R.J., and Levy, F. (2001). Will standards-based reforms improve the education of students of color? *National Tax Journal, 54,* 401–415.

Murnane, R.J., Willett, J.B. and Levy, F. (1995). The growing importance of cognitive skills in wage determination. *Review of Economics and Statistics 77,* 251–266.

National Research Council. (1999). *How people learn: Brain, mind, experience, and school.* Committee on Developments in the Science of Learning. Bransford, J.D., Brown, A.L., and Cocking, R.R. (Eds.). Commission on Behavioral and Social Sciences and Education. Washington, DC: National Academy Press.

National Institute for Literacy. (2000). *Equipped for the future content standards: What adults need to know and be able to do in the 21st century.* Washington, DC: Author.

Parrado, E., and Wolff, E. (1999). *Occupational and industrial mobility in the United States, 1969–92.* New York: New York University.

Secretary's Commission on Achieving Necessary Skills. (1991). *What work requires of schools: A SCANS report for America 2000.* Washington, DC: U.S. Department of Labor.

Zehr, M.A. (1998). Computer giants look to students. *Education Week,* April 15.

6

Creating High-Quality Learning Environments: Guidelines from Research on How People Learn

John Bransford, Nancy Vye, and Helen Bateman*

Not long ago, our local newspaper announced that the state university system was going to offer a number of college degree programs over the Internet. Some people scoffed at the idea and made statements like "here come the diploma mills." However, for a large number of individuals, this was genuinely exciting news. Some had attended college but did not get a chance to finish because they needed to go to work full-time—now they had a chance to get a degree. Others never had the chance to attend college—now they could do so without having to move from their present location. Even if it turns out that many of these people don't have the time to take enough courses to graduate, it can be a wonderful sense of accomplishment to have taken a college course or two.

We applaud the increased access to educational opportunities that new technologies are making possible. Nevertheless, we have been asked to focus on the issue of educational quality rather than access. Ultimately, people need access to high-quality learning opportunities. Issues of quality are important for face-to-face learning environments, totally online environments, and hybrid environments that include combinations of both.

We organize this chapter into three major sections:

*John Bransford is Centennial Professor of Psychology and codirector of the Learning Technology Center at Peabody College of Vanderbilt University. Nancy Vye is senior research associate and codirector of the Learning Center at Peabody College of Vanderbilt University. Helen Bateman is presently a research fellow at the Learning Technology Center, Vanderbilt University. This chapter is based on research funded by the National Science Foundation and the U.S. Department of Education.

- An overview of different ways to think about educational quality.
- A discussion of ways that information about how people learn can guide the design of environments that support high-quality learning.
- An examination of some of the special challenges and opportunities for high-quality learning that accompany new technologies.

SOME WAYS TO THINK ABOUT ISSUES OF EDUCATIONAL QUALITY

People who want to improve educational quality often begin with a focus on teaching methods. We have been approached by a number of professors and K-12 teachers who heard that lectures (whether live or online) are a poor way to teach. "Is this true?" they ask. "Is cooperative learning better than lecturing?" "Do [computers, labs, hands-on projects, simulations] help learning?" For Web-based instruction, we are often asked to identify the most important technology features needed for success, including the relative importance of threaded discussions, chat rooms, availability of full motion video, and so forth.

Questions about teaching strategies are important, but they need to be asked in the context of whom we are teaching and what we want our students to accomplish. The reason is that particular types of teaching and learning strategies can be strong or weak depending on our goals for learning and the knowledge and skills that students bring to the learning task (e.g., see Jenkins, 1978; Morris, Bransford, and Franks, 1977; Schwartz and Bransford, 1998).

The Jenkins Tetrahedral Model

A model developed by James Jenkins (1978) highlights important constellations of factors that must be simultaneously considered when attempting to think about issues of teaching and learning. (See Figure 6-1. We have adapted the model slightly to fit the current discussion.) The model illustrates that the appropriateness of using particular types of teaching strategies depends on (1) the nature of the materials to be learned; (2) the nature of the skills, knowledge, and attitudes that learners bring to the situation; and (3) the goals of the learning situation and the assessments used to measure learning relative to these goals. A teaching strategy that works within one constellation of these variables may work very poorly when that overall constellation is changed. One way to think about the Jenkins model is to view it as highlighting important parameters for defining various educational ecosystems. A particular teaching strategy may flourish or perish depending on the overall characteristics of the ecosystem in which it is placed.

Attempts to teach students about veins and arteries can be used to illustrate the interdependencies shown in the Jenkins model. Imagine that the materials to be learned include a text, which states that arteries are thicker than veins and more elastic and carry blood rich in

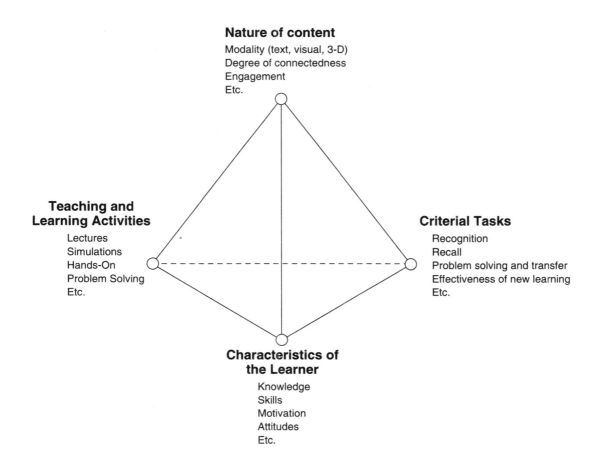

Nature of content
Modality (text, visual, 3-D)
Degree of connectedness
Engagement
Etc.

Teaching and Learning Activities
Lectures
Simulations
Hands-On
Problem Solving
Etc.

Criterial Tasks
Recognition
Recall
Problem solving and transfer
Effectiveness of new learning
Etc.

Characteristics of the Learner
Knowledge
Skills
Motivation
Attitudes
Etc.

FIGURE 6-1: Jenkins Tetrahedral Model.

SOURCE: Adapted from Jenkins (1978).

oxygen from the heart. Veins are smaller, less elastic, and carry blood back to the heart. What's the best way to help students learn this information? The Jenkins model reminds us that the answer to this question depends on who the students are, what we mean by "learning" in this context, and how we measure the learning that occurs.

Consider a strategy that teaches students to use mnemonic techniques. For example, they might be taught to think about the sentence "*Art(ery)* was *thick* around the middle so he wore pants with an *elastic* waistband." The Jenkins framework reminds us that the ability to use this particular technique presupposes specific types of knowledge and skills on the part of the learners (e.g., that they understand English, understand concepts such as elasticity and why they would be useful in this situation, etc.). Given the availability of this knowledge, mnemonic techniques like the one noted above "work" extremely well—given particular assumptions about what it means for something to "work."

Mnemonic techniques "work" for remembering factual content. If asked to state important characteristics of arteries (e.g., thick, elastic), the preceding statement about Art(ery) can be very helpful. If our tests assess only memory, we tend to say that our students have learned. But suppose that we change the goal from merely remembering to learning with understanding. The Jenkins framework reminds us that a change in learning goals and assessments often requires a change in teaching and learning strategies as well.

In order to learn with understanding, students need to understand *why* veins and arteries have certain characteristics. For example, arteries carry blood from the heart, blood that is pumped in spurts. This helps explain why they would need to be elastic (to handle the spurts). In addition, arterial blood needs to travel uphill (to the brain) as well as downhill, so the elasticity of the arteries provides an additional advantage. If they constrict behind each uphill spurt, they act as a type of one-way valve that keeps the blood from flowing downhill.

Learning to understand relationships such as why arteries are elastic should facilitate subsequent transfer. For example, imagine that students are asked to design an artificial artery. Would it have to be elastic? Students who have only memorized that arteries are elastic have no grounded way to approach this problem. Students who have learned with understanding know the functions of elasticity and hence are freer to consider possibilities like a nonelastic artery that has one-way valves (Bransford and Stein, 1993).

Overall, this example illustrates how memorizing versus understanding represents different learning goals in the Jenkins framework and how changes in these goals require different types of teaching strategies. The details of one's teaching strategies will also need to vary depending on the knowledge, skills, attitudes, and other characteristics that students bring to the learning task. For example, we noted earlier that some students (e.g., those in the lower grades) may not know enough about pumping, spurts, and elasticity to learn with understanding if they are simply told about the functions of arteries. They may need special scaffolds such as dynamic simulations that display these properties. As a different kind of example, imagine that we want to include mnemonics along with understanding and one of the students in our class is overweight and named Art. Under these conditions, it would seem unwise to use the mnemonic sentence about Art(ery) that was noted above.

The Importance of Working Backwards

The Jenkins model fits well with a recent book by Wiggins and McTighe entitled *Understanding by Design* (1997). They suggest a "working backwards" strategy for creating high-quality learning experiences. In particular, they recommend that educators (1) begin with a careful analysis of learning goals; (2) explore how to assess students' progress in achieving these goals; and (3) use the results of

1 and 2 to choose and continually evaluate teaching methods. (Assumptions about steps 1 and 2 are also continually evaluated.) When using a "working backwards" strategy, one's choice of teaching strategies derives from a careful analysis of learning goals, rather than vice versa. In the discussion below, we attempt to clarify the importance of working backwards by discussing some imaginary universities that each set different goals for their students. These different goals have strong effects on what and how the universities teach.

Father Guido Sarduci's Plans for Education

One example of working backwards from a well-defined set of goals is illustrated in a wonderful four-minute comedy routine by Father Guido Sarduci from the television program "Saturday Night Live." Father Sarduci begins by looking at the knowledge and skills that the average college graduate remembers five years after he or she graduates. He accepts these five-years-later memory performances as his standard and proposes a new kind of university that will have the same outcomes. His innovation is "The Five-Minute University," which will cost only $20. Father Sarduci notes that $20 might seem like a lot for only 5 minutes, but it includes tuition, books, snacks for the 20-second spring break, cap and gown rental, and graduation picture.

Father Sarduci provides examples of the kinds of things students remember after five years. If they took two years of college Spanish, for example, he argues that—five years postgraduation—the average student will remember only "¿Como esta usted?" and "Muy bien, gracias." So that's all his Five-Minute University teaches. His economics course teaches only "Supply and Demand." His business course teaches "You buy something and sell it for more," and so forth. A video of Father Sarduci's performance demonstrates how strongly the audience resonates to his theme of the heavy emphasis on memorization in college courses and the subsequent high forgetting rates.

Competing with Father Sarduci: Reducing Forgetting

A competitor to Father Sarduci's Five-Minute University might establish the goal of reducing the amount of forgetting that typically occurs five years after students graduate. The competitors' university will have to last longer than five minutes, but the increased retention of what was learned in college should make it worth the students' time. In order to accomplish this goal, the competitor will introduce students to a number of memory techniques.

We saw an example of a memory technique in our earlier discussion of veins and arteries. A teacher in the competing university might introduce it as follows: "OK class. Here's a way to remember the properties of arteries. Think about the sentence *ART(ery) was THICK around the middle but he was RICH enough to afford pants with an ELASTIC waistband.* This will help you remember that arteries are thick elastic and carry oxygen-rich blood. In a minute I'll give you a different sentence for remembering information about veins."

There is a great deal of research about the power of memory techniques and about ways that strategically spaced reminders can decrease the rate of forgetting (e.g., Bjork and Richardson-Klavhen, 1989; Bransford and Stein, 1993; Mann, 1979). The competitor to Father Sarduci's university would probably use these studies as evidence for the "research-based teaching methods" that her school provides.

Another Competitor: Learning With Understanding

A third competitor proposes to move beyond the goal of simply increasing retention. Her university emphasizes the importance of learning with understanding. This not only can help remembering, it can also provide a basis for transfer to new problems that need to be solved. (e.g., National Research Council [NRC],1999a; Bransford and Stein, 1993; Judd, 1908; Wertheimer, 1959). We noted earlier how learning with understanding applies to the veins and arteries example. From this perspective, students need to understand *why* veins and arteries have certain characteristics.

The benefits of learning with understanding include a more flexible ability to transfer to new situations (e.g., to design an artificial artery). The downside is that learning with understanding typically takes more time than simply memorizing. Students need to understand something about the circulatory system and the body as a whole in order to understand the structure and functions of veins and arteries. So our third university is going to have to be longer than the other competitors. But the results should be worth this extra time.

Still More Competitors

We could continue to add more competitors to our existing trio of universities. In addition to a focus on learning with understanding, several competitors might also emphasize problem solving. However, there are many ways to define "effective problem solving," and we would eventually expect new universities to differentiate themselves within this category. For example, one might prepare students to deal with realistic, open-ended problems rather than simply prepare them to solve the kinds of well-specified word problems that are often used in school settings (e.g., see Bransford, 1979; Cognition and Technology Group at Vanderbilt [CTGV], 1997; Hmelo, 1995; Williams, 1992). This will require a change in the kinds of assessments used to demonstrate success (i.e., the use of open-ended rather than simply well-scripted problems).

Still another competing university might promise to accomplish all the preceding goals plus tailor the educational curriculum to the strengths, needs, and desires of each learner. This would include the development of self-understanding (metacognition) as an important goal of learning. There is a considerable amount of data that supports the value of a metacognitive approach to instruction (e.g., see Brown, 1978; Leonard, Dufresne, and Mestre, 1996; Lin and Lehman, 1999; Pressley, 1995; White and Frederiksen, 1998). It includes an emphasis on learning with understanding and on problem solving, but part of the emphasis is on understanding the cognitive and emotional processes involved in these kinds of activities.

Summary: Issues of Education Quality

We began this section by noting that some people approach the issue of defining high-quality learning by focusing exclusively on teaching methods and asking, "which ones are best?" An alternative (and we argue more productive) approach is to focus on what we want students to know and be able to do, and to then work backwards (Wiggins and McTighe, 1997). We discussed the strategy of working backwards in the context of (imaginary) competing universities that try to differentiate themselves by focusing on different learning outcomes. Their choice of outcomes had a major impact on their choice of teaching strategies—including the length of time that students need to spend in their school.

The Jenkins model (Figure 6-1) reminds us that a change in learning goals is only one of several factors that should have an impact on our choice of teaching methods. Other factors include whom we are teaching and what they already know. If we are teaching plate tectonics to novices, or veins and arteries to novices, we probably need to include visuals—preferably ones that show the dynamics of the systems. If our students already know the core workings of the subject, they may well be able to generate the necessary images on their own (e.g., see Schwartz and Bransford, 1998).

Ultimately, the ability to design high-quality learning environments requires that we move beyond a procedural description of strategies such as working backwards (Wiggins and McTighe, 1997) and diagrams such as the Jenkins tetrahedral model. All these authors would agree that we also need to understand the kinds of skills, attitudes, and knowledge structures that support competent performance, plus understand the literature on ways to *develop* competence and confidence. We turn to these issues in the discussion below.

USING INFORMATION ABOUT HOW PEOPLE LEARN

During the past 30 years, research on human learning has exploded. Although we have a long way to go to fully uncover the mysteries of learning, we know a considerable amount about the cognitive processes that underlie expert performances and about strategies for helping people increase their expertise in a variety of areas. Several committees organized by the National Academy of Sciences have summarized much of this research in reports published by the National Academy

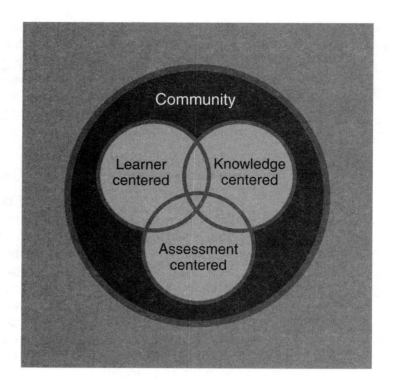

FIGURE 6-2: Four lenses that together make up the How People Learn (HPL) framework.

Press. Some of the key publications that inform our current discussion are *How People Learn: Brain, Mind, Experience and School* (NRC, 1999a) and *How People Learn: Bridging Research and Practice* (NRC, 1999b). These two individual reports have recently been combined to produce an expanded edition of *How People Learn* (NRC, 2000). A more recent report, *Knowing What Students Know* (NRC, 2001), which builds on *How People Learn,* is also relevant to this discussion. Its focus is primarily on assessment.

An organizing structure used in the *How People Learn* volumes (hereafter HPL) is the HPL framework (see Figure 6-2). It highlights a set of four overlapping lenses that can be used to analyze any learning situation. In particular, it suggests that we ask about the degree to which learning environments are:

• Knowledge centered (in the sense of being based on a careful analysis of what we want people to know and be able to do when they finish with our materials or course and providing them with the foundational knowledge, skills, and attitudes needed for successful transfer);
• Learner centered (in the sense of connecting to the strengths, interests, and preconceptions of learners and helping them learn about themselves as learners);

- Community centered (in the sense of providing an environment—both within and outside the classroom—where students feel safe to ask questions, learn to use technology to access resources and work collaboratively, and are helped to develop lifelong learning skills);
- Assessment centered (in the sense of providing multiple opportunities to make students' thinking visible so they can receive feedback and be given chances to revise).

We discuss each of these lenses below.

Knowledge Centered

It seems obvious that any learning situation—whether informal or formal; whether face-to-face, online, or a hybrid—involves the goal of acquiring new knowledge (we include skills within this category). The HPL framework helps us think more deeply about this issue by reminding us to take very seriously questions about *what* should be taught and why. Consistent with our earlier discussion of *Understanding by Design* (Wiggins and McTighe, 1997), an important first step is to ask what we want people to be able to know and do at the end of a course or learning experience. Or at a broader level, what do we want them to know and be able to do once they graduate?

Information about how people learn provides important guidelines for deepening our thinking about knowledge-centered issues. For example, learning goals should not simply be viewed as a list of disconnected "behavioral objectives." A key is to emphasize *connected* knowledge that is organized around foundational ideas of a discipline. Research on expertise shows that it is the organization of knowledge that underlies experts' abilities to understand and solve problems (see HPL [NRC, 1992b], especially Chapter 2).

Bruner (1960) makes the following argument about knowledge organization:

> The curriculum of a subject should be determined by the most fundamental understanding that can be achieved of the underlying principles that give structure to a subject. Teaching specific topics or skills without making clear their context in the broader fundamental structure of a field of knowledge is uneconomical. . . . An understanding of fundamental principles and ideas appears to be the main road to adequate transfer of training. To understand something as a specific instance of a more general case—which is what understanding a more fundamental structure means—is to have learned not only a specific thing but also a model for understanding other things like it that one may encounter. (pp. 6, 25, and 31)

An emphasis on knowledge organization (as opposed to a mere list of behavioral objectives) has important implications for the design of instruction. For example, Wiggins and McTighe (1997) argue that the knowledge to be taught should be prioritized into categories that range from "enduring ideas of the discipline" to "important things to know and be able to do" to "ideas worth mentioning." Thinking through these issues and coming up with a set of "enduring connected ideas" is an extremely important aspect of educational design.

Our earlier discussion of veins and arteries provides a simple contrast between a mere list of fact-oriented behavioral objectives (e.g., be able to list the features of veins and arteries) and an attempt to develop a more coherent, enduring model that explains why veins and arteries have certain properties. As Bruner (1960) argues, taking the time to develop an understanding of key concepts and models is more efficient in the long run (see also Bransford and Schwartz, 1999) because it facilitates subsequent learning. He also states: "One of the principal organizing concepts in biology is the question, "What function does this thing serve?" This question is premised on the assumption that everything one finds in an organism serves some function or it probably would not have survived. Other general ideas are related to this question. The student who makes progress in biology learns to ask the question more and more subtly, to relate more and more things to it (Bruner, 1960, p. 280). Bransford and Schwartz's (1999) discussion of "preparing students for future learning" provides additional examples of this point of view.

Many courses are organized in ways that fail to optimally prepare students for future learning. For example, texts often present lists of topics and facts in a manner that has been described as "a mile wide and an inch deep" (e.g., see NRC, 2000). Taking the time to define and teach the "enduring ideas of a discipline" is extremely important for ensuring high-quality learning. Making this choice is often described as choosing "depth over breadth," but in the long run it is not an either/or proposition.

Learner Centered

There are many overlaps between being knowledge centered and learner centered, but there are differences as well. From the instructor's perspective, an important aspect of being learner centered involves recognition of "expert blind spots." Instructors must become aware that much of what they know is tacit and hence can easily be skipped over in instruction. For example, experts in physics and engineering may not realize that they are failing to communicate all the information necessary to help novices learn to construct their own free body diagrams (Brophy, 2001). The reason is that many decisions are so intuitive that the professors don't even realize they are part of their repertoire. Studies of expertise (e.g., NRC, 2000) show that experts' knowledge helps them begin problem solving at a higher level than novices because they almost effortlessly perceive aspects of a problem situation that are invisible to novices (e.g., Chi, Feltovich, and Glaser, 1981; deGroot, 1965). Shulman (1987) discusses how effective teachers need to develop "pedagogical content knowledge" that goes well beyond the content knowledge of a discipline (see also Hestenes, 1987).

A learner-centered approach includes an understanding of how novices typically struggle as they attempt to master a domain and an understanding of strategies for helping them learn.

Related to the idea of expert blind spots is the notion that students are not "blank slates" with respect to goals, opinions, knowledge, and time. The HPL volume summarizes a number of studies that demonstrate the active, preconception-driven learning that is evident from infancy to adulthood (see also Carey and Gelman, 1991; Driver, Squires, Rushworth, and Wood-Robinson, 1994). In many cases, students develop preconceptions based on their everyday experiences that are at odds with the basic assumptions that underlie various disciplines (e.g., modern physics). If these preconceptions are not addressed directly, students often memorize content (e.g., formulas in physics) yet still use their experience-based preconceptions (which are often misconceptions from the perspective of mature disciplines) to act upon the world.

Other components of being learner centered involve honoring students' backgrounds and cultural values and finding special strengths that each may have that allow him or her to connect to information being taught in the classroom. Unless these connections are made explicitly, such strengths often remain inert and hence do not support subsequent learning.

An article written in 1944 by Stephen Corey provides an insightful look at the importance of being learner centered and attempting to help students connect school learning with other knowledge and skills that are available to them. Entitled "Poor Scholar's Soliloquy," the article is written from the perspective of an imaginary student (we'll call him Bob) who is not very good in school and has had to repeat the seventh grade. Many would write Bob off as having a low aptitude for learning. But looking at what Bob is capable of achieving outside of school gives a very different impression of his abilities.

Part of the soliloquy describes how teachers don't see Bob as a good reader. His favorite books include *Popular Science*, the *Mechanical Encyclopedia*, and the *Sears'* and *Ward's* catalogs. Bob uses his books to pursue meaningful goals. He says, "I don't just sit down and read them through like they make us do in school. I use my books when I want to find something out, like whenever Mom buys anything second hand, I look it up in *Sears'* or *Ward's* first and tell her if she's getting stung or not."

Later on, Bob explains the trouble he had memorizing the names of the presidents. He knew some of them, like Washington and Jefferson, but there were 30 altogether at the time and he never did get them all straight. He seems to have a poor memory. Then he talks about the three trucks his uncle owns and how he knows the horsepower and number of forward and backward gears of 26 different American trucks, many of them diesels. Then he says, "It's funny how that diesel works. I started to tell my teacher about it last Wednesday in science class when the pump we were using to make a vacuum in a bell jar got hot, but she said she didn't see what a diesel engine had to do with our experiment on air pressure so I just kept still. The kids seemed interested, though."

Bob also discusses his inability to do the kinds of word problems found in his textbooks. Yet he helps his uncle make all kinds of complex plans when they travel together. He talks about the bills and letters he sends to the farmers whose livestock his uncle hauls and about how he made only three mistakes in his last 17 letters—all of them commas. Then he says, "I wish I could write school themes that way. The last one I had to write was on 'What a Daffodil Thinks of Spring,' and I just couldn't get going."

Bob ends his soliloquy by noting that, according to his dad, he can quit school at the age of 15 and how he feels like he should. After all, he's not getting any younger and he has a lot to learn.

The story about Bob is as relevant today as it was in 1944. NRC (1999a,b) discusses how all new learning rests on connections to previous learning, yet potential connections are not necessarily made spontaneously. The advantages of helping students make these connections are continuing to be explored (e.g., Moll, Tapia, and Whitmore, 1993).

Sometimes our assumptions about other people are based on hearsay, stereotypes, or interpretations of behaviors that are one sided because we lack other perspectives. The research literature on stereotypes demonstrates the unfortunate ease with which humans make unwarranted assumptions about others based on only superficial cues (e.g., Cole, 1996; Hamilton, Stroessner, and Driscoll, 1994; Jussim, Coleman, and Lerch, 1987; Salzer, 1998). Research by Lin and Bransford (in preparation) shows how efforts to personalize information about people can help fellow students and teachers get beyond their initial stereotypes. Interestingly, in an online world, many identifying characteristics of individuals that might cause stereotyping can remain hidden. Many argue that this can have important benefits.

Community Centered

This aspect of the HPL framework is highly related to being learner centered, but it specifically focuses our attention on the norms and modes of operation of any community we are joining. For example, some classrooms represent communities where it is safe to ask questions and say, "I don't know." Others follow the norm of "Don't get caught not knowing something." An increasing number of studies suggest that—in order to be successful—learning communities should provide their members a feeling that members matter to each other and to the group and a shared faith that members' needs will be met through their commitment to be together (Alexopoulou and Driver, 1996; Bateman, Bransford, Goldman, and Newbrough, 2000).

The importance of creating and sustaining learning communities in which all members are valued can be traced to Vygotsky's theory that culture plays a central role in developmental processes. Vygotsky

(1978) suggested that all learning is culturally mediated, historically developing, and arising from cultural activity. Leontiev (1981) describes Vygotsky's "cultural method of thinking" as developing in a system of human relationships: "If we removed human activity from the system of social relationships, it would not exist. . . . The human individual's activity is a system of social relations. It does not exist without these reactions" (pp. 46-47).

An important implication of this perspective is that providing supportive, enriched, and flexible settings where people can learn is essential. Having strong social networks within a classroom, within a school, and between classrooms and outside resources produces a number of advantages.

First, networks provide students with multiple sources of knowledge. This is very important since different students often vary in what they know about a particular topic and hence need access to additional knowledge that may go beyond what is explicitly taught (Moll and Greenberg, 1995). Second, strong learning communities provide learners with considerable support in obtaining such knowledge by providing settings where students are not afraid to ask questions, to attempt solving difficult problems, and to occasionally fail. Such social networks can be thought of as communities of learners (Bateman, 1998; Bateman, Bransford, Goldman, and Newbrough, 2000; CTGV, 1994). Successful learning communities provide students with multiple opportunities for active participation (Brown and Campione, 1994; Lave and Wenger, 1991; Vygotksy, 1978). Such communities of practice provide learners with intrinsic motivation to move to greater levels of participation in the community, thus becoming active members of the community of learners (Lave and Wenger, 1991).

Although many aspects of community seem intuitively obvious when observed, there is currently considerable debate on defining the term "community"; hence there are numerous definitions of the term. Hillery (1955) was able to identify and analyze similarities among 94 sociological definitions. Poplin (1979), as well as Hillery, concluded that all definitions held the following identifying characteristics in common:

1. a group of people,
2. who share social interaction,
3. who share common ties between themselves and the group, and
4. who share a common "area" for at least some of the time.

McMillan and Chavis (1986) have developed one of the most influential community models to date. They propose that effective communities should provide their members with:

1. Membership—a feeling of belonging and acceptance, of sharing a sense of personal relatedness. Personal investment and boundaries are important elements of membership.

2. Influence—a sense of mattering, of making a difference to a group, and of the group mattering to its members. Influence is bidirectional.
3. Integration and fulfillment of needs—a feeling that the needs of the individual will be met by the community, as well a feeling that the individual can meet the needs of the community.
4. Shared emotional connection—an emotional bond that gradually builds as members of a community share events that require investment of time, energy, and effort. Unlike more traditional "social network" theories, the McMillan and Chavis (1986) model has as its focal point the concept of a person as being both an agent of activity and a member of a community (Lave and Wenger, 1991). This emphasis on the individual as an active agent of the community provides an important perspective when one's goal is helping all students learn.

Studies by Bateman, Goldman, Newbrough, and Bransford (1998) have explored how different approaches to instruction affect students' sense of being in a learning community. They found that when compared to traditional classroom environments, those characterized by a constructivist/collaborative approach to learning were significantly higher in students' sense of community as well as in students' levels of social skills (CTGV, 1994). The goals of constructivist-oriented teachers were to teach for deep understanding and to make students active participants in the learning process. All students were encouraged to develop expertise, and all students were given multiple opportunities to be actively involved in the classroom community. Students were allowed to learn at their own pace, and teachers provided scaffolding that was appropriate to each student's developmental level (Vygotsky, 1978). Students in these classrooms were given multiple opportunities to engage in formative assessment. Student reflection and revision were the focus of the assessment process.

Community building was actively encouraged in the class, with mutual respect for individuality and differences among students as the focal point. Students learned to listen to each other and to the teacher with respect and consideration even if they disagreed with the speaker's point of view. Students were also encouraged to work together in small groups and in pairs, sharing their expertise and understanding with others. When interviewed at the end of the year, most students felt that the opportunities to share, help, and get help from each other were very valuable experiences that contributed to their academic as well as their social development over the school year (Bateman, in press). Students in these strong community classrooms felt that their learning needs as well as their academic needs were being met successfully by their classroom community. They also felt that they had some influence over the learning process (Bateman et al., 1999).

Research also shows that high levels of community in classrooms are associated with high levels of prosocial behavior such as collaboration and cooperation among students and low levels of antisocial behavior such as bullying and fighting (Bateman, 1998; Bateman et al., 1997). Students in classrooms with strong communities also demonstrate higher levels of conflict resolution skills. These classroom communities are also associated with a host of desirable academic outcomes.

Students in these classrooms exhibit higher levels of academic self-efficacy, and higher levels of interest in learning in a classroom setting (Bateman et al., 1999, 2000). Students in classrooms with strong community are unafraid to take chances at occasional failure (Bateman et al., 2000).

Students in classrooms with strong community report higher levels of complex problem-solving ability. Strong classroom communities appear to foster the development of learning goals in students. Students in these classrooms feel free to focus on learning/mastery goals rather than performance academic goals. Focusing on learning/mastery goals facilitates students to become lifelong learners. Overall, these results support the hypothesis that classroom communities that provide stimulating, supportive, and safe environments in which students are not dissuaded from challenging themselves due to fear of failure and ridicule are the classrooms in which students become lifelong learners. The community-centered lens of the HPL framework (Figure 6-2) is designed to remind us of the extreme importance of this aspect of educational effectiveness and design.

Assessment Centered

In addition to being knowledge, learner, and community centered, effective learning environments are also assessment centered. Typically when we think about assessment, we think about the tests that an instructor might give at the end of a unit or class, or about large-scale assessments such as state-mandated achievement tests and certification tests mandated by various professional organizations. The following challenge explores people's perceptions of tests.

A Challenge

During the December holiday season, a local newspaper ran a cartoon showing students in a classroom who had each received a wrapped present from their teacher. Upon opening the present, each student discovered the contents—a geometry test. Needless to say, the students were not pleased with their "gift." People who viewed the cartoon could easily understand the students' anguish. Tests are more like punishments than gifts. However, is there any way that a "test" could be perceived as something positive?

We have presented this challenge to many students and, more often than not, they answer that tests are negative experiences—period. The exception is when they happen to do very well on one—but they don't know this until after the fact.

Consider a slight twist on the preceding scenario. Imagine that the students have all been preparing for some kind of big event they consider very important. They may have been studying to pass the written part of their driver's test, which they have a great stake in passing. They may have been working on a geometry project that involves creating something for the community and doing a presentation for community members—they want to do a great job. They may have a chance for an internship with an architectural firm if they can demonstrate proficiency in design and mathematics. They may simply want to do well on a test that is going to be administered later. The important point is to imagine that the impending big event is significant to students.

Under the preceding conditions, the dreaded test can be transformed into a wonderful gift. Imagine, for example, that the teacher has carefully selected a set of items that help students assess their readiness for their written driver's test, their geometry demonstration, their future employment, or whatever the big event is that is on the horizon. Assume further that the purpose of the test is to help students identify and correct any weaknesses now—prior to the big event. Under these conditions, one can well imagine the students' delight and appreciation as they open their present and find a "test" from their teacher. The tests provide important feedback about their progress—feedback that lets them continue to work on any weaknesses. But these tests have a very different function from the one that was portrayed in the initial cartoon. Their function is to guide learning—to be formative rather than summative.

Formative Assessment

Formative assessments—when coupled with opportunities to revise— provide a number of advantages. They serve a learning function for teachers who can use the information to change their instruction to make it more effective or to target students who are in need of further help. Similarly, students can use feedback from formative assessments to help them determine what they have not yet mastered and need to work on further. Data indicate that providing opportunities for feedback and revision greatly helps students learn (e.g., Black and William, 1998; Barron et al., 1998; CTGV, 1997; Hunt and Minstrell, 1994).

Helping students learn to self-assess (to become more metacognitive) is especially important (e.g., see NRC, 2000). Ultimately, they need to develop the habits of mind to assess their own progress rather than always rely on outsiders. A number of studies show that achievement improves when students are encouraged to self-assess their own contributions and work (e.g., NRC, 2000; Lin and Lehman, 1999; White and Frederiksen, 1998). It is also important to help students assess the kinds of strategies they are using to learn and solve problems. For example, in quantitative courses such as physics, many students simply focus on formulas rather than attempt to first think qualitatively about problems and relate them to key ideas in a discipline (e.g., Newton's second law). When they are helped to do the latter, performance on new problems greatly improves (e.g., Leonard et al., 1996).

Providing frequent opportunities for feedback and revision takes time, and this is a major impediment for teachers. Providing opportunities for formative assessment is an area where new technologies can have major benefits. We discuss some computer-based and Web-based assessments later on in the section on technology. However, it is useful to know that there are also inexpensive wireless classroom communication systems (CCSs) that provide a powerful opportunity to make even large classes more interactive.

A simple version of a CCS allows teachers to show multiple-choice questions during the course of a lecture or demonstration. Students respond by pressing a key on a handheld device. Responses are aggregated and shown as a graph, so all individual responses are anonymous. CCSs provide both students and teachers with immediate feedback about what is and is not being understood.

During its early years, CCS research and implementation efforts were limited by hardwired, relatively costly systems with restricted functionality. The new wireless systems include increasing ranges of functionality, and with several manufacturers there is now competitive pricing. As a consequence, the opportunities for widespread use of these promising tools are greatly increased.

Professors at the University of Massachusetts, Amherst have been using a classroom communication technology called Classtalk for a number of years (Dufresne, Gerace, Leonard, Mestre, and Wenk, 1996; Mestre, Gerace, Dufresne, and Leonard, 1997; Wenk, Dufresne, Gerace, Leonard, and Mestre, 1997). Initially, Classtalk consisted of handheld devices (either Hewlett-Packard palmtop computers or Texas Instruments calculators) that were wired via phone-jack ports to a computer in the front of the room. The existence of multiple phone-jack ports throughout the auditorium allowed students to sign on to the system, with groups of up to four students sharing one handheld device. The software and hardware allowed the presentation of questions for students to work on collaboratively and the collection and anonymous display of students' answers in histogram form. Data indicate that the vast majority of the students felt that, compared to traditional courses, Classtalk improved their abilities to understand the subject matter they were trying to learn (Dufresne et al., 1996; Mestre et al., 1997; Wenk et al., 1997). Systems similar to Classtalk have also been successfully used in K-12 settings (Gomez, Fishman, and Pea, in press; Pea and Gomez, 1992).

The entire HPL framework (Figure 6-2) is useful to keep in mind as a guide for using CCSs. The knowledge-centered lens reminds us to carefully explore the questions being asked. Are they simply fact based or do they develop an understanding of the discipline? The learner-centered lens reminds us to help students understand why certain answers are and are not correct, to make it possible for them to be wrong without being embarrassed, and to provide them opportunities to discuss questions with one another. The community-centered lens reminds us to think about ways to use CCSs to build a learning community rather than simply spark cutthroat competition.

Interviews with students who have used CCSs in their classes (in particular, Classtalk) indicate that its introduction had a number of ripple effects that had an impact on all aspects of the HPL framework. Examples of student interviews are as follows (Bransford, Brophy, and Williams, 2000):

> In class I really don't learn anything by lecture. I'm more of a person that reads.
>
> That's how I learn. I go to class all the time but it's a waste of time. I'll take notes, but when I leave the class I won't have any idea what the professor has just talked about. With Classtalk you're forced to pay attention, you're forced to process all the information right there.
>
> You're not just writing down notes then leaving class; you're actually applying what you're learning as you and others are thinking.

Another student emphasized the benefits of seeing what others in the class were thinking about problems. If many other students were confused, it was nice to see that she wasn't the only one. If she did understand but many others didn't, she could appreciate why the professor needed to take the time to make things clearer to those who needed help. And when different groups explained their reasoning behind different answers, it helped her better appreciate the range of possible ways to think about problems that were posed.

Still another student talked about the bonds formed by working in groups to answer via Classtalk. She then noted how working in groups had helped her meet new people and how her Classtalk group also met outside of class to help one another:

> I think working in groups has helped us meet other people in our major and our classes. It turns out I meet with those same people outside of class. We practice tests together.

Often, one worries that students being interviewed are just being polite. We believe that the students noted above were being quite honest. For example, one began her interview by stating how Classtalk made her physics class exciting. After a moment she amended her statement and, in the process, formulated a potentially important principle about formal education:

> Even with Classtalk that doesn't mean the class isn't going to have its boring moments. I mean, that's impossible. You have to be bored to be in school.

Summative Assessment

Unlike formative assessments, summative assessments are generally used to index what has been learned at the end of a unit, course, or program of study. Issues of summative assessment are also discussed in NRC (1999a,b) and in much more detail in the new National Academy of Sciences report entitled *Knowing What Students Know* (NRC, 2001b). The latter report points out both strengths and a weakness of typical approaches to standardized testing, and recommends that course-relevant formative assessments receive much more attention than they have in the past.

Ideally, summative assessments provide an indication of students' ability to do something other than simply "take tests." Assessments should be predictive of performance in everyday settings. One way to look at this issue is to view tests as attempts to predict students' abilities to transfer from classroom settings to everyday settings. From this perspective, assumptions about the nature of "transfer" affect how we think about assessing what students have learned.

It has been argued that traditional ways of conceptualizing and measuring transfer may be unnecessarily constraining how we think about assessment (Bransford and Schwartz, 1999). Central to traditional approaches to transfer is a "direct application" theory and a dominant methodology, which asks whether people can apply something they have learned previously to a new problem or situation. Thorndike and colleagues' classic studies of transfer utilized this paradigm. For example, in Thorndike and Woodworth (1901), participants took a pretest on judging the area of various rectangles and then received opportunities to improve their performance through practice plus feedback. Following this learning task, participants were tested on the different but related task of estimating the areas of circles and triangles. Transfer was assessed by the degree to which learning skill A (estimating the area of squares) influenced skill B (estimating the area of circles or triangles). Thorndike and Woodworth found little evidence for transfer in this setting and argued that the "ability to estimate area" was not a general skill.

Gick and Holyoak's (1980, 1983) work on analogical transfer provides a modern-day example of a similar paradigm for studying transfer. Participants in their studies first received information about a problem and a solution such as "The General and the Fortress" Problem. They then received a second problem (Dunker's [1945] Irradiation problem) that could be solved by analogy to the first problem. Depending on the conditions of the experiment, participants either did or did not show evidence of applying what they had learned about the general's solution to solve the irradiation problem. In many instances, there was a surprising failure to transfer spontaneously from one problem to the next. Many other researchers use a similar paradigm of initial learning followed by problem solving. Examples include Adams, Kasserman, Yearwood, Perfetto, Bransford, and Franks (1988); Bassok (1990); Brown and Kane (1988); Chen, and Daehler (1989); Lockhart, Lamon, and Gick (1988); Nisbett, Fong, Lehman, and Cheng (1987); Novick (1988); Perfetto, Bransford, and Franks (1983); Reed, Ernst, and Banerji (1974); Thorndike and Woodward (1901); and Wertheimer (1959).

A striking feature of the research studies noted above is that they all use a final transfer task that involves what Bransford and Schwartz (1999) call "sequestered problem solving" (SPS). Just as juries are often sequestered in order to protect them from possible exposure to "contaminating" information, subjects in experiments are sequestered during tests of transfer. There are no opportunities for them to demonstrate their abilities to learn to solve new problems by seeking help from other resources such as texts or colleagues or by trying things out, receiving feedback, and getting opportunities to revise. Accompanying the SPS paradigm is a theory that characterizes transfer as the ability to directly apply one's previous learning to a new setting or problem, which we call the direct application (DA) theory of transfer. Bransford and Schwartz's thesis is that the SPS methodology and the accompanying DA theory of transfer are responsible for much of the pessimism about evidence for transfer.

An alternative to SPS methodology and DA theory is a view that acknowledges the validity of these perspectives but also broadens the conception of transfer by including an emphasis on people's "preparation for future learning" (PFL). Here, the focus shifts to assessments of people's abilities to learn in knowledge-rich environments. When organizations hire new employees, they don't expect them to have learned everything they need for successful adaptation. Organizations want people who can learn, and they expect employees to make use of resources (e.g., texts, computer programs, and colleagues) to facilitate this learning. The better prepared people are for future learning, the greater the transfer (in terms of speed and/or quality of new learning).

As a simple illustration of a PFL perspective on transfer, consider a set of studies conducted by Kay Burgess (Bransford and Schwartz, 1999). In one study, researchers asked fifth graders and college students to create a statewide recovery plan to protect bald eagles from the threat of extinction. The goal was to investigate the degree to which their general educational experiences prepared them for this novel task; none of the students had explicitly studied eagle recovery plans.

The plans generated by both groups missed the mark widely. The college students' writing and spelling skills were better than the fifth graders, but none of the college students mentioned the need to worry about baby eagles imprinting on the humans who fed them, about creating tall hacking towers so that fledgling eagles would imprint on the territory that they would eventually call home, or about a host of other important variables. In short, none of the students—college level or fifth graders—generated a recovery plan that was even close to being adequate. Based on these findings, one might claim that the students' general educational experiences did not prepare them adequately for transfer.

However, by another measure of transfer, the differences between the age groups were striking. We asked the students to generate questions about important issues they would research in order to design effective recovery plans for eagles (see Box 6-1). The fifth graders tended to

**A Categorization of Questions Generated by Fifth-Grade and
College Students About Creating an Eagle Recovery Plan**

FIFTH-GRADE STUDENTS

"Basic" Eagle Facts: How much do they weigh when full-grown? How big are their bodies? What is their wingspan? How big are they? How high do they fly? Are they color blind? What do they look like? How many are there in the U.S.? Why do you call them bald eagles?

Habitat Questions: Where do they live? Where do you find them? What kind of trees do they live in?

Developmental Questions: How do they take care of their babies? How many eggs do they lay at one time? How big are their nests? What age do they fly? How old do they get?

Foraging Questions: How do they find food? What do they like to eat? How do they catch their prey?

COLLEGE STUDENTS

Interdependency Questions: What about predators of eagles and eagle babies? Do other animals need to be recovered in order to recover eagles? Why save the bald eagle versus other organisms? What type of ecosystem supports eagles?

Survival Needs Questions: What are the eagles' daily needs? What kinds of habitat do eagles need to live in, and is there sufficient habitat? Are today's threats like the initial threats to eagles? Are there different types of eagles with different needs?

Human Resource and Impact Questions: What are the laws? What resources (financial and info) are available to support? What are the politics of eagles? What different kinds of specialists are needed for different recovery areas? What facilities are needed and what transport methods? What kind of training is necessary to handle an eagle? What were the detrimental effects of DDT?

Goal- and Plan-Related Questions: What are the goals of current programs? What is the ultimate goal of population recovery (how many needed)? Why is there a belief that the population needs to be doubled? What are the current recovery plans? What are the eagle recovery regions and how are they working? What are the most promising recovery methods? How do people estimate eagle populations? Why are some states more successful? What can be learned from the more successful states?

SOURCE: Bransford and Schwartz (1999).

focus on features of individual eagles. In contrast, the college students were much more likely to focus on issues of interdependence between the eagles and their habitats. They asked questions such as "What type of ecosystem supports eagles?" (reflecting an appreciation of interdependence); "What about predators of eagles and eagle babies?" (also reflecting interdependence); "Are today's threats like the initial threats to eagles?" (reflecting an appreciation of history and change); "What different kinds of specialists are needed for different recovery areas?" (reflecting an appreciation for a possible need for multiple solutions). Because they had not studied eagles directly, the college students were presumably generating questions that were framed by other aspects of biology that they had learned. So, by this alternative form of transfer test, it would appear that the college students had learned general considerations that would presumably help shape their future learning if they chose to pursue this topic (Scardamalia and Bereiter, 1992). In this regard, one would call their prior learning experiences a success.

It is important to emphasize that the PFL perspective on transfer does not assume the existence of a set of general learning skills that are content free. The expertise literature (e.g., NRC, 2000) shows clearly how strategies and knowledge are highly interdependent. Similarly, we discussed earlier how one's knowledge has extremely important implications for the kinds of questions one asks (about eagles and how to help them make a recovery as a species). Broudy (1977) provides an additional example: "The concept of bacterial infection as learned in biology can operate even if only a skeletal notion of the theory and the facts supporting it can be recalled. Yet, we are told of cultures in which such a concept would not be part of the interpretive schemata" (p. 12).

The absence of an idea of bacterial infection should have a strong effect on the nature of the hypotheses that people entertain in order to explain various illnesses, and hence would affect their abilities to learn more about causes of illness through further research and study and the strategies they would use in order to solve new problems. In short, the acquisition of well-differentiated knowledge is crucial for future learning (e.g., NRC, 2000; Schwartz and Bransford, 1998). The more that this knowledge is acquired with understanding, the higher the probability that appropriate transfer will occur.

Relying exclusively on static assessments may mask the learning gains of many students, plus the learning advantages that various kinds of educational experiences provide (Bransford and Schwartz, 1999). Linking work on summative assessment to theories of transfer may help us overcome the limitations of many existing tests.

HPL and Motivation

Many people ask where motivation resides in the HPL framework. We argue that all aspects of the framework are relevant to this issue.

If students know they are learning content and skills that will be important in life, that is motivating. If courses connect with their interests and strengths and provide interesting challenges to their preconceptions, that is motivating (Dweck, 1989). If students receive frequent feedback that lets them see their progress in learning and gives them chances to do even better, that is motivating. And if students feel as if they are a valued part of a vibrant learning community, that is motivating as well.

Summary: Using Information About How People Learn

The How People Learn framework provides a convenient way to organize a great deal of information about the nature of competent (expert) performance and about ways to help people develop their own competence (e.g., NRC, 2000). The framework highlights a set of four overlapping lenses that are useful for analyzing the quality of various learning environments. Balance is particularly important. For example, learning environments can be knowledge centered but not learner centered, and vice versa. In addition, many environments lack frequent opportunities for formative assessment and revision, and many fail to promote a sense of community where learning (which includes admissions of "not knowing") is welcomed. The framework can be useful for analyzing face-to-face environments, online environments, and combinations of the two.

ISSUES AND OPPORTUNITIES SURROUNDING NEW TECHNOLOGIES

In this section we explore some ways that knowledge about how people learn can help us use technology more effectively. It is also noteworthy that new technologies can push our thinking about learning because they provide opportunities that were not possible in the past.

A number of authors and groups have written about the present and possible futures of technology-enhanced learning environments (e.g., Bonk and Wisher, 2000; Palloff and Pratt, 1999; NRC, 2000; Web-Based Education Commission, 2000). Covering this rapidly growing literature is beyond the scope of the present chapter. Our goal is more modest: to provide a few examples of how a combination of new technologies—plus knowledge of how people learn—can help us create new types of learning opportunities.

Bringing Issues of Learning and Teaching to the Forefront

A major benefit of efforts to put courses online is the effect on discussions of teaching and learning. Traditionally, teaching practices have tended to remain private and have been very hard to capture and analyze. If science had been carried out primarily by individual scientists who never made their thinking and work public, it seems clear that progress would have been very slow (H. Simon, personal communication, September 21, 1999).

Even the simple act of putting one's syllabus and reading list on the Web makes it more public. Many instructors are going well beyond syllabi and reading lists and putting major portions of their courses on the Web. We call these courses Web-enhanced because they also involve frequent opportunities for face-to-face learning. Other courses—and even entire credentialing and degree programs—lean more toward being Web based, where face-to-face meetings of students and faculty may be infrequent or nonexistent (Bonk and Wisher, 2000; Stacey, 1999).

The ability to use technology to reach large numbers of students has created financial incentives to market "distance education" programs. Furthermore, new technology has allowed education providers other than existing schools, colleges, and universities to enter the credentialing and degree-granting business. This increased competition, coupled with the increased visibility of the content and teaching strategies used in the online courses, is increasing the national dialogue about effective learning. A number of online sites are devoted to the scholarship of teaching, complete with examples of teaching online (e.g., www.carnegiefoundation.org, www.vkp.org, www.vanth.org, www.cilt.org).

Weigel (2000) notes that the majority of the Web-enhanced and Web-based courses are based on a "port the traditional classroom to the Internet" model: "The result, most often, has been little more than an exercise of posting on the Internet an enhanced syllabus that includes lecture content, reading assignments and practice tests, along with using discussion groups and e-mail to respond to students' questions" (p. 12).

We noted above that even these small changes can be valuable because they make teaching and learning practices more visible, and they add some clear functionalities that can be very valuable (e.g., the ability to rehear or rewatch a lecture on one's own time; the ability for asynchronous communication and discussion via threaded discussions and e-mail, etc.). Nevertheless, research on how people learn suggests that we can improve both the traditional classroom and the "port the traditional classroom to the Internet" model (Duffy and Cunningham, 1996). In the discussion below, we explore several ways to redesign a traditional lesson in order to take advantages of both new technologies and new knowledge of how people learn.

A Challenge Involving a Sample Lesson on Density

Consider the following transcript of a lecture on density that is designed for high school science classes. As you read it, think about how you might improve upon it to teach students about the concept of density.

Young people, I want you to listen to me, and listen very carefully, because the concept of density is very important now. The formula for density is D = M/V.

D stands for density, of course. M stands for the mass of an object. You determine the mass of an object by weighing it. In science, the unit of mass is in metric units such as grams.

V stands for the volume of an object. The volume of a cube is measured by its length times its width times its height. A cube that is one centimeter long, tall, and wide would equal one cubic centimeter.

If an object is irregularly shaped, volume can be measured by an immersion technique where the object is placed in a cylinder filled with water. The volume is equal to the amount of water that the object displaces. Volume is measured in units like cubic centimeters.

Different types of materials have specific densities. The density of lead is approximately 11.2 grams per cubic centimeter. The density of gold is approximately 19.3 grams per cubic centimeter. The density of a cubic centimeter of sand might be around 3 grams, depending on the coarseness of the sand.

Now, young people, listen. This it the essence of the secret of density. I've been around a long time. This is the kind of thing you'll need to know some day.

We have given this challenge to several different groups of individuals and find some high-frequency categories of responses. One is that the lecturer needs to be more interactive—perhaps stopping once in a while to ask students questions and then provide answers. Another is that a lot of information is presented in a small amount of time and, depending on the audience, the lesson might need to be broken into subparts. For example, more time might be taken to teach the subtopic of volume. A third is that some type of memory aid should be suggested for helping students remember the density formulas. A fourth is that it might be important to add practice problems that ask students to find specific densities so that they can practice their skills. In general, people seem to respond to the challenge by drawing on their experiences of how they were taught.

Putting the Lesson Online

What happens when people (in our case, undergraduate and graduate education majors) are asked to generate ideas about creating an online density lesson? Not surprisingly, most adopt a "port the classroom" model (e.g., Weigel, 2000). For example, many note that the lecture could be put online—either as text, audio, video, or as a combination of all of these. Readings and other resources (a resource might include memory techniques for remembering formulas) can be put online as well. In addition, students can contact one another—and ideally their instructor—electronically. (Instructors typically learn to set online office hours rather than have students assume that they are available on a 24/7 basis.) Practice problems can also be provided that ask students to compute new density problems, that are automatically graded, and that provide instant feedback to the users.

Advantages of having the lesson online include the fact that the lecture can be re-viewed on an as-needed basis, students can communicate asynchronously rather than only synchronously, and they can get instant feedback on practice problems they submit. If the course is Web-enhanced rather than Web-based, students also have the advantage of discovering what they don't yet understand by working on the Web and then talking with the professor when they come to class (e.g., Bransford, Lin, and Schwartz, 2000).

Using the HPL Framework to Redesign the Lesson

The HPL framework provides a useful set of lenses for taking the redesign of the density lesson a step deeper than was described above. Please note that the HPL framework is very general and can be used quite flexibly—this is both its strength and its weakness. In the discussion below we provide only *one* of many possible ways to use HPL to think about a redesign.

Knowledge Centeredness

Central to the HPL approach is the issue of clearly defining what we want students to know and be able to do at the end of the lesson. This is consistent with the implications of the Jenkins model (Figure 6-1), with Wiggins and McTighe's (1997) strategy of working backwards, and with Bruner's (1960) arguments about the importance of defining the core ideas in the discipline.

Given the goal of teaching about density, what is it that we want students to know and be able to do when they finish our lesson? Based on the transcript of the lecture presented above, one might conclude that the instructor wants students to be able to calculate the density of various materials. This is very different from a goal such as "to see how the concept of density becomes a powerful tool for understanding a number of mysteries about the world."

In order to take seriously the knowledge-centered lens of the HPL framework, we would need to carefully review the literature on students' preconceptions and misconceptions about the subject (e.g., Carey and Gelman, 1991; Driver, Squires, Rushworth, and Woods-Robinson, 1994) and work closely with content experts who are willing to join our search for the enduring ideas of their discipline. The present authors are far from content experts in the area of density. We know from experience that it is easy to think we know enough about a subject to teach it and to then be surprised when we discuss it with experts in the field (e.g., see Bransford, Zech, et al., 1999).

A simple technique we have devised for gathering content from (busy) experts is to conduct short phone interviews about the important ideas of a topic. These interviews are easy for experts to generate.

They are then digitized, put on a tape or CD, and made available to course designers. They can be played while commuting, on planes, and in other places, and hence are easy to access. This approach to knowledge capture provides a starting point that allows designers to get back to the experts with more specific questions to which they can respond.

As noted earlier, one example of an enduring idea with respect to density might be that different materials have characteristic densities (note the periodic table) and that this information can help us understand many things about the world. But of course, simply saying this to students is not sufficient to help them understand the power of this point.

Learner Centeredness

The learner-centered lens of the HPL framework reminds us to create situations that are engaging and meaningful to students and allow them to test their initial thoughts about some topic or problem. One way to do this is to focus on "challenge-based learning" rather than lecture-based learning. Students' challenges can be anchored in real data and experiences (e.g., Tinker and Berenfeld, 1994); computer simulations (e.g., Edelson and Gordin, 1998; Kozma, Russell, Jones, Marx, and Davis, 1996); videos of real-life problems (CTGV, 1997); and so forth. Medical schools, law schools, business schools, and increasingly K-12 educators have used this general approach under names such as problem-based learning, case-based learning, project-based learning, learning by design, inquiry learning, and anchored instruction (e.g., Barrows, 1983; Kolodner, 1997; CTGV, 1997). Williams (1992) provides an excellent discussion of the similarities and differences among these approaches. They all begin with context-rich problems to be solved that are designed to help students develop a "big picture" for their new learning, plus help them learn to generate their own learning goals.

It is important to note that an emphasis on challenge-based learning does not necessarily rule out lectures. There is a "time for telling" (Schwartz and Bransford, 1998). However, when working with novices in a domain, simply starting with lectures is typically not the right time. Lectures, discussions, and other instructional techniques can be much more powerful *after* students have first attempted to grapple with a problem where they have some intuitions about its importance and some general ideas about how to approach it—even if these ideas are wrong (see Schwartz and Bransford, 1998).

An example of challenge for a density lesson has been developed in conjunction with Bob Sherwood, a science educator at Vanderbilt. It is certainly not the only way to teach about density, but it has been tested enough to allow us to know that it is engaging to students and helps them develop an understanding of density that goes beyond the lecture provided above (e.g., see Brophy, 1998).

The challenge is a short four-minute video entitled *The Golden Statuette* that was filmed very inexpensively with two high school actors. A high school boy decides to paint a lead statue gold and try to sell it to the proprietor of a metallurgy shop as being "pure gold." "Don't you go cutting into it or anything," he says to the proprietor (obviously worried that this would reveal the true nature of the metal). "It's pure gold and real soft."

The proprietor of the store first weighs the statue and then writes down what she found (908 grams). Next she immerses it in a cylinder of water and writes down the overflow (80 cm^3). She then divides the mass by the volume. Finally she looks at (a) a chart of the densities of various metals and (b) a chart of selling prices for these metals. At the end, she gives the boy 10 cents for his statuette. The challenge to the students is to figure out if she was right and, if so, how she knew how much to pay.

We have given this challenge to a number of students—including those who have been in very high-quality high schools. Few know how to solve the challenge. Most could remember learning about density when we explicitly asked them if they had learned it in science, but they had basically been taught formulas rather than helped to understand how the concept of density is a powerful tool for understanding numerous mysteries about the world.

We have also found that once students have grappled with the challenge, they are both more motivated and "cognitively ready" (see Schwartz and Bransford, 1998) to learn about the concept of density. For example, the lecture provided earlier becomes much more interesting and relevant to students because it contains clues for how to solve the challenge that they face.

Assessment Centeredness

This lens of the HPL framework has a number of important implications for redesigning the density lesson. First, the challenge-based approach invites students to make their initial thinking visible. Whether they discuss the challenge face to face or online, many discover that they don't really understand what units such as grams and cubic centimeters are measuring. Often they don't understand why the statuette was placed in the cylinder of water. And many question the boy's statement that gold is soft.

The assessment-centered lens also reminds us to help students engage in a self-assessment of their own thoughts and behavior—both as they considered the challenge and began to discuss it with others. Did they define learning goals or simply cringe at not being able to solve the problem? For example, if they could ask one or two questions about the challenge, what would the questions be? Did they interact with fellow students in ways that supported mutual learning? This emphasis on metacognition has been shown to increase learning in a number of areas (e.g., Brown and Campione, 1994; NRC, 2000; Leonard, et al., 1996; Lin and Lehman, 1999; White and Frederiksen, 1998).

Being assessment centered in this context also reminds us to help students think about multiple problems—not simply the original challenge. For example, "what if" questions can be asked about the original challenge (What if the statue were zinc rather than lead? How much would it be worth if it were really gold? What if the mass had been x grams? Which would weigh more if you picked it up—the solid lead statue or a solid gold statue?) The addition of "what if" challenges to anchoring challenges has been shown to facilitate transfer (e.g., CTGV, 1997; NRC, 2000). A number of tools for online assessments are being devised (e.g., Diagnoser by Hunt and Minstrell, 1994; Immex by Stevens and Nadjafi, 1999).

In addition to "what if" challenges related to the initial golden statuette challenge, formative assessments can invite students to think about new challenges and then get help if they need it. For example, how does the original challenge relate to the story about Archimedes and the King's Crown? How could you predict if gasoline will float on water versus sink? How could you evaluate a design to use five helium-filled balloons to hold up a loudspeaker that weighs x pounds? How can something like gold be both dense and malleable? Ideally, these kinds of formative assessments can be used to help students self-assess their readiness to demonstrate what they have learned.

The HPL framework also reminds us that summative assessments should focus on understanding rather than simply computing the densities of "mystery" entities. One possible assessment is to ask students to generate their own challenges about density for other students. (This is highly motivating and an excellent way to assess students' understanding.) Another is to provide students with different types of transfer problems. One is to use the typical "sequestered problem-solving" paradigm where students have no access to resources other than what they currently have in memory. Another is to use a "preparation for future learning" paradigm (Bransford and Schwartz, 1999) where students have opportunities to formulate learning goals and find relevant resources that can help them solve the problems (e.g., texts, videos, and simulations on the Web or provided among many options in their testing environment). Technology makes it possible to track the resources used by students and to capture their conclusions based on what they consult (Bransford and Schwartz, 1999).

Community Centeredness

The community-centered lens of HPL reminds us to think about this important element. Overall, many features of online environments can make learning more learner friendly than many face-to-face environments. Advantages of going online (either for Web-enhanced or Web-based instruction) include more opportunities for self-paced learning—including revisiting the lecture at one's own pace and pursuing resources on an as-needed basis (e.g., a student may or may not need more help to understand volume). A very important advantage involves getting immediate feedback on homework and practice problems (from automatic homework graders). Opportunities for asynchronous discussions with fellow classmates and professors can be very beneficial as well.

However, there are also downsides of working online. One includes breakdowns in the equipment (this can be very frustrating) or very slow responsiveness due to too much bandwidth for the media and too little for one's Internet connections (also very frustrating). Other difficulties include an inability to get immediate answers to questions because others are not online at the moment or do not have the time to respond.

Perhaps the largest obstacle to effective online learning is the loss of personal interactions with professors and fellow students (e.g., see Hough, 2000; Palloff and Pratt, 1999). Since online discussions are usually text based, there is less personal information available (gestures, smiles, tones of voice) than is typical in face-to-face interactions. This means that people often misinterpret others' intent. Even failures to get responses to one's e-mail can be interpreted negatively. Students who receive no answer to a message can easily assume "no one cares" or "my thoughts must have been stupid." In actuality, people may simply have been too busy to respond.

Interacting with people we do not know can exacerbate the difficulties of interacting electronically. In *The Social Life of Information,* Brown and Duguid (2000) argue that interactive technologies appear to be more effective in maintaining communication among established communities than in building new communities from scratch.

Online courses also often require a level of personal skills of time management that are not as necessary in face-to-face settings when course schedules tend to provide an outside pull that keeps students on track. Keeping students informed that their absences are noticed by the professor (and ideally other members of the community) is very important for successful online learning. Technology such as "knowbots" (J. Bourne, 1998—personal communication, August 10, 1998) have been used successfully to contact students when they have missed an online deadline and ask about their welfare. New versions of course management systems such as Web CT also have the ability to send "personalized" letters to students who need special help. The personalized letters are actually batch processed (e.g., the entire list of students doing poorly on an exam can be put in one batch)—hence saving instructors a great deal of time.

Overall, existing research on how to build and sustain face-to-face learning communities has a number of implications for creating high-quality online courses (Bateman et al., 1999; CTGV, 1994). The data suggest that online learning environments should be designed to enable community elements such as: (a) addressing the learning needs of all participants, (b) enabling participants to be active members in the community, (c) enabling all members to have influence in community processes, (d) enabling all participants to feel important and valued as members of the community, and (e) over time facilitating emotional connections between members of the virtual community.

OVERALL SUMMARY AND CONCLUSIONS

We began by noting that opportunities for Web-based learning are increasing people's access to educational opportunities, and this is an extremely positive development for people's lives and for our nation. We applaud efforts to increase access. By the same token, the goal of our paper is to go beyond issues of access and ask how we might improve the quality of education in any format—be it face to face, Web based, or a combination of both.

In the first section of the chapter, we discussed different ways to approach the issue of high-quality learning. We noted that many people begin with a focus on teaching (e.g., is cooperative grouping better than lectures?) but that it seems more fruitful to focus on learning. We introduced the Jenkins model as depicting some important characteristics of educational "ecosystems" in which teaching and learning strategies operate. The same teaching strategy may be good or poor depending on the rest of the ecosystem. Especially important are the goals for learning and methods of assessing it. We connected the Jenkins model to the idea of "working backwards" in order to design effective educational environments (Wiggins and McTighe, 1997). And we discussed a number of imaginary universities that might compete with one another based on their ultimate goals for their students. Farther Guido Sarduci's "Five-Minute University" was one competitor. He set as his goal the ability to replicate what most college students remember five years after they graduate. Competing universities increasingly raised the bar with respect to what they wanted their graduates to know and be able to do.

Next, we discussed the How People Learn framework (NRC, 2000) and showed how it connects to the Jenkins model and to the idea of working backwards (Wiggins and McTighe, 1997). It is a very general framework that leaves a great deal of room for flexibility, which is both its strength and its weakness. Nevertheless, the framework is useful because it reminds us to analyze situations at a deeper and more complete level than we might do otherwise. In particular, it reminds us to examine the degree to which any learning environment is:

- Knowledge centered (in the sense of being based on a careful analysis of what we want people to know and be able to do when they finish with our materials or course and providing them with the foundational (connected) knowledge, skills, and attitudes needed for successful transfer);
- Learner centered (in the sense of connecting to the strengths, interests, and preconceptions of learners and helping them learn about themselves as learners);

- Community centered (in the sense of providing an environment where students feel safe to ask questions, learn to use technology to access resources and work collaboratively, and are helped to develop lifelong learning skills);
- Assessment centered (in the sense of providing multiple opportunities for formative assessment and revision and providing summative assessments that are carefully aligned with one's learning goals).

The third section of the paper focused on special challenges and opportunities provided by new technologies. We noted that putting courses online has the advantage of making issues of teaching and learning more visible. We also noted that most online courses have tended to look much like "porting" existing classrooms onto the Internet. From the perspective of HPL, neither traditional face-to-face courses, nor their online cousins, represents environments where opportunities for high-quality learning are consistently strong.

We organized much of our discussion in this section around a short lecture-based lesson on density. We have informally asked a number of people to redesign the lesson and found that they can usually make suggestions for improvement. However, for most of them the general lesson format (lecture) remains invariant. When asked to imagine the lesson online, they tend to port their classroom model to the Internet. Many are able to pinpoint some definite advantages to the Internet-based format—like the ability to review the lecture, engage in asynchronous discussions, and get instant feedback on practice problems. Interestingly, very few engaged in the kinds of rigorous "working backwards" strategies that are recommended by theorists such as Wiggins and McTighe (1997).

With some trepidation, we attempted to illustrate how the HPL framework might provide a guide for more fully redesigning the density lecture. We say "with trepidation" because none of us is truly an expert in the area of density. We know something about the concept, but not enough to be truly confident that our decisions are optimal.

The need for deep content knowledge is one of the most important features emphasized in NRC (1999a,b). Especially important is knowledge of key concepts and models that provide the kinds of connected, organized knowledge structures and accompanying skills and attitudes that can set the stage for future learning (e.g., Bransford and Schwartz, 1999; Bruner, 1960; Wiggins and McTighe, 1997). In proposing our redesign, we decided that the best way to make this point was to illustrate that we need this kind of expertise in order to ensure a high-quality lesson. Effective design requires collaboration among people with specific kinds of expertise (content knowledge, learning, assessment, technology). We also discussed a simple technique for capturing expertise that has proven to be very helpful in our work. We do audio interviews with content experts and place them on tapes or CDs so that they can be studied to better understand content issues. They require only about 20 minutes of an expert's time (we can record from the telephone) and provide a starting point for getting back to experts about key ideas and concepts. The experts can hear the other experts as well.

Our (tentative) redesign of the density lesson began with an attempt to say what we wanted students to know and be able to do. The goal of the original density lecture seemed to be "to compute the density of various materials." We wanted students to develop a more fundamental understanding of the power of using concepts of density to explain a range of mysteries in the world.

Our redesign involved a transformation from a lecture-based format to a challenge-based format. We used the term "challenge-based" as a general term for a variety of approaches to instruction that many have studied—this includes case-based instruction, problem-based learning, learning by design, inquiry learning, anchored instruction, and so forth. There are important differences among each of these, but important commonalities as well (e.g., see Williams, 1992).

For our density lesson, we created a challenge around *The Golden Statuette* where a gold-painted statuette was presented to a proprietor as being "solid gold." The proprietor did some measurements, checked some charts, and ended up offering the person 10 cents for the statuette. The challenge for viewers became: Was she right? And if so, how did she know?

We used the HPL framework as a set of lenses for guiding the redesign of the lesson. *The Golden Statuette* challenge was designed to be both knowledge centered and learner centered because it set the stage for understanding the power of understanding concepts of density, and it engaged the students. The challenge was also designed to identify preconceptions about gold, measurements, and other issues. This emphasis on making preconceptions visible was assessment centered as well. Community-centered issues included the development of a climate of collaboration and inquiry where students felt comfortable saying what they didn't know and what they further wanted to understand (e.g., "What does grams stand for?" "Why did she put the statuette in that cylinder of water?").

The HPL framework was used to guide not only the development of our challenge but also the overall instruction that surrounded the challenge. Particularly important were opportunities to make students' thinking visible and give them chances to revise. We also noted the importance of provided opportunities for "what if" thinking, given variations on the challenge (e.g., if the statuette had actually been zinc rather than lead) and for new problems that also involved the concept of density (e.g., explaining the significance of Archimedes' "eureka" moment). Attempts to help people reflect on their own processes as learners (to be metacognitive) were also emphasized. In addition, we discussed issues of effective summative assessments—including the possibilities of moving from mere "sequestered problem-solving" assessments to ones where we track students' abilities to learn to solve new problems because they have been prepared to learn (Bransford and Schwartz, 1999).

Our density lesson is just a small example of the processes involved in rethinking traditional approaches to instruction in order to make them higher quality. A major issue is to help students develop the kinds of connected knowledge, skills, and attitudes that prepare them for effective lifelong learning. This involves the need to seriously rethink not only how to help students learn about particular isolated topics (e.g., density) but to rethink the organization of entire courses and curricula. An excellent model for doing this appears in a book entitled *Learning That Lasts* (Mentkowski et al., 1999). It is not highly technology-based. Nevertheless, it explores issues of high-quality learning that are highly compatible with discussions in NRC (1999a,b), and with new ways to think about transfer as "preparing students for future learning" (Bransford and Schwartz, 1999). All of these issues are relevant to attempts to enhance learning through the effective use of new technologies.

REFERENCES

Adams, L., Kasserman, J., Yearwood, A., Perfetto, G., Bransford, J., and Franks, J. (1988). The effects of facts versus problem-oriented acquisition. *Memory and Cognition, 16,* 167–175.

Alexopoulou, E., and Driver, R. (1996). Small group discussion in physics: Peer interaction modes in pairs and fours. *Journal of Research in Science Teaching, 33(10),* 1099–1114.

Barron, B.J., Schwartz, D.L., Vye, N.J., Moore, A., Petrosino, A., Zech, L., Bransford, J.D., and CTGV. (1998). Doing with understanding: Lessons from research on problem and project-based learning. *Journal of Learning Sciences, (3–4),* 271–312.

Barrows, H.S. (1983). *How to design a problem-based curriculum for the preclinical years.* New York: Springer.

Bassok, M. (1990). Transfer of domain-specific problem solving procedures. *Journal of Experimental Psychology: Learning, Memory, and Cognition, 15,* 153–166.

Bateman, H.V. (1998). Psychological sense of community in the classroom: Relationships to students' social and academic skills and social behavior. Unpublished doctoral dissertation, Vanderbilt University, Nashville, TN.

Bateman, H.V. (in press). Understanding learning communities through students' voices. In A. Fisher and C. Shonn (Eds.), *Psychological sense of community: Research, applications, and implications.* New York: Plenum.

Bateman, H.V., Bransford, J.D., Goldman, S.R., and Newbrough, J.R. (2000, April). Sense of community in the classroom: Relationship to students' academic goals. Paper presented at the annual meeting of the American Educational Research Association, New Orleans, LA.

Bateman, H.V., Goldman, S.R., Newbrough, J.R., and Bransford, J.D. (1998). Students' sense of community in constructivist/collaborative learning environments. In M. Gernsbacher and S. Derry (Eds.), *Proceedings of the twentieth annual meeting of the Cognitive Science Society* (pp. 126–131). Mahwah, NJ: Lawrence Erlbaum Associates.

Bateman, H.V., Newbrough, J.R., Goldman, S.R., and Bransford, J.D. (1999, April). Elements of students' sense of community in the classroom. Paper presented at the annual meeting of the American Educational Research Association, Montreal, Canada.

Bateman, H.V., Goldman, S.R., Newbrough, J.R., Bransford, J.D., and the Cognition and Technology Group at Vanderbilt. (1997, August). Fostering social skills and prosocial behavior through learning communities. Paper presented in the seventh biennial conference of the European Association for Research on Learning and Instruction, Athens, Greece.

Bjork, R.A., and Richardson-Klavhen, A. (1989). On the puzzling relationship between environment context and human memory. In C. Izawa (Ed.), *Current issues in cognitive processes: The Tulane Flowerree symposia on cognition.* Hillsdale, NJ: Lawrence Erlbaum Associates.

Black, P., and William, D. (1998). Assessment and classroom learning. *Assessment and Education, 5*(1), 7–75

Bonk, C.J., and Wisher, R.A. (2000). *Applying collaborative and e-learning tools to military distance learning: A research framework* (Tech. Rep. No. 1107). Alexandria, VA: U.S. Army Research Institute for the Behavioral and Social Sciences.

Bransford, J.D. (1979). *Human cognition: Learning, understanding, and remembering.* Belmont, CA: Wadsworth.

Bransford, J.D., Brophy, S., and Williams, S. (2000). When computer technologies meet the learning sciences: Issues and opportunities. *Journal of Applied Developmental Psychology, 21*(1), 59–84.

Bransford, J., Lin, X., and Schwartz, D. (2000). Technology, learning, and schools: Comments on articles by Tom Carroll and Gerald Bracey. *Contemporary Issues in Technology and Teacher Education* [Online serial], *1*(1). Available: http://www.citejournal.org/vol1/iss1/ currentissues/ general/article3.htm [December 17, 2001].

Bransford, J.D., and Schwartz, D. (1999). Rethinking transfer: A simple proposal with multiple implications. In A. Iran-Nejad and P.D. Pearson (Eds.), *Review of research in education* (vol. 24, pp. 61–100). Washington, DC: American Educational Research Association.

Bransford, J.D., and Stein, B.S. (1993). *The IDEAL problem solver* (2nd ed.). New York: Freeman.

Bransford, J.D., Zech, L., Schwartz, D., Barron, B., Vye, N., and CTGV. (1999). Designs for environments that invite and sustain mathematical thinking. In P. Cobb (Ed.), *Symbolizing, communicating, and mathematizing: Perspectives on discourse, tools, and instructional design* (pp. 275–324). Mahwah, NJ: Lawrence Erlbaum Associates.

Brophy, S.P. (1998). Learning scientific principles through problem solving in computer supported and laboratory environments. Unpublished doctoral dissertation, Vanderbilt University, Nashville, TN.

Brophy, S.P. (2001). Exploring the implication of an expert blind spot on learning. Unpublished manuscript, Vanderbilt University, Nashville, TN.

Broudy, H.S. (1977). Types of knowledge and purposes of education. In R.C. Anderson, R.J. Spiro, and W.E. Montague (Eds.), *Schooling and the acquisition of knowledge* (pp. 1–17). Hillsdale, NJ: Lawrence Erlbaum Associates.

Brown, A.L. (1978). Knowing when, where, and how to remember: A problem of metacognition. In R. Glaser (Ed.), *Advances in instructional psychology,* (vol. 1, pp. 77–165). Hillsdale, NJ: Lawrence Erlbaum Associates.

Brown, A.L., and Campione, J.C. (1994). Guided discovery in a community of learners. In K. McGilly (Ed.), *Classroom lessons: Integrating cognitive theory and classroom practice* (pp. 229–270). Cambridge, MA: MIT Press.

Brown, A.L., and Kane, M.J. (1988). Preschool children can learn to transfer: Learning to learn and learning from example. *Cognitive Psychology, 20,* 493–523.

Brown, J.S., and Duguid, P. (2000). *The social life of information.* Boston: Harvard Business School Press.

Bruner, (1960). *The process of education.* Cambridge, MA: Harvard University Press.

Carey, S., and Gelman, R. (1991). *The epigenesis of mind: Essays on biology and cognition.* Hillsdale, NJ: Lawrence Erlbaum Associates.

Chen, Z., and Daehler, M.W. (1989). Positive and negative transfer in analogical problem solving by 6-year-old children. *Cognitive Development, 4*, 327–344.

Chi, M.T.H., Feltovich, P.J., and Glaser, R. (1981). Categorization and representation of physics problems by experts and novices. *Cognitive Science, 5*, 121–152.

Cognition and Technology Group at Vanderbilt. (1994). From visual word problems to learning communities: Changing conceptions of cognitive research. In K. McGilly (Ed.), *Classroom lessons: Integrating cognitive theory and classroom practice* (pp. 157–200). Cambridge, MA: MIT Press.

Cognition and Technology Group at Vanderbilt. (1997). *The Jasper Project: Lessons in curriculum, instruction, assessment, and professional development.* Mahwah, NJ: Lawrence Erlbaum Associates.

Cole, M. (1996). *Cultural psychology: A once and future discipline.* Cambridge, MA: Harvard University Press.

Corey, S.M. (1944). Poor scholar's soliloquy. *Childhood Education, 33*, 219–220.

deGroot, A.D. (1965). *Thought and choice in chess.* The Hague: Mouton.

Driver, R., Squires, A., Rushworth, P., and Wood-Robinson, V. (1994). *Making sense of secondary science: Research into children's ideas.* London: Routledge Press.

Duffy, T.J., and Cunningham, D. (1996). Constructivism: Implications for the design and delivery of instruction. In D.H. Jonassen (Ed.), *Handbook of research for educational communications and technology* (pp. 170–198). New York: Macmillan.

Dufresne, R.J., Gerace, W.J., Leonard, W.J., Mestre, J.P., and Wenk, L. (1996). Classtalk: A classroom communication system for active learning. *Journal of Computing in Higher Education, 7*, 3–47.

Duncker, K. (1945). On problem-solving. *Psychological Monographs, 58* (5, Whole No. 270).

Dweck, C.S. (1989). Motivation. In A. Lesgold and R. Glaser (Eds.), *Foundations for a psychology of education* (pp. 87–136). Hillsdale, NJ: Lawrence Erlbaum Associates.

Edelson, D., and Gordin, D. (1998). Visualization for learners: A framework for adapting scientists' tools. *Computers and Geosciences, 24*, 607–616.

Edelson, D., Pea, R., and Gomez, L. (1996). Constructivism in the collaboratory. In B.G. Wilson (Ed.), *Constructivisit learning environments: Case studies in instructional design* (pp. 151–164). Engelwood Cliffs, NJ: Educational Technology.

Gick, M.L., and Holyoak, K.J. (1980). Analogical problem solving. *Cognitive Psychology, 12*, 306–355.

Gick, M.L., and Holyoak, K.J. (1983). Schema induction and analogical transfer. *Cognitive Psychology, 15*, 1–38.

Hamilton, D.L., Stroessner, S.J., and Driscoll, M. (1994). Social cognition and the study of stereotyping. In P.G. Devine, D.L. Hamilton, and T.M. Ostrom (Eds.), *Social cognition: Impact on social psychology* (pp. 292–316). San Diego, CA: Academic Press.

Hestenes, D. (1987). Toward a modeling theory of physics instruction. *American Journal of Physics, 55*, 440–454.

Hillery, G.A. (1955). Definitions of community: Areas of agreement. *Rural Sociology, 20*, 11–123.

Hmelo, C.E. (1995). Problem-based learning: Development of knowledge and reasoning strategies. In *Proceedings of the seventeenth annual conference of the Cognitive Science Society* (pp. 404–408). Pittsburgh, PA: Lawrence Erlbaum Associates.

Hough, B.W. (2000). Virtual communities of practice in teacher education: Assessing reflection in computer-mediated communication environments. Unpublished doctoral dissertation, Vanderbilt University, Nashville, TN.

Hunt, E., and Minstrell, J. (1994). A cognitive approach to the teaching of physics. In K. McGilly (Ed.), *Classroom lessons: Integrating cognitive theory and classroom practice* (pp. 51–74). Cambridge, MA: MIT Press.

Jenkins, J.J. (1978). Four points to remember: A tetrahedral model of memory *experiments*. In L.S. Cermak and F.I.M. Craik (Eds.), *Levels of processing and human memory*. Hillsdale, NJ: Lawrence Erlbaum Associates.

Judd, C.H. (1908). The relation of special training to general intelligence. *Educational Review, 36*, 28–42.

Jussim, L., Coleman, L.M., and Lerch, L. (1987). The nature of stereotypes: A comparison and integration of three theories. *Journal of Personality and Social Psychology, 52*(3), 536–546.

Kolodner, J.L. (1997). Educational implications of analogy: A view from case-based reasoning. *American Psychologist, 52*(1), 57–66.

Kozma, R., Russell, J., Jones, T., Marx, N., and Davis, J. (1996). The use of multiple, linked representations to facilitate science understanding. In S. Vosniadou, R. Glaser, E. De Corte, and H. Mandl (Eds.), *International perspectives on the psychological foundations of technology-based learning environments* (pp. 41–60). Hillsdale, NJ: Lawrence Erlbaum & Associates.

Lave, J., and Wenger, J. (1991*). Situated learning: Legitimate peripheral participation*. Cambridge, UK: Cambridge University Press.

Leontiev, A.N. (1981). *Problems in the development of mind.* Moscow: Progress.

Leonard, W.J., Dufresne, R.J., and Mestre, J.P. (1996). Using qualitative problem-solving strategies to highlight the role of conceptual knowledge in solving problems. *American Journal of Physics, 64*(12), 1495–1503.

Lin, X.D., and Bransford, J.D. (in press). People knowledge: A missing ingredient in many of our educational designs. Unpublished manuscript, Vanderbilt University, Nashville, TN.

Lin, X.D., and Lehman, J. (1999). Supporting learning of variable control in a computer-based biology environment: Effects of prompting college students to reflect on their own thinking. *Journal of Research in Science Teaching, 36*(7), 837–858.

Lockhart, R.S., Lamon, M., and Gick, M.L. (1988). Conceptual transfer in simple insight problems. *Memory and Cognition, 16*, 36–44.

Mann, L. (1979). *On the trail of process: A historical perspective on cognitive processes and their training.* New York: Grune and Stratton.

McMillan, D.W., and Chavis, D.M. (1986). Sense of community: A definition and theory. *Journal of Community Psychology, 14*, 6–23.

Mentkowski, M. et al. (1999). *Learning that lasts.* San Francisco: Jossey-Bass.

Mestre, J.P., Gerace, W.J., Dufresne, R.J., and Leonard, W.J. (1997). Promoting active learning in large classes using a classroom communication system. In E.F. Redish and J.S. Rigden (Eds.), *The changing role of physics departments in modern universities: Proceedings of international conference on undergraduate physics education* (pp. 1019–1036). Woodbury, NY: American Institute of Physics.

Moll, L.C., and Greenberg, J.B. (1995). Creating zones of possibilities: Combining socialcontexts for instruction. In L.C. Moll (Ed.), *Vygotsky and education: Instructional implications and applications of sociohistorical psychology* (pp. 319–348). Cambridge, UK: Cambridge University Press.

Moll, L.C., Tapia, J., and Whitmore, K.F. (1993). Living knowledge: The social distribution of cultural sources for thinking. In G. Saloman (Ed.), *Distributed cognition* (pp. 139–163). Cambridge, UK: Cambridge University Press.

Morris, C.D., Bransford, J.D., and Franks, J.J. (1977). Levels of processing versus transfer appropriate processing. *Journal of Verbal Learning and Verbal Behavior, 16*, 519–533.

National Research Council, (1999a). *How people learn: Brain, mind, experience, and school.* Committee on Developments in the Science of Learning. J.D. Bransford, A.L. Brown, and R.R. Cocking, (Eds.). Commission of Behavioral and Social Sciences and Education. Washington, DC: National Academy Press.

National Research Council. (1999b). *How people learn: Bridging research and practice.* Committee on Learning Research and Educational Practice. M.S Donovan, J.D. Bransford, and J.W. Pellegrino (Eds.). Commission on Behavioral and Social Sciences and Education. Washington, DC: National Academy Press.

National Research Council (2000). *How people learn: Brain, mind, experience, and school, Expanded edition.* Committee on Developments in the Science of Learning. J.D. Bransford, A.L. Brown, and R.R. Cocking (Eds.), with additional material from the Committee on Learning Research and Educational Practice. Commission on Behavioral and Social Sciences and Education. Washington, DC: National Academy Press. Available http://www.nap.edu. [December 12, 2001].

National Research Council. (2001). *Knowing what students know: The science and design of educational assessment.* Committee on the the Foundations of Assessment. J.W. Pellegrino, N. Chudowsky, and R. Glaser (Eds.). Board on Testing and Assessment, Center for Education. Division of Behavioral and Social Sciences and Education. Washington, DC: National Academy Press.

Nisbett, R.E., Fong, G.T., Lehman, D.R., and Cheng, P.W. (1987). Teaching reasoning. *Science, 238,* 625–630.

Novick, L. (1988). Analogical transfer, problem, similarity, and expertise. *Journal of Experimental Psychology: Learning, Memory and Cognition, 14,* 510–520.

Palloff, R.M., and Pratt, K. (1999). *Building learning communities in cyberspace: Effective strategies for the online classroom.* San Francisco: Jossey-Bass.

Pea, R.D., and Gomez, L.M. (1992). Distributed multimedia learning environments: Why and how? *Interactive Learning Environments, 2,* 73–109.

Perfetto, G.A., Bransford, J.D., and Franks, J.J. (1983). Constraints on access in a problem-solving context. *Memory and Cognition, 11,* 24–31.

Poplin, D.E. (1979). *Communities: A survey of theories and methods of research* (2nd ed.). New York: MacMillan.

Pressley, M. (1995). *Advanced educational psychology for educators, researchers and policy makers.* New York: Harper Collins College.

Reed, S.K., Ernst, G.W., and Banerji, R. (1974). The role of analogy in transfer between similar problem states. *Cognitive Psychology, 6,* 436–450.

Rheingold, H. (2000). *The virtual community.* Cambridge, MA: The MIT Press.

Salzer, M.S. (1998). Narrative approach to assessing interactions between society, community, and person. *Journal of Community Psychology, 26*(6), 569–580.

Scardamalia, M., and Bereiter, C. (1992). Text-based and knowledge-based questioning by children. *Cognition and Instruction, 9*(3), 177–199.

Schwartz, D.L., and Bransford, J.D. (1998). A time for telling. *Cognition and Instruction, 16*(4), 475–522.

Shulman, L.S. (1987). Knowledge and teaching: Foundations of the new reform. *Harvard Educational Review, 57,* 1–22.

Slevin, J. (2000). *The Internet and society.* Cambridge, UK: Polity Press.

Stacey, N.G. (Ed.). (1999). *Competence without credentials.* Washington, DC: U.S. Department of Education, Office of Educational Research and Improvement.

Stevens, R., and Nadjafi, K. (1999). Artificial neural networks as adjusts for assessing medical students; problem solving performances on computer-based simulations. *Computers and Biomedical Research, 26,* 172–187.

Thorndike, E.L., and Woodworth, R.S. (1901). The influence of improvement in one mental function upon the efficacy of other functions. *Psychological Review, 8,* 247–261.

Tinker, B., and Berenfeld, B. (1994). *Patterns of U.S. global lab adaptations.* Hands-on Universe, Lawrence Hall of Science, University of California, Berkeley. Available: http://hou.lbl.gov [December 12, 2001].

Vygotsky, L.S. (1978). *Mind in society: The development of higher psychological processes*. Cambridge, MA: Harvard University Press.

Web-Based Education Commission. (2000). *The power of the Internet for learning: Moving from promise to practice*. Washington, DC: Author. Available: http://www.webcommission.org [December 12, 2001].

Weigel, V. (2000). E-learning and the tradeoff between richness and reach in higher education. *Change, 32*(5), September/October, 10–15.

Wenk, L., Dufresne, R., Gerace, W., Leonard, W., and Mestre, J. (1997). Technology-assisted active learning in large lectures. In C. D'Avanzo and A. McNichols (Eds.), *Student-active science: Models of innovation in college science teaching* (pp. 431–452). Philadelphia, PA: Saunders College.

Wertheimer, M. (1959). *Productive thinking*. New York: Harper and Row.

White, B.C., and Frederiksen, J. (1998). Inquiry, modeling, and metacognition: Making science accessible to all students. *Cognition and Instruction, 16*(1), 39–66.

Wiggins, G., and McTighe, J. (1997). *Understanding by design*. Alexandria, VA: Association for Supervision and Curriculum Development.

Williams, S.M. (1992). Putting case-based instruction into context: Examples from legal and medical education. *The Journal of the Learning Sciences, 2*(4), 367–427.

Appendix A

Workshop Agenda

THE NATIONAL ACADEMIES

DIVISION OF BEHAVIORAL AND SOCIAL SCIENCES AND EDUCATION

CENTER FOR EDUCATION

THE IMPACT OF THE CHANGING ECONOMY ON THE POSTSECONDARY EDUCATION SYSTEM

Foundry Building, Room 2004
1055 Thomas Jefferson Street, NW
Washington, DC

Monday, May 14th

8:00 a.m.   **Continental Breakfast**

8:30 a.m.   **Welcome and Introductions**
Patricia Albjerg Graham, Harvard Graduate School of Education

Barbara Torrey, Division of Behavioral and Social Sciences and Education

8:45 a.m.	**The Economy as the Context for the Workshop** Moderator: *Arne Kalleberg*, University of North Carolina
	A View from The World Bank *Charles Abelmann*, The World Bank
	A View from Wall Street *Brandon Dobell*, Credit Suisse First Boston
	A View from Higher Education *David Breneman*, University of Virginia
	A View from America's Workplaces *Peter Cappelli*, The Wharton School of the University of Pennsylvania
10:30 a.m.	**Break**
10:45 a.m.	**Demographic and Educational Trends in Postsecondary Education** Moderator: *Martha Darling*, Private Consultant Presenter: *Lisa Hudson*, National Center for Education Statistics, U.S. Department of Education
12:30 p.m.	**Luncheon Speaker** **On Being Savvy About Segments, Markets, and Missions** *Robert Zemsky*, University of Pennsylvania
2:00 p.m.	**Changes in Two-Year, Four-Year, and For-Profit Postsecondary Institutions** Moderator: *David Breneman*
	Community Colleges in the 21st Century: Challenges and Opportunities
	Presenter: *Thomas Bailey*, Teachers College, Columbia University Discussant: *David Stern*, University of California
	The Impact of the Changing Economy on Four-Year Institutions of Higher Education
	Presenter: *Carol A. Twigg*, Center for Academic Transformation, Rensselaer Polytechnic Institute Discussant: *William H. Graves*, Eduprise

The Public Interest and the Emerging Postsecondary Market

Presenter: *Brian Pusser*, University of Virginia
Discussant: *Estela Bensimon*, University of Southern California

5:00 p.m.   **Adjourn**

Tuesday, May 15th

8:00 a.m.   **Continental Breakfast**

8:30 a.m.   **Learning About IT with IT: A Case Study of Cisco Networking Academies**
Moderator: *Ronald Latanision*, Massachusetts Institute of Technology
Presenter*: Richard Murnane*, Harvard University
Discussants: *Clifford Adelman*, Office of Educational Research and Improvement, U.S. Department of Education
Lisa Lynch, Tufts University

9:30 a.m.   **The Learning Sciences in Cyberspace**
Moderator: *Michael Feuer,* Center for Education
Presenter: *John Bransford*, Vanderbilt University
Discussants: *Irving Hamer*, New York City School Board of Education
Thomas Duffy, Cardean University

10:30 a.m.   **Break**

10:45 a.m.   **Summary of the Workshop**
Patricia Albjerg Graham

12:30 p.m.   **Lunch**

Adjourn

Appendix B

Workshop Participants

Richard Apling
Congressional Research Service
E-mail: rapling@crs.loc.gov

Robert Bednarzik
U.S. Department of Labor
E-mail: Bednarzik-Robert@dol.gov

Amy Beeler
National Alliance of Business
E-mail: beelera@nab.com

John Beverly
U.S. Department of Labor
E-mail: jbeverly@doleta.gov

Steve Brint
University of California, Riverside
E-mail: brint@mail.ucr.edu

Nancy Brooks
U.S. Department of Education
E-mail: nancy.brooks@ed.gov

Ann Clough
Senate Committee on Health, Education, Labor and Pensions
E-mail: ann_clough@labor.senate.gov

Kristin Conklin
National Governors Association
E-mail: kconklin@nga.org

Linda DePugh
The National Academies
E-mail: ldepugh@nas.edu

Pasquale DeVito
The National Academies
E-mail: pdevito@nas.edu

Denis P. Doyle
Schoolnet
E-mail: denis@schoolnet.com

Susan Duby
National Science Foundation
E-mail: sduby@nsf.gov

Peter Eckel
Kellogg Projects on Institutional
    Transformation
E-mail: peter_eckel@ace.nche.edu

Karolyn Eisenstein
National Science Foundation
E-mail: keinsenst@nsf.gov

Michael Feuer
The National Academies
E-mail: mfeuer@nas.edu

Gerri Fiala
U.S. Department of Labor
E-mail: gfiala@doleta.gov

Saul Fisher
The Andrew W. Mellon Foundation
E-mail: sf@mellon.org

Antoine M. Garibaldi
Educational Testing Service
E-mail: agaribaldi@ets.org

Evelyn Gazglass
National Governors Association
E-mail: eganzglass@nga.org

Michael Goldstein
Dow, Jones & Albertson
E-mail: mgoldstein@dlalaw.com

David Goodwin
U.S. Department of Education
E-mail: david.goodwin@ed.gov

James A. Griffin
Office of Science and Technology Policy
E-mail: jgriffin@ostp.eop.gov

Janet S. Hansen
Committee for Economic Development
E-mail: janet.hansen@ced.org

Lucy Hausner
National Alliance of Business
E-mail: hausnerl@nab.com

Gregory Henschel
U.S. Department of Education/OERI
E-mail: gregory.henschel@ed.gov

Ricardo Hernandez
U.S. Department of Education
E-mail: ricardo.hernandez@ed.gov

Margaret Hilton
The National Academies
E-mail: mhilton@nas.edu

John Jackson
National Science Foundation
E-mail: jajackso@nsf.gov

Janet Javar
U.S. Department of Labor
E-mail: jjavar@doleta.gov

Julie Kaminkow
CISCO
E-mail: jkaminko@cisco.com

Paula Knepper
U.S. Department of Education
E-mail: paula.knepper@ed.gov

Jay Labov
The National Academies
E-mail: jlabov@nas.edu

Mark A. Luker
EDUCAUSE
E-mail: mluker@educause.edu

Angela Manso
American Association of Community Colleges
E-mail: amanso@aacc.nche.edu

Hans Meeder
National Alliance of Business
E-mail: meederh@nab.com

Jeanne Narum
Project Kaleidoscope
E-mail: pkal@pkal.org

Erin Nicholson
National Alliance of Business
E-mail: nicholsone@nab.com

Samuel Peng
U.S. Department of Education/NCES
E-mail: samuel_peng@ed.gov

Ronald Pugsley
U.S. Department of Education
E-mail: ronald.pugsley@ed.gov

Sahar Rais-Danai
U.S. Department of Labor
E-mail: srais-dana@doleta.gov

Jane Richards
International Labor Affairs
E-mail: richards-jane@dol.gov

Stuart Rosenfeld
Regional Technology Strategies, Inc.
E-mail: rosenfeld@rtsinc.org

Gerhard L. Salinger
National Science Foundation
E-mail: gsalinge@nsf.gov

Claudio Sanchez
National Public Radio
E-mail: csanchez@npr.org

Margot Schenet
Congressional Research Service
E-mail: mschenet@crs.loc.gov

Charlotte Schifferes
U.S. Department of Labor
E-mail: cschifferes@doleta.gov

Merrill Schwartz
Association of Governing Boards
E-mail: merrills@agb.org

Karen Sheingold
Independent Consultant
E-mail: ksheingold@mindspring.com

Nevzer Stacey
The National Academies
E-mail: nstacey@nas.edu

Adam Stoll
Congressional Research Service
E-mail: astoll@crs.loc.gov

Hong W. Tan
The World Bank
E-mail: htan@worldbank.org

Elizabeth Teles
National Science Foundation
E-mail: ejteles@nsf.gov

Barbara Torrey
The National Academies
E-mail: btorrey@nas.edu

Monica Ulewicz
The National Academies
E-mail: mulewicz@nas.edu

Betsy Warner
U.S. Department of Education
E-mail: betsy.warner@ed.gov

Pamela Wilson
Department for Professional Employees
E-mail: wilsonpj@workmail.com

Robert Wisher
U.S. Army Research Institute
E-mail: wisher@ari.army.mil

Patricia Wood
ERIC Clearinghouse on Higher Education
E-mail: pwood@eric-he.edu

Terry Woodin
National Science Foundation
E-mail: twoodin@nsf.gov